BUFFALO GAP FRONTIER

Pioneers, Ranchers, and Oglala Lakota
all shared the same landscape in a tenuous peace

Bernie Keating: from Buffalo Gap

With:
Tom Norman: rancher from the Cheyenne River,
and Pat Cuny: Oglala Lakota from the Pine Ridge Indian Reservation

ISBN: 978-1-57579-371-9

Library of Congress Control Number: 2008922624

First Edition

Printed in the United States

PINE HILL PRESS
4000 West 57th Street
Sioux Falls, SD 57106

TABLE OF CONTENTS

ILLUSTRATIONS

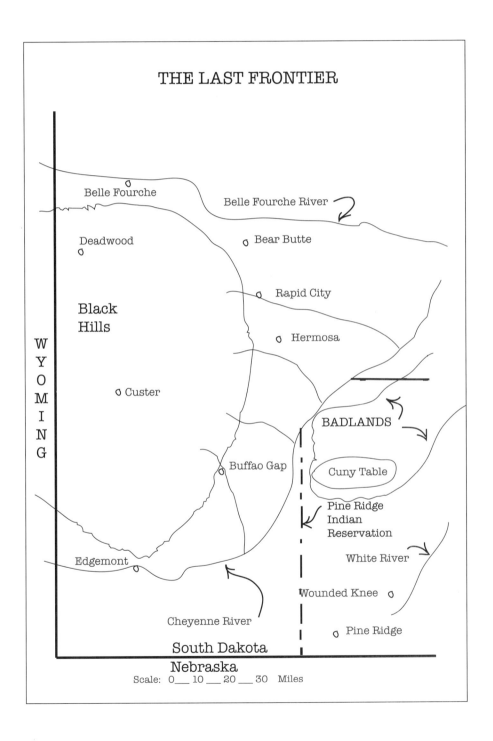

This is the opening at the edge of the Black Hills called Buffalo Gap. It was a natural route for buffalo that summered in the mountains to travel onto the plains where they wintered.

Lakota Indians pitched their tipis here and killed the buffalo that provided them their winter supply of meat, hides for tipis, and capes to ward off the bitter winds that swept over the plains of Dakota.

Then gold was discovered and Buffalo Gap became a passageway for stagecoaches and the rush of gold seekers into the Black Hills.

The town of Buffalo Gap was located alongside the little stream that flowed onto the plains and emptied into the Cheyenne River.

INTRODUCTION

The Buffalo Gap frontier was a caldron during the 19th century when Indian and white men clashed, and it gradually became a melting pot where the three cultures of Indian, cattlemen, and townspeople came together in a tenuous peace. This was the last frontier of the American West.

An opening at the edge of the Black Hills called Buffalo Gap was a focal point of conflict. It was a natural route for buffalo that summered in the mountains to travel onto the plains where they wintered. With the first snows, the Oglala Lakota Indians pitched their tipis at Buffalo Gap, and killed the buffalo that provided their winter supply of *PAH-pah* (jerky) and hides for tipis and capes to ward off the bitter winds that swept over the plains of Dakota.

Then gold was discovered, and Buffalo Gap became a passageway for stagecoaches into the Black Hills. This invasion by white men created a clash with Indians who fought to defend their territory. With the support of the U. S. Cavalry, the white men prevailed, however, and the Oglala tribe of the Lakota Nation was relegated to the Pine Ridge Indian Reservation, a few miles east of Buffalo Gap.

Soon cattle herds then arrived from Texas, passing Buffalo Gap on their way to the northern grasslands. Some cowboys grew tired of the hard life of trailing a herd, found the Cheyenne River country to their liking, and stayed. They collected a few head of cattle, laid claim to a piece of the prairie, constructed a sod dugout cabin, and patrolled the unfenced perimeter of their ranch on horseback, fighting off all predators with rifle and grit.

The stagecoach station at Buffalo Gap grew into a rip-roaring town that rivaled Deadwood for it notoriety. It had gunfights, dozens of saloons, "sporting houses," blacksmith shops, and became home to three thousand people who lived in tents and shacks along dirt streets. When a desperado named Charley Fugit came to town and announced his intention to kill the local lawman, Marshal Arch Riordan met him on the street in front of a saloon, challenged him, and Fugit was buried on Boot Hill. The railroad was extended north in 1885 with its terminus at Buffalo Gap, which quickly became a major shipping point for cattle to the markets of Omaha and Kansas City.

The heydays of the 19th century came to an end as the gold fields played out. The Lakota struggled for survival on the reservation, and cattlemen faced the reality of ranching on a marginal landscape barely suitable for anything other than a hardy buffalo herd -- but buffalo were now nearly extinct. The railroad was then extended north to Belle Fourche which became the new shipping terminus, leaving Buffalo Gap without enterprise, and then in November 1891 most of the business establishments caught fire and burned to the ground. Buffalo Gap died. The few remaining inhabitants resigned themselves to living in a "ghost town."[1]

The grandparents of our trio: Pat Cuny, Tom Norman, and Bernie Keating, had come to the frontier during the tumult of the 19th century. Pat Cuny's Oglala grandmother was one of the first to live on the Pine Ridge Indian Reservation. Her grandfather was a French fur trader who lived on the western frontier when it belonged to France, married a Lakota, and was absorbed into the Indian culture. Except for his time as a staff sergeant fighting across Europe in World War II, Pat Cuny spent his life ranching on the reservation. Tom Norman's grandmother became a single parent raising her son alone in a dug-out cabin along the banks of the Cheyenne River. Her husband grew tired of frontier hardships and Indian scares and fled back to the east; deserting her. Tom was raised on a Cheyenne River ranch where he and his Dad rode the fenceless territory onto the Indian reservation where their cattle pastured. My grandfather came to the Black Hills to work in the Cuyahogo Gold Mine before the turn of the 20th century. My Dad was raised as a hillbilly who hunted to put food on the table, worked in a few gold mines, and became a frontier banker. Pat Cuny, Tom Norman, and I were boyhood friends in the 1920s and 1930s. We lived in the three different cultures of Indian, cattlemen, and townspeople sharing the same landscape, and we three boys rode our horses together as saddle pals across the plains and down the buttes to the Cheyenne River.

This is a story about the intermingled cultures of that last frontier as we remember it. We will not call it a history, because then no one under the age of forty would read it. It is not biographical in the sense that no publisher wants a book about three "nobodies," nor will we claim it is entirely factual, because we cannot attest to stuff that took place before our time. We will only talk about the Buffalo Gap frontier as we found it in our youth of nearly eighty years ago, or heard about it from our parents, grandparents, or next-door neighbors.

Now, a word about how this memoir progresses: it starts with the story of the warrior, No Water. As a boy in Buffalo Gap during the 1930s, I knew this elderly man who often came off the reservation to sit under a cottonwood tree next to his tipi, while his family worked on the Sewright ranch across from our home. No Water's grandson was my playmate for the summer, and we spent many hours alongside a campfire, while No Water talked about his years in the nomadic tribe of Sitting Bull-- telling us stories that no one else wanted to listen to. I was not aware until recent years that No Water's wife, Black Buffalo Woman, had been involved in a love affair with Chief Crazy Horse, and a jealous No Water had shot and nearly killed the great chieftain. No Water never told me about that, and perhaps it was a part of his life he wanted to forget. Crazy Horse carried the facial disfigurement that resulted for the rest of his life.

There are only a handful of us left whose parents came to the Buffalo Gap frontier during the last half of the 19th century, and we are all around eighty. Pat Cuny, Tom Norman and I are still around -- then there are descendents and a few neighbors. That is the sum and total of the few survivors who can reach back to the Buffalo Gap Frontier.

My thanks to Lois (Wilson) Rapp, Anita (Degnan) Gallentine, Ed Streeter, Nellie Cuny, Freda Yeager, Dick Sewright, Hazel (Bondurant) Krutsch, and Will Keating, all lifelong friends who contributed their stories; also to the next generation of mixed-blood ranchers: Doug Temple of the White River country, Frank Rapp of the Cheyenne River country, and Dave Cuny of Cuny Table. Thanks to Sandra Lowry, librarian at Fort Laramie National Historic Site, Fort Laramie, Wyoming, who made the extensive historical archives available to me.

Also, thanks to Editor Beverly Pechan who has contributed extensively to Black Hills historical literature, and to Dave Strain of Dakota West Books, both of whom have assisted me along the way.

— *Bernie Keating*

1
MY LAKOTA FRIEND, NO WATER

<u>1935: AT BUFFALO GAP</u>

George No Water, Billy Thompson, and I rode our ponies down the ravine to Beaver Creek, waded across it with the water knee deep to the horses, and entered the No Water encampment at the edge of the cottonwood grove on the Sewright ranch. The Lakota grandfather, No Water, reclining against a log in the shade alongside his tipi, watched as we dismounted and turned our horses loose. The old man wore a solitary eagle feather in his hair, which hung long and straight, smiled and said something in Lakota to his grandson.

"What did he say, George?" I asked.

"He said in the old days when they lived here with Sitting Bull, he had a pinto mare exactly like yours. He's always talking about the old days and the crazy things they worshipped. It's boring. Come on. Let's go over to the hay barns and play."

George No Water and Billy were my playmates for the summer. Buffalo Gap was my home -- a town named for the valley that created a passage for the buffalo from the prairie into the Black Hills. The Pine Ridge Indian Reservation was a few miles east on the Dakota prairie. My family lived across from the Sewright ranch, and I spent most hours of the summer over there. Sewright hustled any way he could; a strug- gling rancher barely keeping his head above water during the rough Depression years of the 1930s. One of Sewright's enterprises was to butcher sheep and cows during the wintertime and take them to the In- dian reservation to sell. But he didn't actually sell anything, because the destitute Indians had nothing. It was a bartering process. He'd give them meat and potatoes, and in return they'd agree to work on his ranch the following summer, where he'd supply them with food and a place to stay. The Francis Stands family of four spent the summer living in an abandoned railroad box car that had been moved to the vacant lot across from our house. Their two children were playmates of my younger sister and brother. Several males, Pursey Kills-A-Warrior, Comes Again, and John Sitting Bull, would come without their families and live in a shack that was once a hay barn. They had been warriors in the Battle of the Little Bighorn. The No Water family pitched a tipi alongside Beaver Creek that meandered through the ranch. George No Water's father drove a team of workhorses to pull mowing machines during the haying season. The grandfather (I never knew if he had a first name, we just called him No Water) was an old man in his eighties -- long past the age of working on a ranch, and so he sat all day in the shade under the cottonwood trees near his tipi. While he understood English when he wanted to, he seldom spoke anything but Lakota, and gradually I learned some of it. When we boys struck his fancy, he would tell us stories about the old days. Often I'd linger with him by the campfire, someone who would listen to an old man with many memories about life on the plains that no one else wanted to hear.

No Water had been raised as a member of Sitting Bull's tribe which had roamed this country as nomads, living in tipis and following the buffalo herds. This gap in the mountains was their camping place while the buffalo herds were leaving the Black Hills with the first snows, and moving onto the plains where the snows were lighter. The Indians pitched their tipis along the creek in these cottonwood groves and feasted on the plentiful buffalo. Then later in winter, the tribe would move with the meandering herd out onto the plains and hunker down in protected ravines, sheltered from the blizzards that blew around the north end of the Black Hills.

No Water was a survivor. He too had been with Sitting Bull at the Little Bighorn when Custer's men attacked their village. That was sixty years earlier, when he was twenty years of age. It was a confused battle with women, children, warriors and soldiers everywhere. After the battle, No Water fled with Sitting Bull into Canada, and a few years later, he returned with his wife and children to the reservation. There, they began a life of survival in a meager existence in the Badlands of Dakota.

Stories of his nomad life were told to me over the campfire as No Water turned hunks of meat on a crude spit. When he felt like talking, words came forth in a combination of Lakota and his blend of English. I understood most of it, and George translated the rest.

"Did he ever go up into the Black Hills when he was a boy?" I asked. The answer was a resounding no. The Black Hills was a hostile place where few Indians ventured, except in an armed hunting party. It was full of bears and other prey that attacked them and spooked their horses -- and then there was the thunder and lightning. The old warrior's eyes closed in remembrance as he mumbled something about great spirits. Once he had climbed the mountain we call Bear Butte. There, No Water was close to those spirits, and he saw visions of the White Buffalo. A cloud came, and the thunder cracked as lightning struck the trees. He fled in fear down the mountain in the rainstorm, never to return. No Water was telling me of this vision and these spirits as he continued to turn the spit over the fire. George's father returned from his day on the ranch and told me I must go home before my parents worried, because another thunderstorm was on the way.

The storm hit.

Were these No Water's angry spirits?

Lightning bolts glanced off the high peaks, turning night into day. Thunderclaps shook the foundations of our house as the rain fell and the wind uprooted trees which crashed to the ground outside my bedroom window. Was No Water's vision of a White Buffalo his symbol of hope? A God? I felt I could believe in them just as I did in the white man's church God I heard about on Sundays.

The storm passed and I snuggled under my warm blankets and dreamed about No Water and his tipi village here in Buffalo Gap. I wondered what it was like back then.

1866: NO WATER ENCAMPMENT AT THE BUFFALO GAP

When morning came, No Water awakened in a silent world except for the breathing of his *WEEN-yon* ("Woman"). [2] (See endnotes) Black Buffalo Woman and their baby huddled together under the buffalo robe in a darkened tipi while outside, the world was encased in snow and bitter cold at the beginning of the Dakota winter season. Inside the tipi, it was still warm from last night's fire, made of sweet- smelling pine from the nearby Buffalo Gap.

No Water and his small band of Hunkpapa Lakota warriors had arrived here yesterday with their families, carrying their rolled-up tipis and possessions on travois' behind their horses. They knew buffalo would be on the move with the first snow of winter, migrating from the mountains of *pah- HA SAH-pah* (Black Hills) down through this gap, leading onto the plains where buffalo spent the winter. No Water and his Lakotas would intercept them at the narrow pass. By driving small herds to the south up a bluff, they could stampede the herd, driving them over the backside of a steep embankment, called a buffalo jump. As the injured buffalo tumbled down, warriors would be waiting at the bottom, using arrow and tomahawk to kill the struggling animals. No Water's tribe could feast on fresh meat; the women would dry *PAH-pah* (jerky) for travel, skin and scrape the buffalo hides for capes and tipi covers, and prepare for the rest of the long winter ahead.

Buffalo Gap was a favorite place No Water's band returned to each year when the buffalo were on the move -- both in the spring as the buffalo migrated through the gap up into the cool *pah- HA SAH-pah*-- and again in the fall when they migrated down through the gap with the first snowfall. A little stream with beaver dams flowed though the gap and out onto the plains where it meandered in and out of cottonwood groves, and eventually flowed into the Cheyenne River.

Now, with the first feast of the early winter completed, the women pulled down the tipis, loading all their possessions on travois' behind their horses. Moving a day's travel to the east, a new encampment was set up in a ravine near the Cheyenne River, where the buffalo herds also spent the winter.

No Water was happy. He had a beautiful wife. Black Buffalo Woman was the niece of Red Cloud -- the great chieftain of the Oglala tribe. Even though No Water was from the Hunkpapa tribe, the two Lakota tribes were friendly and inter-marriage was permitted. No Water was a fierce warrior, and some day he would become chieftain of his small band, replacing his own father. Black Buffalo Woman would bear him many sons, and yes, he knew, they would enjoy the buffalo feasts every spring and fall alongside the Beaver Creek that flowed down through Buffalo Gap.

When spring came, they would travel three days north to *mah- TOH pah-HA* (Bear Butte), the center of their tribal culture, and there they would parlay with other tribes of Lakota. Sitting Bull, the medicine man chieftain of the Hunkpapa would be there, and also Red Cloud with his tribe of Oglala. They would discuss many things, but the urgent subject would be the travel of white men though their Indian lands. Wagons of white men now traveled along the Platte River, and they must discuss with other tribes what should be done. This was Indian land and white men had no right to travel and disturb the buffalo herds. Should they fight and kill the white man?

Then, after the peace pipe had been smoked and the parlay of chieftains was completed, the feast began and was followed by dances that continued around the huge fire until early morning. It was a time of celebration in the shadow of *pah- HA SAH-pah*; their beloved Black Hills homeland.

1869: NO WATER ENCAMPMENT ON THE POWDER RIVER

No Water was now chieftain of his small band of forty warriors, as part of Sitting Bull's Hunkpapa tribe. His father, with advancing age and infirmities, had passed the mantle of leadership to his son. Black Buffalo Woman had borne No Water three children. Their tipi encampment was in the Powder River country in Wyoming Territory, where the Lakota activity had moved to the vicinity of Fort William (later becoming Fort Laramie), which had become the trading post of Campbell and Sublette, a French fur trading company. [3] The Indians assisted the French fur trappers in their quest of beaver pelts and buffalo hides, and the French men traded guns, gunpowder, jewelry, and liquor in return.

While the Indians welcomed French traders, it was not the case with the white pioneers who drove covered wagons following the Platte River, heading to California. These white men, they felt, disturbed the buffalo herds and left the landscape bare. Then the white man's *e-SON hon-ska* (cavalry) arrived to take over the fort from the French fur trading company and stationed a regiment of blue coats at the post. Meanwhile, the Frenchmen continued to conduct their business at the fringe of the fort. Occasional skirmishes occurred between the *e-SON hon-ska* and Indians, and it was only a tentative peace. Then the troopers began to ride north into Indian country where they had no right to be and the level of fighting increased.

Both the Hunkpapa and Oglala tribes co-existed in the Powder River country. Occasional contact between these tribes was not unusual, since they both lived as nomads following the buffalo herds. But now they were joined together fighting a common enemy -- the white man and their *e-SON hon-ska* in blue coats. In the aftermath of a joint Indian battle against the mounted troopers, the Hunkpapa tribe of No Water was visited by the young rising star of the Oglala, Chief Crazy Horse -- a handsome warrior with light brown-colored hair. His mother was a Brul'e, and he had been raised in that tribe, but was now in the Oglala tribe of his father. There was much celebration because the Indian warriors had been victorious, and the people chanted their praises -- particularly toward the hero of the day -- Crazy Horse, who sat motionless, embarrassed to be pushed forward in this way. "The light-haired man of the Oglala lifted his eyes and then he saw Black Buffalo Woman, No Water's wife, looking straight and upon him ... upon him alone." [4] Their encounter was brief and involved no conversation, only a brief glance between the two, but it fueled the beginning of a torrid romance.

A few weeks later, Crazy Horse and his warriors stopped again at No Water's camp. After feasting and smoking, they were asked to stay for the evening's dancing. Black Buffalo Woman and her friends teased Crazy Horse about being an Old Lone One (a bachelor). He was already twenty-four, and still standing off by himself while the others danced to the girls and back again. As the dancing ended and the others moved away, Black Buffalo Woman and Crazy Horse remained alone together in the darkness. What transpired is not known. If No Water noticed the encounter, he made no mention, but there was talk amongst the women in his camp.

Then shortly afterward, Crazy Horse visited the camp again, saw the faces watching him and knew the talk of the women; but not even the frowns of an annoyed husband could keep him from walking across the camp circle with Black Buffalo Woman, making a few words for only her ear .... "And saying all the silent things for which there were no words, things of the time past and the time to come." [5] Black Buffalo Women now had a third baby bound in the cradleboard. Crazy horse's frequent visits continued, and the women of the village wondered about his visits to her tipi when No Water was away in hunting parties.

One evening, when Crazy Horse returned to his camp from a visit to Black Buffalo Woman, he found his father, Worm, waiting for him along with two other warriors. Worm spoke to his son, Crazy Horse:

"They will not let you have Black Buffalo Woman. She is the niece of Chief Red Cloud, the wife of the brother of Black Twin, and they say they will not let her go." [6]

"Hah! They will not let her go!" Crazy Horse cried out, his anger breaking his silence as a flood sweeps through a beaver dam. "Like the white man they come saying what others cannot do." A violent argument ensued, and there were possibilities that this could lead to trouble between the Hunkpapa and Oglala tribes. Then a few days later, the improbable happened. Someone was missing from the Hunkpapa lodge circle. Black Buffalo Woman had put her three children out among relatives and was gone. Everyone knew she was gone because she and Crazy Horse had openly ridden out of camp together as members of a small war party to go into the Yellowstone area. On the second night the little party came to several small bands camped at a timber-lined creek. Suddenly, there was shouting and noise in the camp. No Water stood before them with eyes as red as an angry grizzly and he looked across the fire.

"My friend, I have come," he cried, as he aimed his revolver at Crazy Horse and fired. The bullet crashed through Crazy Horse's upper jaw and he fell unconscious across the fire. Before anyone could put a hand on him, No Water was gone; convinced he had killed Crazy Horse. He fled first to his Hunkpapa camp, and then hid in the mountains.

But Crazy Horse lived.

Gradually he recovered from the wound, but was left with a scar at the corner of his nose. A few weeks later he began his hunt for No Water, and "Chased him clear across Wyoming to the Yellowstone River. He would have caught him there, but No Water plunged his sweating buckskin straight into the river and swam across it to safety." [7] In a few days, a meeting of Lakota chiefs from various tribes was called to consider what Crazy Horse had done. He was found to have endangered the peace among the tribes, and as punishment had to return the ceremonial shirt received for prior bravery. That finished the affair between Crazy Horse and the wife of No Water.

Chief Crazy Horse did recover physically, emotionally, and politically within his Oglala Lakota tribe. In an arranged marriage, he took as his *WEEN-yon* a beautiful woman, Black Shawl, who was nearly as old as his own twenty-eight years. "They started their life together, Crazy Horse with his brown hair hanging loose as always, his rifle across his

horse before him, a bow and quiver at his back. Behind him rode Black
Shawl on her spotted pony, her buckskin dress deep-yoked in beads,
her saddle hanging long-fringed and beaded too, in the design of her
family." [8] No, she was not Black Buffalo Woman, his first love, but she
was his *WEEN-yon*, the wife of the great chieftain of the Oglala Lakota,
Chief Crazy Horse. That was in the year of 1872, and Black Shawl and
Crazy Horse were to have five years together before he was killed by
a white soldier at Fort Robinson. Black Shaw was at his side when he
died, as was the army surgeon, Valentine McGillycuddy.

This complex man had another love triangle in the final year of his
life, when he took a second wife, Nellie Larrabee, who was an eighteen
year-old mixed-blood daughter of an army scout. Nellie may have been
given to Crazy Horse as an attempted bribe to quit fighting the white
man--but he never did. [9] She was elsewhere when he was killed, and
later married a man named Greasing Hand, who then took the name of
Crazy Horse. Black Shawl never remarried and lived nearly fifty more
years into the late 1920s. [10]

During those five years from 1872 to 1877, Crazy Horse was to
distinguish himself as one of the greatest leaders of Indian people. Although he was killed, he was never captured, never defeated in battle,
and never stopped fighting for his lands. Crazy Horse's leadership was
recognized during his day by Indians and cavalry generals alike. Today, the huge mountain carving *in pah- HA SAH-pah*, his beloved Black
Hills, is testimony to this greatness.

After the love triangle with Crazy Horse was ended, Black Buffalo
Woman had no alternative but to return in submission to her husband,
No Water. For her, it would be a time of great disappointment, but shame
was not a part of their culture. She was his *WEEN-Yon*, and mother of
their three children. They returned with their Hunkpapa tribe to the Dakota plains east of the Black Hills. It was another cold winter.

In the spring, Sitting Bull called his band together and said they
could no longer believe in the white man's promises, so they must leave
the reservation and flee beyond *pah- HA SAH-pah* where some buffalo
still remained. Moving quickly before the cavalry men could react, the
WEEN-yon pulled down the tipis and prepared the village for the move.
Using their tipi poles for the travois that the ponies would drag, they
loaded their buffalo robes and hides -- the only possessions they had

-- and trudged along behind the ponies as the caravan moved away in a long line that included several hundred warriors and their families.

Heading north to skirt *pah- HA SAH-pah* along its eastern edge, they arrived at the base of *mah-TOY-SAH-pah* (Bear Butte). In better times, all the Indian chiefs of the Lakota nations met here in tribal counsels with the Cheyenne and Arapahos to smoke the peace pipe. Here they worshipped their spirits of lightning and thunder and witnessed their visions of the White Buffalo; a God that would protect their hunting grounds. But no more. They must flee to the west to join other tribes in the Powder River country, where they could band together with enough strength to fight the *e-SON hon-ska* (cavalry) with their *yu-SHO-shay* (rifles). A full moon later, they had arrived at a stream called the Little Bighorn River, where they found the Indian villages of many other tribes: Mineconjous under Fast Bull, Sans Arcs under Red Bear, Cheyenne under Ice Bear, Santee and Yanktonais under Red Paint, Blackfoot under Scabby Head, Oglala under Crazy Horse, and his own tribe of Hunkpapa under Sitting Bull. Many of these were tribes No Water had never encountered before; some had formerly been enemies of the Hunkpapa Lakota, but not now as they banded together for mutual defense against possible slaughter, and to escape starvation on their reservations. These combined villages consisted of eighteen-hundred buffalo hide lodges and four hundred wickiups -- a lodge made from small poles and willows. This gathering of tribes numbered ten-thousand, and the villages stretched for three miles along the river.

Sitting Bull chose for himself a small bluff near the southern edge of the tribes to establish his Hunkpapa village on the western side of the river. The tribes were independent of each other, but Sitting Bull was seen as the most powerful leader. The *WEEN-yon* dismantled the travois' and helped each other place the poles in their pyramid arrangement, pulling the buffalo hides up to form the tipi walls. Inside, they placed rocks in the center for the fire and buffalo robes to cover the ground. This tipi was their home --the only home they had ever known, and they had performed this task many times before. Then the women began their hunt on the hillsides and along the small stream looking for roots or stalks they could gather to feed their families.

No Water rode his pony with Sitting Bull and other warriors along the creek to visit other tribes. Sitting Bull smoked the peace pipe with each and talked about what they should do for protection against the *ska-we cha-SKA* if he should come again to force them onto a reservation where they did not want to go. These tribes in years past had raided neighboring villages, killing warriors and taking women and children as captives. How many women in these other villages had once been *WEEN-yon* of one of their own Lakota warriors? But a common threat now brought these former enemies together at this place; they pledged peace with each other for the security that strength in numbers could provide.

The Little Bighorn River which normally could be waded became swollen with spring rains and the days became warm.[11] No Water emerged into the daylight where his *WEEN-yon* was working on a buffalo hide, making it soft for use on the ground inside their tipi. It was a quiet morning, with the sun already high in the sky; there would be little to do. Hunting parties must travel far to the west to search for buffalo, and even then, few were found. Black Buffalo Woman found a few roots of plants amongst the willows near the little stream, and she pounded them into a mush that they could chew and swallow. But that would provide little nourishment and they must search elsewhere for food or they would perish.

The Indians knew they must always be ready to fight the white man. Crazy Horse left earlier with a large war party, traveling south to the Rosebud River. There he defeated a large force under General George Crook, who scattered and retreated to the south from which direction they came. No Water was still jealous of Crazy Horse, but he kept these things to himself.

Suddenly, No Water heard gunfire of the kind made by the *e- SON hon-ska*. There was excitement throughout the camp. "Boys were rounding up horses from the pack herd; barking dogs and excited children were everywhere underfoot; and hundreds of women milled about, uncertain whether to stay or flee. Confusion became pandemonium when a line of soldiers on gray cavalry mounts -- Custer's troopers -- appeared along the crest of the low hills across the river."[12] No Water grabbed his bow and arrow and ran to his pony. With the other warriors he raced south in the direction of the gunfire. Approaching the river, he saw a dust cloud created by the horses of the *e-SON hon-ska* riding in his direction at full speed. Chaos prevailed among the disorganized Lakota and Cheyenne as they rushed ahead with bow and lances toward the enemy. The men in blue stopped, dismounting to kneel on the ground and to shoot at the oncoming foe. No Water saw many warriors fall alongside him. At the sound of a bugle, the enemy remounted their horses and fled in retreat across the river from where they had come -- with the Indians following them. Many of the frightened horses stumbled and fell as they plunged into the swollen river. The Indians slew many with tomahawks and arrows. Then, as the remaining enemy raced up the bluff, the Indians caught and killed them one-by-one as the men in blue reeled in panic. When the enemy reached the crest of the hill, they stopped to fight. The Indians returned to the stream as word arrived of a new enemy further north. [13]

Then No Water raced with others to fight a new force that was attacking a village further north. He arrived to see a side hill littered with dead soldiers and others firing from behind a ring of downed horses. Over the hill from the other side came Chief Crazy Horse, leading warriors for the final charge to overcome and kill the enemy.

Suddenly it was all over. The white intruders lay scattered over the hillside and in the river. The warriors used their lance points to touch and make coup on the still quivering bodies, and then dismounted to collect their scalps. Lt. Colonel George Armstrong Custer, with his golden hair, blood-stained buckskin uniform and bloodied sword in his grip, was lying there among his fallen comrades. The *WEEN-yon* pulled off the bloodied uniforms, and the soldiers were lying naked now with their white bodies; the *WEEN-yon* disfigured and made sport of these enemies who had come to kill them and their families; to destroy their village and their way of life. [14]

It was all over before No Water realized that he had been in a battle with the *e-SON hon-sha*, and that all the men in blue had been killed. He returned to his tipi village. Now it was a time of new panic; what would happen? They had won this battle, but what next? Other enemy must be nearby; they would come with new horses and *yu-SHO- sha* (rifles) that the Indians could not match. At the signal from Sitting Bull, all the villages were to disband and flee. The *WEEN-yon* quickly pulled down the tipis, loaded the travois', and within the hour, the caravan was hurrying away under the cover of smoke from a prairie fire they had started. By nightfall the landscape was empty -- except for all the naked dead bodies. The Little Bighorn River was red with the blood of enemy and Indian alike, and this river flowed through a valley that was now devoid of human life.

After the Battle of the Little Bighorn, Sitting Bull asked all the tribes to split up into smaller groups so they would be more difficult to pursue, and so they could more efficiently hunt the few remaining buffalo. Eventually, he took his Hunkpapa tribe into Canada. Crazy Horse remained with his Oglala tribe in the area north of the Black Hills. They fought skirmishes in the Slim Buttes area, but were in turmoil as they were constantly pursued by more troopers in blue coats. It was a losing cause.

A final chapter of the No Water love triangle came when the jilted husband was finally able to get his revenge against Crazy Horse. The government had recruited scouts among the remnants of the Indian tribes, and offered $200 for anyone who could capture Crazy Horse. Lieutenant W. P. Clark at Fort Robinson was surprised at the co-operation he got from No Water, one of the scout leaders they sent to catch the hostile chief. Clark reported to his superiors that No Water, who had charge of one party of twenty-five scouts, had killed two ponies in his efforts to overtake and capture the hostile chief. Riding with his men, No Water saw Crazy Horse in the distance with Black Shawl and two other warriors, and a chase began that lasted through an entire day. Never once did he get within shooting range. He rode the two horses to their deaths from exhaustion under the sting of his rawhide whip.

Finally, Crazy Horse reached the safety of his own camp and then turned himself in at the Spotted Tail Agency. From there he was taken to Fort Robinson. "Quietly, his blanket folded over his arm as though he were going to his lodge, Crazy Horse was taken past soldiers with bayonets and then in through a door. There he saw barred windows, the men with chains on their legs, and he realized it was the iron house." [15] The final melee of events is unclear and Indian scouts may have been implicated in his death, but what is undisputable is that Crazy Horse was bayoneted by a soldier and given a fatal wound. [16]

Crazy Horse's father, Worm, was brought to the bare, dusky room where his son lay, saying, "Son, I am here." Then the son saw him, "Ahh-h my father," he whispered. "I am bad hurt. Tell the people it is no use to depend on me any more now."[17] Soon the great Chief Crazy

Horse was dead.

The legacy of Crazy Horse was to grow as the Indians found themselves captives assigned within the borders of a reservation. It was Crazy Horse who foresaw that fate and tried to convince Red Cloud and other Indian leaders that they should fight for their land and not negotiate with the white man. [18]

Crazy Horse was just another tribal chieftain among many during his lifetime, but he has become a symbol that now fills a mountain. As a twelve-year-old boy named Curly, Crazy Horse was with his Brul'e mother when the U.S. Cavalry raided their village, killing old people, women and children, then took the few survivors as prisoners to Fort Laramie. In that cruel experience, Curly learned to hate the white man. He was raised as a Brul'e, fought alongside the Mineconjous, Cheyenne, and Blackfoot, and called himself an Oglala -- the tribe of his father. At the Battle of the Little Bighorn, he led the final charge that killed Custer. He was a strange man -- an enigma even to his own people -- but he was the kind of which legends are made, and in death became even bigger than in life. Crazy Horse has become a symbol for all Native Americans in their hope for better times to come.

Sitting Bull's small tribe of Hunkpapa would endure four long seasons of terrible winters and starvation. The band he brought into Canada kept melting away, until four years later he had only 185 followers left. Many were his relatives; most were elderly, all longed for their old home. They were hungry. Sitting Bull led the remnants of his followers toward Fort Buford, seventy miles south of the border and near the Dakota-Montana line. [19] They lost hope and had nothing. Theirs was a male-dominated society -- yet it was the strength of the *WEEN-yon* that kept these Lakota families together. Whenever the warriors lost heart, it was the women who kept the vision of a new future. It was the *WEEN-yon* who made the difference.

Five decades later, as a little boy in Buffalo Gap, I knew the elderly No Water. He came with his son who worked on the Bill Sewright ranch and his grandson, George, was my summer playmate. We listened to the stories of the old man, but he never talked to me about Black Buffalo Woman, or about Crazy Horse. Perhaps it was a chapter of his life he wanted to forget. Or maybe it was just the foggy memory of an old man who had spent too many years living on the Dakota prairies.

Sometimes in the late afternoon, I would see him sitting in the shade under a cottonwood tree, eyes half-closed in a sort of daydream, and I've often wondered what it would be like to enter into one of those dreams.

2
THE EARLY FRONTIER

Buffalo Gap's frontier was part of the grand finale of our nation's expansion; a caldron where all the elements came together in a meltdown: Indian, cavalry, gold rush, stagecoach, pioneer, cattle drive, and the Wounded Knee Massacre.

Everyone on the frontier came from somewhere else. The earliest white men were French fur traders in the 18th century who traveled the rivers north from New Orleans when this central part of North America belonged to France. The Lakota (Sioux) who had been chased westward into Minnesota by other tribes crossed the Missouri River in 1776, subsequently subdued and replaced the other Indian tribes living in the Black Hills region. Then a hundred years later, gold-seekers arrived after color was discovered by the Custer Black Hills expedition in 1874. Cattlemen arrived soon after with herds driven up from Texas headed to the grasslands of Montana Territory. Each of these peoples brought their own unique culture into the area, established claim to the land, and fought to keep it.

We three contributors represent the protagonists of that era. Pat Cuny's male ancestors were some of the earliest French fur traders who ventured into the unexplored Western lands when it still belonged to France, married Indian women, raised mixed-blood families, and guided early explorers like Fremont and Kearney. Pat's grandmother was an Oglala Indian married to a Frenchman who was killed. She then fled with her small children from a hostile military environment and was herded onto the Pine Ridge Indian Reservation. Tom Norman's grandmother was a pioneer rancher along the banks of the Cheyenne River. She shot a Brul'e Indian warrior who was rustling horses from her corral during the Indian scare of the 1890s. My grandfather came as a gold miner to the Black Hills, and my family lived in the town of Buffalo Gap with elderly white pioneers and Indian warriors who spent their last years sharing the same territory.

We three -- Pat, Tom, and I, were on the scene when the vestiges of the frontier culture finally came to an end. But before we talk about the end-point, let's start back at the beginning. The story about the killing of American Indians by Europeans and later by the U.S. Government must be understood to place the Buffalo Gap frontier and the lives of Pat, Tom, and myself in its historical perspective.

The Pamunkey, Mattapony, Powhatana, and Chickahominy tribes of Virginia and the Massachuset tribe of New England who fought the invading Europeans early in the 17th century were eventually all killed and became lost in the pages of history, as are so many other tribes of that early era. Those not annihilated entirely were assimilated into the white man's culture. Then the conquest spread westward across the continent to other tribes such as the Potawatomi, Kickapoo, Cherokee, and Pawnee; today the names of some former Indian tribes are remembered only as places on our maps: Omaha, Kansas, Iowa, Yankton, Waco, Yuma, and Cheyenne. When the Oregon Trail and Lewis and Clark water routes were opened, permitting white settlers to bypass troubled areas and tame the West, the Nez Perce, Klamath, Mono, and Ute became the victims.

Early native people in the Black Hills region were the Mandan and Arikara. They were eventually driven out by other tribes and moved into Dakota lands further north. The Cheyenne were also in the region at the time, and they became the dominant tribe for several centuries. The first white men into the new territory were French -- when this central area of North America belonged to France. As early at 1739 -- and long before the United States came into existence -- a French fur trader -- Joseph Bissonette -- who was Pat Cuny's great-grandfather, ventured into the unexplored area of present-day Nebraska and Colorado, married an Indian, and lived there with his mixed-blood family. During those same early years, four Frenchmen, guided by Mandan Indians, traveled from the Missouri River and visited the Black Hills and Bear Butte. They left engraved plates to confirm the claim of France to the region.

During this era, the Lakota had lived in the regions of Minnesota and Wisconsin where they had been driven by white expansion. Then in 1776 (the same year that the United States came into existence with the Declaration of Independence), the Lakota tribe of the Sioux Nation crossed the Missouri River and occupied the plains of Western Dakota. The prairies were covered with buffalo, and these nomads followed their migration. While the Lakota and Cheyenne normally shared the same territory in a non-warlike manner, the Lakota gradually gained dominance.

The Lakota Indians belonged to the Ocetic Sakowin-- or Council of Seven Fires -- that today is commonly called Sioux. However, the word "Sioux" means "snake", and was a derogatory name applied to them by an adversary Indian tribe and later by early French traders. The word "Lakota" is truly the tribal name used in the Teton dialect, and it means "allies" or "friends." [20] We will use the name Lakota rather than the former reference: Sioux. At an early time, the Lakota began to fight among themselves and broke into three sub-groups: the Dakotah -- also called the Santee – who remained east of the Mississippi River; the Yanktonai lived east of the Missouri River in southeastern Dakota Territory, and the Lakota, also known as the Teton, moved west of the Missouri River. [21] The Lakota subdivided into seven tribes: Oglala, Hunkpapa, Mineconjous, Brul'e, Two Kettles, Sans Arcs, and Blackfoot, and were nomadic in lifestyle. [22]

Names like Colorado, Wyoming, Dakota, and Nebraska did not yet have a geographic meaning to the Lakota tribes moving through this region. Their boundaries were determined by the topography of mountains and rivers and by the enemies that existed on their perimeters -- the Crows to the west, Pawnees and Arapaho to the south, and the white man to the east.

"Even the idea of belonging to a tribe not by bloodline but by affinity is less vague than it sounds. Some Indians preferred to live with bands or tribes other than the one they were born into. An Oglala of one band might move with his mother's relatives among another band … Santee Sioux might journey west from Minnesota and join an Oglala … A Sioux might be adopted into Cheyenne or Arapaho." (Ian Frazier describes this in his book *On The Rez*.) [23]

"The political situation of the Oglala Lakota tribes during the early 19th century is unclear, but they may have been in the process of consolidating their loosely governed bands into a single tribal organization under one or two dominant leaders. Clearly, Smoke and Bull Bear combined numerous *tiyospaye* under their leadership." (Gregory Gagnon and Karen White Eyes discuss this in their book *Pine Ridge Reservation*.) [24] Smoke was the more powerful, and the many small bands that collectively made up his tribe usually ranged in the Lakota lands south of their Lakota base at Bear Butte and the southern regions of *PAH-ha SAP-ha* and in present day Nebraska, along the Platte River. It was there on the banks of Blue Creek, near where it meets the Platte River that Red Cloud was born in 1821. He was the son of Smoke's sister, and one day would replace Smoke as the dominant leader of the Lakota. [25] Other Lakota tribes that roamed the Dakotas were those under the chief Bull Bear. They normally ranged north of Bear Butte in regions to the north, east, and west of *PAH-ha SAP-ha*. While the tribes of Smoke and Bull Bear co-existed sharing the same lands, intermarriage occurred. The two leaders were reasonably friendly, often meeting at Bear Butte to smoke the peace pipe – still they were wary rivals. Ultimately, years later, they openly quarreled and the young warrior, Red Cloud, shot and killed Bull Bear. The event added to the reputation of the young warrior -- but it also created a rift between the two Oglala tribes that was to remain for many years. The quiet man named Crazy Horse was later to replace Bull Bear as Oglala chieftain, taking over his tribal role. (Red Cloud saw as a rival and a threat, and was rumored to be compliant in the eventual capture and murder of Crazy Horse.)

In 1803, the new United States government purchased this entire section of central North America from France, whose leaders were willing to sell because of their problems on the European continent. President Thomas Jefferson then sent an expedition led by Captains Meriwether Lewis and William Clark to determine exactly what he had bought, and to see if they could find a satisfactory route to the Pacific Ocean. Lewis and Clark's party traveled on the Missouri River into Montana, well to the north of the Black Hills, thereby avoiding the plains of western Dakota where the hostile Lakota dominated.

During this era and as previously stated, the heart of Lakota activity was centered at Bear Butte and its vicinity, which extended west to Devil's Tower in the northern region of the Black Hills. [26] "Oglala traditions describe this area as a crucial site in the practice of traditional Vision Quests and annual Sun Dances … And the Cheyenne Indian nation also considers Bear Butte as the geographic location of their origins."[27] Then in the mid-1800s, the center of Oglala activity shifted several hundred miles southwest to the confluence of the North Platte River and Laramie River as a result of new trade with the Frenchmen.

"William Sublette realized that the junction of the North Platte and Laramie Rivers, where numerous Indian nations had camped and traded for generations, was an ideal point for a trading post. He foresaw that the fur trade would soon concentrate on buffalo hides as beaver were trapped out." [28] Sublette built Fort William, and then sent messengers north to encourage the Oglala to trade at his new establishment. Bull Bear moved four thousand of his tribe from the region of Bear Butte to the vicinity of Fort William in the year 1840; this established a new center of Oglala activity that was to continue for another forty years. Smoke's band followed within the year, and the Oglala then drove all other Lakota and Cheyenne tribes from the new center of the Oglala Empire. "It was here that all the Oglala *tiyospaye* dominated their portion of the Lakota territory, disciplined invaders, and lived the life romanticized by the 1990 film *"Dances With Wolves."* [29]

After the U.S. Government bought Louisiana Territory from France, this huge region became a part of the new America and the westward course of the empire followed three main prongs: the Missouri River, the Santa Fe Trail, and the Platte River Road. By all standards, the most important of these was the Platte River Road -- the great highway for the covered wagon migrations to Oregon, California, and Utah. During this era, as mentioned earlier, the government in 1843 established Fort Laramie, and stationed a cavalry force there to maintain order throughout the region. Fort Laramie was the undisputed capital of the vast territory between Denver and Santa Fe to the south and the chain of Missouri River posts to the north, as well as the last significant outpost of civilization on the Great Platte River Road; being the principal way-stop for the thousands of emigrants on their way west. Until its demise in 1890, Fort Laramie continued to be a key military installation on the Northern Plains. [30]

Many young Frenchmen at the fort married Lakota women and by doing so, became quasi-Oglala themselves. Pat Cuny's grandfather, Adolph Cuny, arrived there as an immigrant, ran a business at the fort, married an Oglala Lakota *WEEN-yon* and became known as a "French squaw man" -- reflecting the new bloodline added to the Lakota ancestry. [31]

During the first half of the 19th century, some American white men did venture into this hostile area in armed parties. The Henry-Ashley Party of 1823 visited the northern Black Hills in the vicinity of Bear Butte, and a second party under the leadership of Jedediah Smith explored the southern hills, entering through Red Canyon near present-day Edgemont. Another party of seven men -- named the Ezra Kind Party -- explored the northern portion of the hills in 1833 and managed to leave a sandstone plaque as a historical marker before being killed by Indians. Then a few years later, gold was reportedly found by several men -- also in the Black Hills -- so rumors of gold persisted for four decades before Custer's expedition exploited the fact. [32]

Finally, after the close of the Civil War, the warlike Lakota had become the most troublesome of the hostile Indian tribes, and they occupied the western Dakota Territory in what was the last remaining major pocket of Indian resistance to the United States. General Phil Sheridan commanded the army forces, which included all the areas that surrounded these hostile Indians. He had forts in the south along the Platte River and forts along the Missouri River to the east and north to protect the river route to the Northwestern region of the nation. Dakota Territory in the center and occupied by the hostile Lakota Tribes presented a problem. It was already inevitable that an expanding nation in need of more land and resources would find some means to tame and occupy this land.

The tribes of the Great Sioux Nation signed treaties in 1824, 1851, and 1868 with the United States. "The Black Hills region was a part of the Great Sioux Reservation created by the Sioux treaty of 1868," as stated in Collier's Encyclopedia. [33] That treaty established borders which in essence gave the land north of the Platte River in the center of Nebraska and west of the Missouri River in the center of the Dakota Territory to the Sioux Nation. The only way this land could become occupied and owned by the white man was by some sort of subterfuge and illegal invasion. In 1980, the U.S. Supreme Court affirmed a ruling by lower courts that the 1868 treaty was valid and the Indian had been wronged, but ruled the remedy should be only some form of compensation. [34]

Strong "special interest" forces were at work in the political climate after the end of the Civil War. "In the early 1870s the depression dried up the financing of railroads headed into the west and Indian country through Kansas and the Dakotas. It was hoped that new gold strikes would lure reluctant investors," said Mari Sandoz. [35] And there were "rumors" of gold in the Black Hills.

Under President Ulysses S Grant, the military had a major voice. Inevitable downsizing came at the close of the war, when career officers jockeyed to retain their commissions. "Ambitious officers were driven to jockeying for honors and victories to raise their rank and position ... To this end, by 1867 the Plains had become a gaming field, a hunting ground for military trophies – victories over the Indians, particularly over bands with women and children, for warrior parties were difficult to locate and more difficult to strike, to defeat. Even with the avowed Extermination Policy of the government, there was usually some protest over the slaughter of helpless Indians and demands that the real culprits, the hostile warriors, be punished," said Mari Sandoz. [36] The western frontier was the only game in town, and it drew Civil War leaders such as generals Sheridan, Crook, Terry, and Custer.

Military officers hoped to further their ambitions in Indian warring and led unbelievably brutal forays: the Sand Creek Massacre of two hundred Cheyenne -- mostly women and children; Reynold's bloodbath; Custer's slaughter of a sleeping village of Cheyenne women and children at the Washita; and Merritt's butchering of Indians hunting for food "a band of tame Cheyenne, mostly women and children and old men, a band peaceful enough to have remained this long around a hungry agency." [37] The American public, exposed to so much carnage during their recent Civil War, paid scant attention to this barbaric extermination since it only involved "ignorant savages" [term used by Benjamin Franklin]. [38]

In 1874, General Sheridan recommended to Washington officials that a military post be established in the Black Hills in order to obtain better control over the Indians, and he obtained approval for a military reconnaissance, since little was known about the area. [39] Sheridan sent a force of 1000 men under the command of Lt. Colonel George Custer, who had been a temporary Brevet General during the Civil War and was still referred to as General Custer. This army force left Fort Abraham Lincoln on the Missouri River in the Dakota Territory at Bismarck, in what is now North Dakota. A prospector accompanying the army dis-

covered gold. General Custer personally accompanied scout Charlie
Reynolds out of the Black Hills to the Cheyenne River, sending him
through hostile territory to carry this news to the outside world.

Arriving at Fort Laramie, scout Reynolds told his listeners of the
discovery. The news flew out by telegraph, and in August of 1874, the
gold rush to the Black Hills began. Prior discoveries of gold in California, Nevada, Montana, and Colorado led to outbursts of people rushing
to seek their fortunes. This new discovery of gold in the Black Hills saw
the same frenzy, but it had a new dimension --the gold was located in the
midst of hostile Indian country.

You probably have heard much of this history before, but let me
set the record straight with some actual facts as Tom, Pat and I remember them, heard stories from our parents, had conversations with Indian
warriors and white pioneers, or utilize some history documented by others. Tom, Pat, and I knew each other as boyhood friends. Now we tell
our stories and those of our parents and grandparents as we relive those
years. The three cultures of Buffalo Gap, the Cheyenne River, and the
Oglala Lakota Reservation are truly the last frontier in our nation's history.

The Pat Cuny Oglala Lakota heritage began at Fort Laramie in the
1840s, then moved to the Pine Ridge Indian Reservation in the 1870s,
and Pat has lived his eighty-four years on the Reservation. Tom Norman's grandparents arrived with the first white settlers in the Cheyenne
River country, and Tom has lived his eighty-two years ranching alongside the river. My grandfather arrived at the turn of the last century to
work in a gold mine, and my parents lived in Buffalo Gap -- a frontier
town on the stagecoach route to the gold fields.

Gold was discovered in the summer of 1874, and by the following spring, a gold rush to the Black Hills was too great for the army to
contain -- not that they tried very hard. The initial favored route into
the Black Hills was to take the train to Cheyenne in Wyoming Territory
and then take a stagecoach north past Fort Laramie through semi-desert
country. Stagecoaches left Cheyenne for twice-a-week trips to Custer
City.

Fredrick Heidepriem (whose son was my father's classmate in
Custer) paid $75 for a stagecoach fare from Cheyenne to Custer and had
to walk the entire distance of one hundred-eighty miles alongside the

stagecoach, because there was no room inside. [40] The fare was for the protection that an armed stagecoach provided against the Indians and highwaymen along the route. Making approximately twenty miles per day, nights were spent at stage stations strung along the route. Traveling through Wyoming, coaches crossed the Cheyenne River along the southwestern edge of the Black Hills, traveled up through Red Canyon near present day Edgemont, and then headed on to Custer.

Gold findings were sparse at Custer City, and soon a bonanza was found forty miles north at Deadwood. The favored route to Deadwood was to leave the railhead at Sidney, Nebraska, heading north to the stagecoach station at Buffalo Gap. This was hostile territory and encountered numerous Indian attacks. At the Buffalo Gap, the route passed through a natural opening into the Black Hills and on to Custer to the northwest. As the action shifted to Deadwood, coaches would travel along the eastern edge of the hills, rest at a station at Rapid City, and then continue on to Deadwood.

A Buffalo Gap pioneer, Gus Haaser, traveled this route, but like Heidepriem, he also had to walk most of the way -- since it was the rainy season and his services were required to scrape the sticky gumbo from the wheels of the stagecoach. Haaser halted his journey to the gold fields at the Rapid City stage station, however, to start a new career as a cowboy.

The Lakota watched this activity through their lands, becoming increasingly angry and restless. Bands of marauding Indians began attacking settlers on the prairies surrounding the Black Hills; they assaulted stages, raided stock from cattle herds, killed and scalped herders, and burned freight outfits.

The Commissioner of Indian Affairs admitted that the "experience of the past summer proved the utter impracticability of keeping American citizens out of a country where gold exists by fear of a cavalry patrol or by any consideration of the rights of the Indians." [41] How many white men pushed their way into the Black Hills during the two years subsequent to the discovery of gold will never be known, but it was estimated to be in the tens of thousands. Early in December of 1875, the commissioner of Indian Affairs ordered Indian agents along the Missouri River to notify Indians in unceded territory that if they did not come into the agencies before January 31, 1876, they would be designated "hostiles."

The message was hampered by winter snows, however, and the Indians remained in their camps and did not come into the agencies as ordered.

Meanwhile, in Deadwood, gold fever ruled the day. Saloons were crowded and a spirit of lawlessness prevailed. In actual fact, the only law was the gun that each man carried in his holster. Wild Bill Hickok "while playing poker in a saloon in Deadwood, holding a pair of aces and a pair of eights, now known as 'the dead man's hand,' was shot in the back by Jack McCall on Aug. 2, 1876." [42]

Everyone in Deadwood and Buffalo Gap was an unlawful trespasser on Indian land, but the cavalry remained for the most part in the comfort of their forts along the Platte and Missouri Rivers.

Historical accounts of that era talk much of Deadwood, but seldom mention Buffalo Gap. Still, nearly everyone in Deadwood -- including Wild Bill Hickok and Calamity Jane -- had passed through Buffalo Gap, and most had spent time there. The Buffalo Gap stage station came into existence coinciding with the discovery of gold in 1874, and was operated by George and Abe Boland, who provided rooms, meals, and a bar. George also served as postmaster. When a postal inspector arrived by stagecoach and complained about running a bar in the same facility as the post office, George threw the wooden beer crate out the door which held incoming and outgoing mail, and announced, "There is your goddamn post office!" [43]

Buffalo Gap became a conduit through which people from the east had to pass on their way to the Deadwood gold fields, and was a boisterous frontier town with four blacksmith shops, twenty-three saloons, seventeen hotels and restaurants, two large "sporting" houses and -- numerous smaller ones -- four Chinese laundries, three livery barns, and a couple general stores. Church services were held in tents. At the height of this period there were three thousand residents in Buffalo Gap, plus all the additional hundreds of migrants passing through. [44] Buffalo Gap's prosperity was to go on for nearly fifteen years.

In 1885, the railroad was extended from Chadron, Nebraska, with its terminus at Buffalo Gap, and the town became the jumping-off point from rail to stagecoach for everyone heading to the diggings. Strangers frequented the saloons, visited the "sporting houses," stayed overnight in the Alexander Hotel (which my Dad would own 50 years later) across from the depot, and then catch the next stagecoach to Rapid City and

Deadwood. A stock pen built on a siding alongside the depot became the shipping point of cattle destined for markets in Omaha and Kansas City.

Maintaining law and order in Buffalo Gap was Marshal Arch Riordan. A kindly and peaceful man, he carried a pistol in his holster to add stature to the badge he wore. When Charley Fugit, a hired gun, showed up in town announcing he would kill the Marshal, Riordan who faced him on Main Street, out-drew and killed him. Fugit was buried in the local Boot Hill cemetery.

While all this activity was taking place in Buffalo Gap, the Lakota continued to make life difficult for travelers on their way to the Black Hills. Indian agencies ordered all Indians to their confinement on the reservations that had been designated for them, and while some submitted peacefully to the promise of provisions by the government, others did not. When the provisions didn't arrive and hostility increased, Chiefs Sitting Bull and Crazy Horse led their tribes of Hunkpapa and Oglala around the north end of the Black Hills into Montana. There they joined forces with Mineconjous, Sans Arc, Cheyenne, and Yanktonai. This combined enclave of Indian villages extended for three miles along the Little Bighorn River. Villages consisted of eighteen-hundred buffalo hide lodges, four hundred wickiups, and a collection of tribes that numbered ten thousand. [45]

The refusal of Chief Sitting Bull "to go on reservation led General P.H. Sheridan to initiate a campaign against him which resulted in the annihilation of Lt. Col. George A Custer's troops on the Little Bighorn," as stated in the encyclopedia. [46]

In the spring of 1876, General Sheridan ordered his three-pronged attack against the Indian rebellion, designed to force them back to the reservations from which they came. The strategy was to avoid major combat with the Indians, and anticipated that once they saw themselves surrounded by major army forces, they would submit peacefully and return to their homes. Custer was sent ahead to reconnoiter the situation along the Little Bighorn River and report back to General Terry the position and strength of the Indians. But in characteristic fashion, he decided instead to attack the village he found. Unfortunately for him and the 225 men in the regiments under his direct command, thousands of armed warriors responded, and on June 25, 1876, the Indians wiped out most the Seventh Cavalry. [47]

After the battle, Sitting Bull and his band of Hunkpapa fled to Canada, but in 1881 after four years of freezing cold and starvation, he surrendered and spent the rest of his life on the Standing Rock Indian Reservation hating white men. [48] Gradually all the remnants of the various Indian tribes were forced back to the reservations as a result.

This is where the Josephine Cuny story starts: after her husband was killed in 1878 at Fort Laramie, Pat Cuny's grandmother, Josephine, fled to the Oglala reservation because of the growing hostile anti-Indian climate prevailing at that time on the frontier. [49]

News of the Custer disaster hit the nation much like the *9/11/2001 World Trade Center* disaster of New York City. Not only was it on the eve of a national election, but also on the eve of the nation's celebration of its first century of independence.

Does the Battle of Little Bighorn sound like ancient history?

Well, it wasn't all that far back. When we were boys, Tom Norman, Pat Cuny, and I all knew Lakota warriors who fought in that battle where General Custer and his men were killed.

My boyhood friend, George No Water's granddad, an old man when I knew him in the 1930s, was in his twenties at the time he fought against Custer in the battle. The interval of sixty years from that battle until I knew him was the same as the time from World War II until today. Pat Cuny was a U.S. Army staff sergeant who fought in World War II, and sixty years later he is still ticking pretty well, except for old age and scars from wounds he carries from that war.

"Isn't that right, Pat? Since you still ride a horse as announcer at all the local rodeos, I guess you are still ticking fairly well"? I asked.

"Yes, I suppose you could say that," Pat responded. "But with two bad knees, I'd need some sort of crane to lift me up to the saddle. Riding a golf cart around the rodeo arena would not go over well on the Indian Reservation."

Over the next dozen years after the Battle of the Little Bighorn, the government floundered as it sought ways to cope with disgruntled Indians, and how to reconcile them to a life on the reservation. In 1887, the U.S. Congress passed the Dawes General Allotment Act. Its stated intention was to entice Indians to move away from a nomadic tribal concept to the private ownership of reservation land. This act was designed to give the head of each Oglala household 160 acres. Any un-allotted land was to be opened for non-Indian homesteaders. A few Indian families, such as the Cuny's, took advantage of it and became landowners. But the Allotment Act was not widely or successfully promoted on the reservation, and few Indians saw possibility in the opportunity afforded by the Act.

Unfortunately with the Dawes Act, the subterfuge of the white man continued. The act permitted a rush by non-Indians to come onto the reservation and establish homesteads, so the end result was that a substantial portion of reservation lands to which the Indian had been herded and squeezed into during the 1860s and 1870s suddenly evaporated in 1890 and became owned by white ranchers. Today, whites own nearly one half of this reservation land, and "these areas are not considered part of the reservation by the federal and state governments. Many Oglala lost their land because they did not understand the concept of land as a commodity that could be bought, sold, and taxed." [50]

The land the Cuny family acquired with the allotment program was on a high plateau surrounded by badlands where few others ventured because of the harsh topography of cliffs and nearly impassable landscape that surrounded it. The plateau became known as "Cuny Table," named for Charles Cuny, Pat's father, and it is still called that today. Here the family maintained their cattle camps. It had fertile soil, but little water.

Pat Cuny was born on Cuny Table in 1922, and at the age of eighty-four he is the lone survivor of Adolph's grandchildren. During World War II, the government moved everyone off Cuny Table and converted it into a bombing range where air force planes could train for combat. It was twenty-five years later before the original residents were allowed to move back. Pat Cuny continues to actively ranch there, along with several of Adolph's great-grandchildren -- a remarkable family dynasty on the Indian reservation that stretches back five generations on Cuny Table.

Times in the aftermath of the Battle of the Little Bighorn remained tense. In Buffalo Gap and along the Cheyenne River well-armed men dealt with the Indian unrest. Stagecoach drivers who pulled into the Buffalo Gap stage station carried shotguns; cowhands wore side arms and carried a rifle in the boot of their saddle. Bill Hudspeth, a reputed gunslinger chased out of Texas by the Texas Rangers, had arrived even before the battle to live on the Pine Ridge Indian Reservation, married an Indian, and began his career as rancher there. Several other early pioneers like Fredrick Heidepriem and Gus Haaser had arrived to establish their presence on the frontier before the time of the Little Bighorn battle. Afterwards, other pioneer friends of ours arrived: Tom and Jim Wilson, General Warren Shedd, William Sewright, Sheriff Riordan, and Deputy Sheriff Gene Griffis. Tom Norman's father arrived with his parents to begin ranching in the Cheyenne River country at the edge of the reservation, and my grandfather arrived a few years later to work in the Cuyahogo Gold Mine near Custer City.

Beginning in 1880, cattle drives from Texas that passed through the Cheyenne River country dominated the local scene. Originally these drives had stopped at railheads down in Abilene, Kansas, for shipment of beeves to eastern markets. As the government became obligated to supply beef to various Indian reservations, the drives continued further north into this wild Dakota Territory. [51] Cattle drovers experienced trouble with settlers whose land they passed over and devastated -- and also with the Indians --whose land they passed through. [52] Roving bands of Indians would ride up to a herd and hold aloft one, two, three or more fingers indicating they wanted that many beeves from the herd before it passed peacefully. Soon they learned, also, to see to it that it wasn't the scrawniest, boniest longhorns that were cut out of the herd for their use. Federal and State authorities stepped in, establishing some order by designating a three-mile wide strip that cattle drives had to stay within. This was known as the National Trail. It extended north through Oklahoma to Ogallala, Nebraska. From there the drives entered the no-man's land of Dakota Territory. These cattle drives normally crossed the Cheyenne River just east of Buffalo Gap and further north, passed through Hermosa in a funnel created by the Black Hills to the west and the Badlands to the east.

Moving large herds encountered many hardships, such as Indian raids, but the hardest was the lack of water. Sometimes distances of fifty -- and even a hundred miles would have to be traversed in hot, dry weather without benefit of water. Often traveling would be done by night for some relief. If traveling against a breeze, a herd might be urged on by the smell of water, which some have claimed cattle could detect as much as forty miles away. But disastrous results might develop if the wind should suddenly veer completely around and the smells of life-giving water reached them from sources they had passed days before. Stampedes would sometimes occur.

It is difficult to estimate the numbers of cattle that came up the trails from Texas during the ten years of cattle drives beginning in 1880 and the impact on the local ranchers which would cut both ways. With Bill Hudspeth ranching near the cattle drive trail and looking to increase his herd, I suspect, knowing him as I did, that he may have occasionally done some nighttime riding. Then also, it was a burden to local ranchers to keep their own herds pastured in fenceless land with large herds on the move, passing nearby.

Gus Haaser was hired by a group of local ranchers to be stationed in Hermosa to review every herd and cut back any cattle he found from local ranches. In the two years of 1888 and 1889 when he worked there, a total of 180,000 cattle passed through the Hermosa station.

Can you imagine the challenge of reviewing the brands on all those cattle, then attempting to cut out any with certain brands?

Mind you, all this was accomplished in an environment where everyone wore side arms and many cowboys were mean-tempered. Gus Haaser was a peculiar and ornery cuss -- and that was a requirement for the job.

Cattle fattened on the northern pasture and ready to be shipped, would be driven to a railhead. Prior to 1886, the nearest would be in Nebraska. Then the railroad was extended north to Buffalo Gap, where shipping occurred from stock pens built alongside the rail siding, and the town's economy surged ahead. The town's gradual decline began a year later when the railroad was extended on to Belle Fourche, which then became the principal cattle shipping point. That same year, a disastrous fire destroyed the post office and other businesses, and several years later, a second fire destroyed most of the rest of the business district. Recovery never occurred. Buffalo Gap, which had hosted thousands, dwindled to a couple hundred struggling souls -- mostly those in support of the nearby ranching community.

But relative quiet suddenly grew angry in 1890 during a two-year period known as the "Indian Uprising of 1890." Several events led to great unrest among the Indians on the reservation. Provisions promised by the U.S. Government were often inadequate. Political appointees assigned as Indian agents were sometimes crooked and others were not competent to handle the complex job of running a reservation. Graft ruled the day, often diverting the resources that had been destined for the Indians. Chief Crazy Horse had already been assassinated. Indian police in the employ of the agency killed Chief Sitting Bull, living on the Standing Rock Indian Reservation in 1890. The Indian people lost hope.

Then, a phenomenon known as the *Ghost Dance*, which was imported from Nevada, became popular on the Pine Ridge Indian Reservation. A revivalist religion, it incorporated some Indian religious traditions from the past, promising the return of the old way of life and the defeat of the white man. It was their belief that the white man would disappear and that with the next greening of the grass, dead relatives and friends would return. Dressed in special shirts, the Indians engaged in a circular dance for days until they became dazed and trance-like. These dances were often held at a place called the "Stronghold," located near the present day ranch of Pat Cuny, adjacent to Cuny Table. The Ghost Dance was a craze with great appeal, and during its short life span it spread havoc and fear throughout the Cheyenne River country and Buffalo Gap environs.

Tom Norman's grandmother lived across the Cheyenne River from the reservation, and often the frightened mother rushed her children at night to lie in a potato patch, hidden under a quilt until daylight hours and safety, as starving Lakota sent warriors off the reservation to find cattle and other foodstuffs on area ranches. During one raid, their house was burned to the ground, and Joe's mother moved with her two children into the town of Hermosa.

As all of these elements built to a crescendo, there came the inevitable clash between Indians and the U.S. Cavalry; who were rumored to be still bitter about their defeat at the Little Bighorn. [53] But I am ahead of myself in relating the story about the *Ghost Dance* and Wounded Knee Massacre. The story of that disaster must wait for a later chapter in the book.

3
THE BISSONETTE / CUNY FAMILY

Family histories can often be lost when parents fail to hand down their stories to later generations. This was particularly true among the Lakota, because Teton was a spoken language and so the absence of documentation was a problem. After the government herded the Lakota onto reservations, they also attempted to rid the Indian of their tribal culture and force them to adopt the new ways of the white; much rich heritage was lost in the process. Children were discouraged from speaking the language of their parents and made to learn English, and religious practices of the Indian were forbidden, while Protestant and Catholic missionaries were brought in to proselytize. Schools with tables and desks were built so Indian children could learn the white man's grammar and arithmetic, and some children were separated from their families and sent to "Indian Schools" in Rapid City and elsewhere, while Indian men were taught how to plow up the land and plant corn.

The Cuny family is legendary on the Pine Ridge Indian Reservation. They go back to the earliest days of the Pine Ridge Agency when Dr, Valentine McGillycuddy was the Indian Agent and Chief Red Cloud was the leader and spokesman for the Oglala Lakota. Even if their Indian reservation experiences were the only story, that in itself would be enough to confer such status on the Cunys. However, that is only the final chapter of a rich family history that had its roots in the wild western lands of North America long before John Hancock affixed his signature to the Declaration of Independence.

Agent Valentine McGillycuddy even built Chief Red Cloud a four-room frame house with a kitchen, so he could move from his tipi and serve as a role model for other Oglala to do the same. The end result of these white-man's initiatives was that the rich Lakota culture and much of their history became lost.

When I asked Pat Cuny about his early family history, he knew that his grandfather, Adolph Cuny, was a Swiss who came in the early days to Wyoming, was killed there, and his grandmother, Josephine (Bissonette) Cuny was an Oglala Indian with possible early roots in Colorado. Another member of the extended Cuny family, Dave Cuny, has become the family historian and had a notebook with scraps of information passed down from his father, Chat Cuny. Dave spent time in the archives at the Wyoming State Capitol in Cheyenne to pursue the family story, but it remained fragmentary. The one vital clue was that the Cuny family had spent time at Fort Laramie.

So I traveled to the Fort Laramie National Site and visited with Sandra Lowry, park librarian and keeper of the historical archives. She showed me her file on the Cuny family and my mouth dropped open. The file was one-and-one-half inches thick. Not only had Cuny ancestors spent time in the region, they were some of the dominating personalities in early Wyoming Territory history. The hills near the fort are named the Cuny Hills. Bissonette and Cuny were "movers and shakers" of that era. Adolph Cuny, his partner, Jules Ecoffey -- who was also his brother-in-law -- and Joseph Bissonette, his father-in-law, were three people who had a major impact on early Wyoming and Colorado development. As a result of the documentation preserved at the Fort Laramie National Site Library, these important records have been saved for us.

French traders were the first white men to go into the Western wilderness and they survived because they traveled in peace. They married Indian women and raised mixed-blood families, which then became their passport to safety. These Frenchmen made alliances with the Indian tribes who became their allies and they established a cooperative relationship with the American agents who ran the Indian agencies. Because they traveled both the red and white roads, they successfully interfaced with the uniformed cavalry forces which came and went. The story of these early French traders and their mix-blood Lakota families is a colorful part of the history of the opening of the West.

1739: THE BISSONETTE ORIGINS

Pat Cuny's ancestors are traced back into the eighteenth century when the region west of the Mississippi River to the Continental Divide belonged to France, the region in the southwest belonged to Spain and the United States of America did not yet exist. That was over a half-century before President Thomas Jefferson negotiated with France for the Louisiana Purchase and the expedition of Lewis and Clark to "discover" the West. Much earlier than this, Pat Cuny's ancestors -- the Bissonette family of French traders with their Indian wives and mixed-blood families -- were living in lands later to be named Kansas, Colorado, Wyoming, and Dakota.

This is from the Fort Laramie documentation by John D McDermott in *Mountain Men*, contained in the Fort Laramie National Site file CIN 17-1:

> *The first Joseph Bissonette to move into the Mississippi valley from Canada was a smith by profession who settled in Kaskaskia. Records mention him as early as 1739. The first Bissonettes to migrate to St. Louis were Louis and Francois, brothers who became dissatisfied with British rule following the French and Indian War. They arrived in 1767, a year after the beginning of the original settlement. Louis had two sons, Louis and Joseph, and it appears that the latter may have been the father of the Fort Platte trader. Both Louis and Joseph became traders of note and worked for the Missouri Fur Company, among others. Joseph apparently retired from the fur trade in about 1820, but Louis remained active until his death in 1836.* [54]

The Joseph referred to was the great-grandfather of Pat Cuny.

One of the chroniclers of this history was Charles E. Hanson, Jr., who wrote this item contained in Ft Laramie File CIN-60:

> *We can safely make the following statement regarding the Bissonette family: They were the first of the French families, later identified with the history of Fort Laramie, who moved west of the Mississippi and lived in Missouri under the Spanish Regime. ...*
>
> *The Luis Visonet (Bissonette) who was granted a license to trade with the Indians by Don Francisco Cruzat on November 28, 1777, was one of the earliest of the French who lived in Missouri to be given this privilege by the Spanish authorities, he being authorized to trade with the Osage Indians.* [55]

In 1764, Rene Auguste Chouteau and Pierre Laclede established a settlement to trade with the Osage Indians that was later named St. Louis. While St. Louis belonged to France, much of the southern territory west of the Mississippi and south of the Arkansas River belonged to Spain. French fur traders commonly traveled up the Arkansas River by canoe to trade with the Indian tribes in Southern Colorado. Other French traders traveled up the Missouri and Platte Rivers to reach the Rocky Mountains and they established the semblance of a trading post alongside the Cache La Poudre River near present-day Ft. Collins. These French trappers married Indian women, raised their mixed-blood children in the Indian culture, spoke the Teton language and remained in the West for a lifetime, except for occasional travel back to St. Louis to sell their pelts and obtain new provisions.

Hanson also wrote the following in Ft Laramie File CIN-60:

> By 1800 some important changes had taken place in the Indian population of the area between the Missouri and North Platte rivers. The Oglala Sioux had crossed the Missouri and reached the Black Hills by about 1776 in a great migration westward from the Minnesota country. The Brul'e Sioux came last, moving up the White River to its headwaters by 1810. In these migrations the southern Teton displaced the Cheyenne, Arapaho, and Crow, who had in turn pushed earlier tribes to the south .... The Teton now had horses and were nomads following the buffalo. [56]

Shortly after the Lakota crossed the Missouri River in 1776 and reached the Black Hills, Pat Cuny's great-grandfather, Joseph Bissonette, began living in the western lands. Further from the Fort Laramie file CIN 17-1 by McDermott :

> Joseph Bissonette was born in St. Louis, Missouri, in 1818. At the age of 18 he headed west to seek his fortune like his ancestors before him. Except for occasional visits to St. Louis to sell furs and buy supplies, Bissonette turned his back on civilization and spent the rest of his life in the Rocky Mountain West. He quickly formed an alliance with the Sioux by marrying into the tribe. His first wife, an Oglala, presented him with seven children, and his second, a Brul'e, bore him twice that number. As the years passed his interests

*became those of the Indians with whom he traded and some-
times lived.'* [57]

While the documentation for support is rather sparse, Joseph Bissonette apparently spent time with the French fur traders on the Cache
La Poudre River where it flowed down from the Rocky Mountains in
present-day Colorado. Here they engaged in trade with the Indians, and
gathered their beaver pelts for transportation back to civilization by canoe down the South Platte River. When the center of French fur trading moved to an establishment further north -- at the confluence of the
Laramie River with the North Platte -- named Fort Platte, Bissonette
moved there and became a trader, guide and interpreter for army forces
entering the area.

This also from the McDermott's Fort Laramie documentation in file
CIN 17-1:

> *By 1842 at the age of 24 he had become one of the princi-
> pal traders for Sybiulle and Adams, the owners of Fort Platte.
> ... It was here that John C Fremont found him and engaged
> his services as a guide and interpreter.* [58]

The first government expedition into the area was led by this explorer, Frem'ont, in 1842. Crossing Wyoming via the South Pass, he tried to
navigate the Platte, and recommended building forts along the Oregon
Trail of the Platte River to protect emigrant travel. What role Bissonette performed in these various expeditions is not known in detail, but
it is documented that he was a guide and interpreter. Of course, by the
time Frem'ont arrived for exploration, Joseph Bissonette and his mixed-
blood family had already been living in the region for many years.

It took ingenuity and grit to survive in the complex and hostile environment of the Frontier West. Further Fort Laramie National Site documentation suggests that Bissonette was adept at working all sides of the
street, and was not above doing whatever was necessary to survive in
the complex world of Indians, Government agents and soldiers. McDermott wrote:

> *Fort Platte traders used liquor extensively in their barter
> with the Northern Plains Indians, and the post soon earned
> a reputation for lawlessness and debauchery. ... Bissonette
> met his second military leader in June 1845, when Colonel
> Stephen Watts Kearney arrived. ... Bissonette interpreted the*

address Kearney delivered to the Sioux gathered near Fort John. He may have choked on a few words, since Kearney warned the Indians against the evils of drinking alcohol (The liquor that Bissonette had sold them). [59]

Bissonette was successful in various ventures. He traded cloth goods, hardware, and staples to the Indians in the winter and sold them to emigrants traveling the Oregon Trail along the Platte River in the spring and summer. He continued to raise, buy, and sell horses. He ferried emigrants across swollen streams in May and June. He farmed on the side -- a few miles above Fort Laramie-- and in 1853, he became a partner in a bridge building venture. Joseph Bissonette also sold liquor to all comers -- including civilians, cavalry troopers and their officers -- and the Indians. In addition to running his enterprises, Bissonette was also a politician, becoming a friend of Thomas Twiss, the new Government Indian agent for the Upper Platte, and was appointed interpreter for the Indian Agency located near Fort Laramie.

As a result of controversy with the cavalry commander, Twiss relocated the agency a hundred miles to the west to the mouth of Deer Creek, and Bissonette followed with his family. There, in addition to his interpreting duties, Joseph Bissonette opened a business at this new location and employing fourteen clerks and teamsters -- and by peddling liquor along with the rest of his merchandise -- he cornered the agency trade.

Engaging in various shady enterprises encountered frequent controversy. The Indians complained they had been swindled out of part of their annuity. The agent Twiss was ordered to investigate and Bissonette was accused of unloading six of seventeen wagons that arrived in August in his own warehouse; the Sioux claimed they had to trade for the goods that were rightfully theirs.

Bissonette declared that none of the goods had been traded; they belonged to the Crows, and he was only holding them until the Crow, he said, could be located (but they never were). His friend, Twiss, found Bissonette innocent. President Abraham Lincoln removed the Agent Twiss from office in 1861 for gross dishonesty, and with his "hole card" gone, the fortunes of Bissonette had reached their zenith and began to decline.

Further from McDermott's Fort Laramie file CIN 17-1:

By 1861 the army established a sub-post at Deer Creek,
which meant that Bissonette could not openly sell liquor to the
Sioux. Then later he lost seventy horses to marauding Sioux
and Arapaho. Bissonette had had enough. His resources de-
pleted and his life endangered, the trader fled with his family
back to Fort Laramie. It soon was apparent that an era had
come to an end. The once mighty fur traders of the Laramie
region were now destitute and humble. The beaver were al-
most gone; the buffalo were disappearing; and the building
of the Union Pacific Railroad marked the end of emigrant
trade along the North Platte. Crowded around Fort Laramie,
the old traders banded together to write the Commissioner of
Indian Affairs for help in the form of a petition. Nothing came
of the proposal. [60]

Moving backward to the time when Joseph Bissonette left St Louis to head into the western wilderness, he did not travel alone. He was married to an Oglala woman named Julia (maiden name is unknown), and they had a daughter born in 1835 named Josephine Bissonette. She was to become the grandmother of my friend, Pat Cuny. Josephine was the oldest of seven children born to Joseph's first wife, who died in 1855. [61] He later married a Brul'e Indian woman, Nellie Plenty Brothers, and he had fourteen children with her. [62]

During the American Civil War, few cavalry troops were assigned to the West, and during their absence the Lakota became a dominating force. Previously, the Indians had been relatively peaceful, but became increasingly hostile by this opportunity as they saw the invasion by white pioneers through their lands. The Bozeman Trail up the Powder River Country through Wyoming into Montana was of particular concern to them. In the mid-1860s, they began a merciless war on encroaching whites that was led by Chief Red Cloud, and it was referred to as the Red Cloud War. A treaty at Fort Laramie terminated this war in 1868, under which the U.S. Government abandoned the Bozeman Trail and the forts built to protect it. Red Cloud became known as the only Indian leader ever to win a war against the United States Army.

During these Civil War years of hostility with the Lakota, Bissonette's first wife, Julia, died, and he began a quiet life with a new family. Finally in 1868, Joseph Bissonette was to have one more opportunity

-- and it probably came about because he was now married to his second wife, a Brul'e, and living in their community of tipis near Fort Laramie.

This from the Fort Laramie documentation:

> *The Peace Commission that was established at the end of the Red Cloud War to negotiate a treaty with the Sioux, appointed Bissonette as a special interpreter for the Brul'es. After Spotted Tail and his followers signed the treaty at Fort Laramie, Bissonette received an appointment to act as an interpreter and accompany the Brul'es to their new home on Whetstone Creek, a tributary of the Missouri. He continued to live with the Brul'es, following them to northwestern Nebraska in 1871 when the agency changed location. He held a number of positions at the agency, including those of sub-agent and assistant farmer.*
>
> *Bissonette became one of the principal advisors to the leaders of the reservation Sioux. In 1875 he went to Washington with Red Cloud and Spotted Tail as an interpreter. Near the end of the decade, Bissonette moved to Pine Ridge Agency and finally settled on Wounded Knee Creek. He farmed a little, but government rations were his primary means of support. To the very end he continued to agitate for the payment of Indian claims filed years before. Joseph Bissonette died of natural causes in August 1894,* said McDermott. [63]

During his 76 years, Joseph Bissonette saw first-hand much of the opening of the West. He was a trapper, trader, explorer, interpreter, entrepreneur, builder, opportunist, scoundrel -- and apparently a fine family man -- who helped two wives raise a total of 21 children of mixed-blood French and Lakota ancestry. As previously mentioned, the oldest of his children was Josephine (Bissonette) Cuny, Pat Cuny's grandmother.

Let us follow his trail of genes into the Cuny family that was to follow.

1835-1877: THE JOSEPHINE AND ADOLPH CUNY STORY

When I first met Grandmother Josephine (Bissonette) Cuny, she was already one hundred years of age. That was in 1935 -- a year before her death at the age of 101. She was a wrinkled-up old lady, but even then I could see the facial structure of what must have been a gorgeous Oglala Lakota maiden in her youth. I could personally relate to those ancestral beauty genes, because her great-granddaughters, Norma and Evelyn Cuny, were classmates of mine in Buffalo Gap. I was sweet on Norma, but she carried a haughty, aristocratic attitude that indicated she had little use for anyone in only the seventh grade. No doubt, Norma's great-grandmother as a girl displayed those same traits around the Lakota warriors, French traders, and cavalry troopers who lived at Fort Laramie.

At a hundred years of age, this lady had seen a century that transitioned from her life in a French fur trader's family in the unexplored American West to life on an Oglala Indian Reservation and then to driving an auto to Buffalo Gap to shop. When her father, Joseph Bissonette, left St Louis in 1835 to head into the western wilderness, he did not travel alone. His passport for safe passage through Indian lands was Julia -- his Indian wife -- and she carried a papoose strapped to her back named Josephine Bissonette. It is not documented how they traveled, or where they initially went, but since he was a fur trapper they no doubt traveled in a canoe laden with beaver-trapping supplies, provisions, trinkets and liquor for trade with the Indians.

Julia was more than her husband's interpreter and ambassador; she was also his handmaiden. More than a pretty face and bed partner, Indian wives were helpers who performed a majority of the family work, while the man engaged in his enterprise. And the children followed suit. At an early age the little girl, Josephine, would have assisted her mother in skinning the beaver pelts and tying them to frames for drying. They may have lived in a tipi, but more likely it was some sort of lean-to tent that could be transported in a canoe as the family moved from place to place.

Even though where they went is unknown, there were only two major routes available to carry them to the eastern slopes of the Rocky Mountains where beaver were found. One was up the Arkansas River, through miles of desert prairie land to the region near present-day Pueblo and Colorado Springs, through lands that belonged to Spain. Permission from Spanish authorities was necessary to insure a safe journey. The other route was up the Missouri River into the Platte River and its tributaries. Traveling further west on the North Platte River would carry one past the region where Fort Laramie was later established. Voyaging southwest on the South Platte River would take one to the region near present-day Fort Collins. A tributary here was named *Cache La Poudre* by some Frenchmen who established the semblance of a trading post there. Bissonette may have opted for the Cache La Poudre area -- which is where Josephine found her childhood home -- because many years later when fleeing endangerment, that is where she initially headed.

Josephine's father was not just a simple trapper. He had considerable grit, intelligence, ambition, and was an opportunist, exploiting every opportunity to further his cause. By the time Josephine was six and he was twenty-four, he had become *"one of the principal traders for Sybiulle and Adams, the owners of Fort Platte. ... It was here that John Charles Fremont found him and engaged his services as a guide and interpreter,"* said McDermott. [64]

Josephine, a beautiful girl of mixed Oglala and French blood, was no doubt a prime catch for any newly arriving young Frenchman destined for a life in the wilds of Wyoming.

Let us now turn from Josephine to the story of Adolph Cuny:

When and how Adolph Cuny arrived in North America has not been documented. Family history notes maintained by Dave Cuny suggest that he traveled across Canada. We know he was Swiss, however, and can speculate about some events, because he may have arrived with the Ecoffey brothers who arrived at New Orleans in 1854 from Switzerland. Jules Ecoffey and his brother, Frank, had been educated at the University of Freiburg in western Switzerland, in the region of Lake Geneva. This area had been conquered by Napoleon and became French and Catholic. Even though Napoleon was later defeated, the area remained with a French culture and the language spoken was French, and is essentially still that today. So while the Ecoffey brothers and Adolph Cuny called themselves *Swiss*, they were really of the French culture and language, and passed among the Indian tribes as Frenchmen, who were welcomed everywhere as friends.

Adolph Cuny, the son of Heinrich (Cuoni) Cuny, was born in Switzerland, during an era when this region was essentially French, and he lived in this culture and spoke French. In the southern European tradition, the oldest son would inherit his father's estate; the second son would be sent to the seminary to become a priest, and the other sons were left to fend for themselves in the outside world. Adolph was the youngest of a family of eleven children. As soon as he reached the age of sixteen, he left home to seek a new life in America, arriving on a boat -- either in New Orleans or in Quebec -- with other Frenchmen, and then joined the company of French fur traders traveling into the wilderness lands west of the Mississippi sometime before 1860. Actually, some of this is speculation, because little documentation exists for the early days of Adolph Cuny.

However his name is listed in 1857 as one of the early inhabitants of Denver.

Some documentation exists in the files at the Fort Laramie National Site library to suggest Adolph Cuny initially lived in the region of Colorado. This was an era of gold-seekers, as gold had been discovered earlier in Montana and then in 1859 in Colorado.

Here are two documents that relate to Adolph Cuny's ventures in Colorado. This from the Fort Laramie file CIN 17-23x:

> *It is reported that in the early days Cuny and Jules ran a stage line from Julesburg (Colorado) on the Union Pacific to Virginia City, Montana Territory. They built several stage stations of sod which they later sold.* [65]

The following from the Fort Laramie file CIN 17-28 is a hand-written letter of Batiste (Baptiste) Gene Pourier, and some portions of the letter are difficult to read, as it contains numerous mis-spellings. One interpretation of the letter would suggest that Cuny was one of the 35 Frenchmen who were building the original town of Denver in 1857.

> *John Richards made his fourth trip to St Louis in 1859. John and the 35 French men were building Denver on the so called Cherry Creek. My Gr. and father build [sic] his first house the same place, stores, blacksmith shop, saloons, (?) houses; so John Richard Sr is the first man to build a house in Denver in 1857. His Partners, also Jre Bisnett, Joe Farnie, Nick Janis, Jule Ecoffee, Adolph Cuny, Dave Rich (??) Don't know the right way to spell their names.* [66]

When Adolph Cuny arrived in the vicinity of Fort Laramie in about 1860, Josephine Bissonette was living with her family a hundred miles west of Fort Laramie at the Indian Agency located on Deer Creek in an

Indian tipi village. Her Oglala mother, Julia, died when she was twenty. Her father lost his job as interpreter when President Lincoln fired the Indian Agent, R.S. Twiss. Joseph's resources gradually dwindled, and in 1864 he returned to the Indian village in the vicinity of Fort Laramie with his children. Josephine was now in her twenties, and as the oldest of seven children with the mother gone, she was busy as surrogate mother. Her father, Joseph Bissonette, once one of the most prominent civilians at Fort Laramie saw his fortunes were now in decline.

When Josephine was still in her mid-twenties she met the young French trader, Adolph Cuny, who was an acquaintance of her father. Cuny was tall and handsome, and she was a rare beauty. They immediately fell in love. He was Catholic, and they were married in 1861 by a Jesuit priest who traveled through the area. Adolph immediately became a member of the Oglala tribe, adopted their culture, and spoke the Teton language in their home. Their mixed-bloodline is not unlike many other reservation Indian families, and a Lakota with a pure Indian bloodline is a rarity today. (Even the second wife of Crazy Horse, Nellie Larrabee, was a woman of mixed-blood.) [67]

After Adolph Cuny married Josephine, they probably lived among the Indian population that surrounded the army post. Since Josephine was busy during their life together having babies and raising a family, it is unlikely that she inter-related much in his various business activities, and scarcely knew what he did for a living. This lack of business knowledge was to haunt her later after Adolph was killed at an early age, leaving her with a large family, an extensive business establishment, and unable to cope with a complex pioneer business environment.

Adolph was already a successful businessman when he and Josephine were married and one of the most prosperous in the area. Fort Laramie was on the stagecoach lines, and so Adolph Cuny and his partner, Jules Ecoffey, built business establishments nearby to service civilians and off-duty troopers. These included a general store, blacksmith shop, billiard hall and corral. His activities at Fort Laramie are well documented by the author Agnes Wright Spring in her acclaimed book about that era.

When business became slack in 1874, they decided to add new attractions and for that purpose constructed eight two-room cottages to be occupied by women. They sent to Omaha

*and Kansas City and other places and in a short time had
their houses occupied by ten or more young women, all of
whom were known as sporting characters. Among this bunch
was Calamity Jane.* [68]

So it seems possible that it was Adolph Cuny who introduced Calamity Jane to the Western frontier.

To do an accurate description and full justice to the life of Adolph Cuny at Fort Laramie is difficult. He was certainly one of the most prominent men of that era at the fort. One could probably describe him as gritty, brilliant, industrious, aggressive, shady, a scoundrel, opportunist, and perhaps none of those descriptions are completely accurate because, like Bissonette, he seemed to work all angles. Perhaps it is best to review more of the documentation that has been preserved at the Fort Laramie, and then one can decide what description to assign to him.

Cuny was a big rancher, and apparently his herd had been obtained in Texas and driven up to his ranch near Fort Laramie. Here is an entry from the *Annals of Wyoming* which contained portions of a letter by Denman, Supt. Indian Affairs, dated August 8, 1868 in which he was asking for approval of some vouchers and included a summary of the cattle owned by various ranchers.

"Adolph Cuny, North Platte 1000 head of Stock Cattle." [69]

During the American Civil War, the Lakota became increasingly bold, since few cavalry troops were assigned to western forts. The Lakota had always been resentful of the invasion of their lands by white men, but could do little about it because they were scattered tribes, often with ineffective leadership. The Bozeman Trail had been a route of white settlers and cattle herds up through central Wyoming along the Powder River into Montana, before Red Cloud became a strong leader of his people. With the cavalry now undermanned, Red Cloud led his warriors in open hostility in a determined effort to close the Bozeman Trail, and as stated earlier, he was successful, and the government agreed in 1868 to shut down this route. In the Fort Laramie treaty of that same year, the Indians allegedly agreed to some terms involving ownership of Indian lands and reservations that remain in legal conflict to this day. The issues are too complex and extensive to explore in this discussion. The following are portions of a letter contained in Fort Laramie file CIN 17-7x *Upper Platte River Letters* to "Chas. E. Mix, Commissioner of

Indian Affairs, dated Omaha, June 4th 1868, and signed by Brig Gen. Wm. S. Harney, President pro tem Indian Peace Commission (at the conclusion of the Red Cloud War)."

> *I have the honor to report that on the 25th of May we con-cluded a treaty of peace with the Ogallala [sic] Sioux. Thirty six of their chiefs and leading Warriors signed the treaty. ...We therefore now believe that quiet and peace is secured on the plains. ... It was determined by the commission that to maintain peace, and preserve and civilize the Indians, it was necessary that all the charities of the government should be dispensed, and all its efforts to civilize these Indians made at a point as far removed as possible from the great lines of land travel across the plains. ... Our treaty with the Sioux des-ignates the country between the Northern line of Nebraska and the forty sixth parallel and the Missouri River and the one hundred and fourth Meridian as the ultimate home of the Indians of that nation. ... Adolph Cuny was placed in charge of transportation, to move Indians to the Missouri River, with authority to use five large ox teams to each one hundred per-sons moved, with the understanding that the compensation would be made by the government at the rate of ten dollars per day for each wagon and thirty days allowed to make the trip.*
>
> *... The Ogallala [sic] [70] Chiefs who signed the treaty ex-pressed an earnest desire that the absent chiefs and warriors should have an opportunity to sign also. I accordingly left a copy of the treaty with General Slemmer, commanding Fort Laramie. ... [71]*

A follow-up letter to Adolph Cuny with additional authorization for moving the Indians, dated May 27, 1868:

> *Transportation for the Half Breeds and Indians about to move to the Missouri River has been approved. Ten wagons for this purpose have been engaged of Mr. Bordeau, and five from Mr. Bissonette. ...*

This is a letter from John Sanborn, President pro tem of the Peace Commission to Mr.James Bordeau, dated May 27, 1868.

> *Sir: The white men of this country legally incorporated*

with the Indians and quite a large number of the Ogallala [sic] and Brul'e Indians are about to remove to the Missouri River. ... Mr. Adolph Cuny has been placed in charge of transportation, and you are hereby placed in charge of all subsistence. Thirty five days rations for all persons will be taken. You will obtain the supply from the special Indian agent so far as he may have supplies and the balance will be obtained, if possible, from the Commissary of subsistence at that post. ... Sefroy Jott and Joseph Bissonette have been appointed interpreters, and will aid you in the discharge of your duties. Respectfully yours,

John Sanborn, Pres. Pro. Tem. Peace Commission. [72]

A couple months later, apparently after transportation of the Indians had been completed, the following letter from H. B. Denman, Supt. Ind. Affairs to the Commissioner of Indian Affairs in Washington, dated August 8, 1868, asked for approval of the following vouchers:

Sir: I have the honor to transmit herewith papers pertaining to accounts of the late Special Agent, Chamblin, (etc) To W.H.Brown, for $680 for feeding the Chiefs of the different tribes, to John Finn for $7317 for beef furnished the Indians, and $2046.80 to Adolph Cuny for presents purchased for the Indians. [73]

I wonder what presents purchased for the Indians by Cuny were? (Perhaps liquor supplied by his father-in-law Joseph Bissonette?)

The economic conditions in the Wyoming area took a definite downturn during the Civil War and the Red Cloud War that followed. Frenchmen with their mixed-blood Lakota families came into hard times. Beaver were diminishing, buffalo had mostly been slaughtered by whites, military forces were reduced to a scant few, and the new railroad through the territory reduced travel of emigrants along the Oregon Trail to a minimum. Therefore, much of the economic base for these early mixed-blood families had evaporated, and this is reflected in the following portions of a petition dated November 16, 1867 to the Congress of the United States:

The undersigned petitioners respectfully represent that they are residents of Dakota Territory in the vicinity of Fort Laramie and are each and all heads or members of Indian families, that they have resided in said Country many years, and came to it originally under the auspices of the old North-western Fur Company and for many years depended solely upon said Company for support, (etc) ... That the construc-tion of the Rail Road across the Plains has so changed busi-ness and travel that all ostensible means of support along the North Platte are destroyed, that they are anxious to locate with their families upon some good agricultural land in the Indian Country and commence farming. ... [74]

They then indicated the land they desired the government to convey them ownership of. This petition was signed by seventy three persons, which included:

Adolph Cuny, Jules Ecoffey, Frank Ecoffey, Alfred Ecof-fey, J. Bissonette, & R.S. Twiss (the Government Agent fired by President Lincoln)

This petition was ignored in Washington.

A noted chronicler of that frontier era was Charles W. Allen whose memoirs are contained in the book, *From Fort Laramie to Wounded Knee.* Allen's early employment was for the Cuny and Ecoffey Freight-ing and Contracting Company at Fort Laramie. He wrote extensively about the company, but in his autobiography did not feel it was neces-sary to mention the brothel at the ranch headquarters.

It was at this time that Allen met Cuny's young niece, Emma Hawkins. She was the daughter of Susan Lunan, a mixed-blood Lakota woman, and Henry Hawkins, a Fort Laramie trader. Charles Allen and Emma were wed in 1873. ... He made a defense of mixed-blood unions and especially the character of white men who married Indian women. It is apparent Charles carried resentment for having been called a "squaw man." [75]

The couple was married for over fifty years and had twelve chil-dren.

The company of Ecoffey and Cuny apparently engaged in many moneymaking activities in support of Fort Laramie. Here is a notation in the Fort medical record book for the month of August 1872:

Hobbs expects to complete the foundation in about two weeks. The contracts for lime and stone have been let to Ecof-

*fey and Cuny, 2000 bus. Lime at 72 ½ cents per bushel, and
200 perches stone at $2.82 ½ delivered on the spot.* [76]

The following account is by John D. McDermott, National Park,
as quoted in the *Annals of Wyoming*:

*Three Mile Ranch, by John D. McDermott, National
Park.*

*Early in 1872, Adolph Cuny and Jules Ecoffey constructed
a number of buildings just beyond the borders of the military
reservation on the bank of the Laramie River. In the beginning, the proprietors apparently planned a simple facility for
travelers, but in a few years they decided to add some feminine attractions. Importing women from Omaha and Kansas
City, Cuny and Ecoffey catered to soldiers from Fort Laramie
who sought companionship and escape from the doldrums of
garrison life. Soon the Three Mile Ranch received the oppro-
brious title of "Hog Ranch". ...*

*According to John Hunton, in its heyday the Hog Ranch
consisted of a concrete dwelling, storehouse, bunkhouse, ice
house, six cottages of two rooms each, and a sod corral one
hundred feet square and twelve feet high ...*

*... Lt John G. Bourke visited the Hog Ranch in January
1877, and said he did not think much of its inhabitants:*

*"Three miles from Fort Laramie there was a nest of ranch-
es, Cuny and Ecoffey's and Wright's tenanted by as hardened
and depraved a set of witches as could be found on the face
of the globe. Each of these establishments was equipped with
a rum-mill of the worst kind and each contained from three
to half a dozen Cyprians, virgins whose lamps were always
burning brightly in expectancy of the coming of the bride-
groom, and who lured to destruction the soldiers of the garrison. In all my experience I have never seen a lower, more
beastly set of people of both sexes." ...*

*... According to one author, however," the meals were
good and could be purchased for fifty cents."* [77]

Placing these events at Fort Laramie in a historical perspective, it
was at this time in 1874 that the Custer expedition discovered gold in
the Black Hills and sent scout Charlie Reynolds traveling overland to

Fort Laramie as the telegraph line now reached to Fort Laramie.

Chronicler John Hunton maintained a diary during the Fort Laramie years that is often quoted, and the following is from his diary.

> On the north side of the Fort Laramie, almost directly op-
> posite the old well, is the later site of the Three Mile, now part
> of the John Yoder ranch ... According to John Hunton, the
> structure was built in 1874 by Ecoffey and Cuny. Mr. Hunton
> recalls that these gentlemen found business slowing down at
> the trading post, saloon and road ranch that summer and de-
> cided to add new attractions. They built several such cottages
> and recruited ten or more broad-minded young women from
> Omaha and Kansas City to make headquarters there. Among
> them was the fabled Calamity Jane. [78]

Further, on page 111, speaking about Calamity Jane:

> I am not sure when I first saw her, but I think it was in
> 1875, about the time Col. [Richard Irving] Dodge was get-
> ting ready to go to Jenny's stockade ... She went out with the
> Dodge expedition in 1875 (dressed as a man) and remained
> with them until detected when she was ordered to remain with
> the wagon train until it returned to Fort Laramie ... She then
> resumed her old life at the Cuny and Ecoffey ranch and other
> places of similar character at Fort Laramie and Fort Fetter-
> man.

Everyone, it seems, wanted to write about the Fort Laramie Hog Ranches. Here is another article written at the time by J.W. Vaughn:

CIN-17-23x <u>The Fort Laramie Hog Ranches</u>, by J.W.Vaughn

> ... Ecoffey and Cuny, as the partnership was known, had
> been engaged in many enterprises. Both men were married
> to Indian women. This was probably the reason these men
> were able to engage in business in this area when others were
> forced to leave. Cuny was described as a pretty tough char-
> acter who, with his partner, had been implicated in several
> shady pieces of business ... It is reported that in the early
> days, Cuny and Jules [Ecoffey] ran a stage line from Jules-
> burg on the Union Pacific to Virginia City, Montana Terri-
> tory. They built several stage stations of sod which they later
> sold. Frank Ecoffey was employed at Fort Laramie as clerk

for the interpreter, Bissonette, while Jules was a trader with the Sioux about the post. When Red Cloud Agency was established, Jules was appointed agency trader and was a collaborator with Red Cloud, the Oglala Sioux chief. In 1873, he had trouble with the Indians over a half-gallon of whiskey which he later claimed for his own use. As Red Cloud was absent at the time, Jules was dislodged from the agency and his trader's license was revoked. … In the fall of 1871, Ecoffey and Cuny moved their herd of about 600 cattle from Deer Creek. … Several years later the cattle were sold and it is possible that the proceeds were used to erect the new buildings at the new Three Mile Ranch … Cuny was buried in the citizens' cemetery at Fort Laramie. Although only forty-two years old, he was said at the time to be one of the oldest pioneers in Wyoming. [79]

The following are a series of letters that relate an incident at the Ecoffey and Cuny establishment in which a riot occurred by cavalry troopers. The first is a portion of a letter to the U.S.A. Adjutant General by Lt. Col. Litchfield, and forwarded on by Brig. General William J. Palmer:

Sir: An occurrence took place near here … some twelve or fourteen men of the command received passes to be absent from the Post for the Day and the greater part of them went to a ranch some five miles below kept by Jules Ecoffey and Adolph Cuny … A soldier was shot and killed by a civilian … An officer was sent to investigate, and he sent a party consisting of three noncommissioned officers and about twenty men in pursuit. The party arrested a man and while on their return, the ranch where the murder was committed was entered by the returning party, shamefully pillaged, and then burned … All members of the party were placed in confinement awaiting a General Court Martial now in session … It may not be out of the way here to state that the ranch where the murder was committed was a vile den, the resort of the worse characters in the country. It was a grog shop, faro bank, and billiard saloon. [80]

Then the following was a news account that appeared in the Rocky

Mountain News newspaper on July 12, 1867 about the riot:

> *Without any preliminaries I would say that five miles below Fort Laramie is situated the ranch of Ecoffey & Cuny, which is general headquarters of citizens in that country; in fact it being the only place where traveler or resident can obtain any accommodation, outside scanty provision that one may be able to obtain of the military authorities of the post. Here on the morning of the Forth of July congregated some twenty or thirty soldiers ... All was quiet until dinner was announced, when soldiers made a rush for the dining room, and while dinner was progressing they (the soldiers) commenced a series of abuses in which pistols were drawn and a good deal of loud talk. Soon a general stampede was made into the store of Ecoffey & Cuny, and demands made for more whiskey, which was refused ... The soldiers then drew their revolvers and commenced to climb the counter, pistols in hand. Here a general disturbance commenced, in which firearms were freely used by both parties. The soldiers were finally worsted and driven from the house, with one of their number killed and several soldiers and citizens wounded. The soldiers made a hasty retreat to the post and told their exaggerated story, whereupon a detachment of eighty men under command of a Lieutenant were ordered to the place of disturbance. When they arrived they proceeded to arrest some nine or ten citizens, who were stopping there and employees of the firm. They also arrested Mr. Cuny, one of the proprietors of the ranch. It might be well to state that Messrs. Ecoffey and Cuny are one of the most responsible firms west of the Missouri River, and are government contractors to the amount of one half million dollars.* [81]

Here is another account of the foray by a soldier, Second Cavalry:

> *... As far as the description of Messrs. Ecoffey and Cuny being responsible citizens, I do not doubt the truth of the statement, but there is another ranch close belonging also to Messrs. Ecoffey and Cuny, but rented by one Lowe. This was a billiard saloon, grog shop, monte and faro bank. This saloon -- this saloon -- the proprietor being a professional gam-*

bler -- was the resort of all the gamblers, horse thieves, and cut throats in the territory, where a man's life was not safe if he were known to be possessor of fifty dollars, and where to my own knowledge six or seven atrocious murders have been committed since last December. ... [82]

The following are portions of letter from the Fort Laramie commanding officer:

The commanding officer directs that until further orders you station a picket guard of one noncom. Officer and three privates at the East end of the bridge over the Laramie River ... He will inspect all wagons and arrest and send to the provost marshal's office all persons who may be deemed suspicious or attempt to introduce liquors into the Post with their wagons. ... [83]

These were perilous times in central Wyoming along the Platte River forts. In June, 1876, General Crook left Fort Kearney heading north to help intercept an Indian force encamped on the Little Bighorn River. Crook was the southern flank of the army force to surround a large Indian encampment on the Little Bighorn River, with forces under General Terry and Colonel Gibbons coming down from the north to surround the hostiles and force them peacefully to disband and return to their reservations. Before General George W. Crook got there, however, his force was soundly defeated in a battle under Chief Crazy Horse at the Rosebud River, several hundred miles north of Fort Laramie. Crook's forces retreated in disarray, then on June 26, 1876, the Battle of the Little Bighorn occurred in which General George Custer and his cavalry forces were wiped out. As the Indian tribes scattered in all directions after the battle, it was a dangerous time to be traveling in Wyoming or Dakota. Nearly all the stagecoach stations on the Cheyenne-to-Deadwood route were torched by Indians and burnt to the ground. During this turbulent era, apparently Cuny continued to provide freight services to the army, for here are portions of a letter from the Post Quartermaster dated February 1, 1877 concerning the trip of Cuny to carry provisions to the small cavalry camp [Camp Collier] at the mouth of Red Canyon near present-day Edgemont, South Dakota:

Sir: The commanding Officer directs me to inform you that Adolph Cuny's train to Red Canon turned over to the

*A.A.W.M. at that camp ten (10) sack of grain short, and that
this shortage occurred by feeding the grain to the train animals. The price of the grain should be deducted from the
freighters pay.* [84]

A month later a letter dated March 24th, 1877, was sent to Mr. Cuny,
Deputy Sheriff Laramie Co. by the Post Adjutant. Cuny now carried the
title of Deputy Sheriff:

*Sir: The Commanding officer directs me to inform you that
there are two citizens in the post guard house charged with
horse stealing. They were turned over by a citizen who said
they were caught in the act. These prisoners will be released
today unless you receive them. The citizen who brought them
here said you would receive them yesterday.* [85]

Cuny was now operating his business alone, since his partner, Ecof-
fey, was killed a few months before. Here is a mention of the death of
Jules Ecoffey by Agnes Wright Spring in *The Cheyenne and Black Hills
Stage and Express Routes*:

*Jules Ecoffey died on November 26, 1876 as a result of
injuries inflicted by a man named Stonewall, who had attacked him some three months previous. His funeral was held
at Dyer's hotel in Cheyenne, and burial was in the Cheyenne
Cemetery.* [86]

And here is a brief notation in the *John Hunton Diary* concerning
Cuny's trip to Cheyenne to bury his friend:

*November 27, 1876: Cuny stayed at Maxwell's last night
on the way to Cheyenne with the remains of Jules Ecoffey.
Nice day, a little cold.* [87]

The period after the Battle of the Little Bighorn meant uncertain
times in Wyoming, and Cuny lived in that danger. He was hauling
freight to cavalry camps along the Cheyenne River at the edge of the
Black Hills through two hundred miles of Indian infested country, in
addition to running his business at Three Mile and wearing the badge of
the Sheriff of Albany County.

The hazardous life caught up to him, too, and is reflected in the following account by Hunton:

Adolph Cuny, 42, was killed on July 22, 1877 by Clark

Pelton, Alias Billy Webster, a road agent. Cuny was buried in the citizen's cemetery at Fort Laramie. He was said, at the time, to be one of the oldest pioneers in Wyoming. Cuny was shot when he was deputized by the Sheriff of the adjacent Platte County to assist in the arrest of a gang of road agents that included Pelton. … "Kid" Pelton was tried for killing Cuny, and found guilty of manslaughter and sentenced to from one to four years' incarceration. [88]

The time and place of death certainly makes a difference in funeral and cemetery arrangements. After his partner, Jules Ecoffey, died, Cuny took his body to Cheyenne for a funeral and burial and had a tombstone placed over the grave. Adolph Cuny died eight months later, and was buried in an unmarked grave at Fort Laramie.

And still another brief account found in the Fort Laramie files was written in 1934 by someone named Ed Kelley, who is passing on memories fifty-seven years later about Fort Laramie:

The next place we stopped was three miles southwest of Fort Laramie where the old saloon and dance hall are still standing. It was a lively place in the early days, and over the door of the old saloon is printed "Pay today and Trust tomorrow." This place was located by Cooney [sic] and Coffey [sic] about 1865. … A man called Posey Ran bought the log building and moved it up the river where he located his ranch. Coffey died about 1874 and Cooney, who became a deputy sheriff, was killed at Six Mile a little later. … Charles Charleton married Cooney's widow and thus became owner of the place. About 1877 he sold it to Charlie Owens who used to run a livery stable in Cheyenne. In 1880, Owens sold it to Henry Ritchling who owned it for about 35 years, selling to C.A Guernsey, who a few years ago sold to A.J. Glade. [89]

(Author's note: Personally I don't know what to make of the above memory that was passed along so many years later by someone concerning the marriage of Cuny's widow, but I am inclined to discount it for several reasons: the account sounds fuzzy and does not match other historical facts concerning the later owners, and the family has no knowledge of any second marriage by their grandmother.

Adolph Cuny's son, Charles, was born in 1862 and was fourteen-years-old when his father was killed; he was the oldest of eight children, and a set of twins were only one-year-old. The previous notation claiming that Adolph's widow remarried after his death is probably untrue, but it does underscore the peril she found herself in. She was suddenly in charge of a complex business that she knew nothing about and was unprepared to run.)

Before we live through Josephine Cuny's epic journey to find safety for her family, we will take a look at the hostile environment she faced while living in the shadow of a cavalry fort where Indians had become "persona non grata."

JUNE 25, 1876: THE BATTLE OF THE LITTLE BIGHORN

When my boyhood Lakota playmate, George No Water, and I ventured into the cavalry encampment behind the schoolhouse in Buffalo Gap the summer of 1936, George represented the enemy in the Battle of the Little Bighorn. His grandfather was a warrior sixty years before in that very battle. [90]

While some people think of that event as ancient history, it was still contemporary for us in Buffalo Gap. I knew a half-dozen elderly Sioux who were teenage warriors when the cavalry charged into their village on that fateful day.

It is one of the most analyzed battles in American history, perhaps right up there with Gettysburg and the Alamo, and has been the subject of many books and a Hollywood movie. It occurred just prior to the anticipated Centennial Celebration of the United States scheduled for a week later in July, 1876. When the news reached the public that the popular hero, General Custer, was wiped out together with all the men in his regiments, it was a national shock similar to that of our modern day 9/11 Twin Tower Disaster.

A detailed story of the battle is beyond the scope of this book, and it is mentioned here only to portray in its aftermath the impact on the Cuny family.

The frontier became a hostile environment for any Indian not already on a reservation. When Adolph Cuny was killed by a road agent shortly after the battle, Josephine Cuny found herself and her eight small children in grave danger. She was an Indian, and they were now the enemy of the U.S. Cavalry.

1877: THE JOSEPHINE CUNY FAMILY STORY OF SURVIVAL

As mentioned earlier, Josephine was the wife of Adolph Cuny, a white man who was one of the most powerful men on the western frontier, and as owner of the largest civilian establishment at Fort Laramie, he had access to the commanding officer, who frequently sought his counsel, held civil power with the title of Deputy Sheriff, and often dined at the officer's mess with Josephine at his side.

Then he was killed.

In that instant, Josephine became nothing: -- *worse* than nothing. She was a Lakota Indian, and at Fort Laramie they were now the hated. All Lakota were ordered to go immediately to the reservation in the Dakota Territory; Josephine was no exception. We can only imagine the state of confusion, anguish, and fear Josephine Cuny found herself in: her beloved husband -- a lawman – was murdered by one of the many brigands in the area, where more enemies lurked like vultures. Little time for grief by a new widow!

The Cuny business establishments meant nothing now; they were only stone buildings. Former white friends evaporated, never to reappear. Cavalry officers hated all Indians more than ever. Yes, Josephine was alone with eight small children -- the oldest barely a teenager -- and a set of twins less than a year old.

Go to the Indian reservation! Why? How?

The three hundred miles from Fort Laramie to Pine Ridge were some of the most hostile on the frontier. Roving bands of renegade Oglala, Brul'e, Blackfoot, Cheyenne, were in turmoil and being pursued by cavalry who shot on sight.

Josephine put her family in a wagon -- her only tangible resource. A herd of horses driven by her young sons and daughters -- headed south into Colorado to the safety of Cache La Poudre, where she had been raised amongst Frenchmen. When she got there, she was in even greater peril than on the Wyoming frontier, as the Frenchmen were long gone. Colorado had since become a state and their first order of business was to rid themselves of all Indian populations. Most tribes were in the process of being herded with the help of U.S. Cavalry down into Oklahoma Territory. Josephine soon found she was not welcome to remain in Colorado and would be made part of that movement if she stayed. So she fled north again, realizing her only alternative was life on the Pine Ridge Indian Reservation, where her Oglala people were destined.

This gritty lady was resolved to survive and would do what was necessary to do so. Lessons she learned from her father and mother in a canoe along the South Platte River and from her husband along the North Platte River, helped her determine she would fight any enemy and persevere -- not only for herself -- but for her Oglala family.

Turbulent times rolled throughout the frontier; particularly for Indians. Cavalry troops were mean-tempered and would not hesitate to attack and kill anyone they identified as hostile. The hundreds of covered wagons continuing to travel along the Platte River to California were now even more frequently under attack by Indians. Stagecoaches brought hundreds of gold-seekers and settlers north into the Black Hills, where road agents and renegade Indian bands preyed on them. Everyone on the frontier was heavily armed and ready to fight.

Josephine headed north with a wagon that required a roadbed, so she must follow the trail established by the stagecoach companies from Cheyenne to the Black Hills. We can imagine her thoughts as she passed the Six Mile Station where her husband had been killed only weeks before, and as she proceeded farther north, she also passed the Three Mile Station that had once belonged to them -- perhaps the stone buildings still belonged to her. In the darkness of early morning, Josephine drove beyond Fort Laramie before reveille would awaken the cavalry. Continuing on, she recognized those stagecoach stations she knew by heart. Formerly run by friends of hers, now most were abandoned or set afire by roaming bands of hostile Indians. [91]

Josephine crossed the Platte River, heading north along the familiar stagecoach route, over undulating hills and prairies to the Ten Mile Station. Old Woman's Fork was perilous, according to General Dodge in 1875, "No where do the rains cut more deeply. ... There the beds of most of the streams are quagmires, or the most tenacious quicksand. Banks are to be cut down, narrow strip ridges to be leveled off." [92]

Josephine and her party crossed safely.

Then next came Raw Hide Buttes -- a stage station that the Sioux had burned to the ground. No Indians were welcome there. It was a long distance of many miles to the next station on the Niobrara River near present-day Lusk, Wyoming – a place called Running Water. A few miles further north, the trails divided and the tiny Cuny expedition followed the one heading east that would pass along the southern edge of the Black Hills. The stage station called Hat Creek, like the others, had also been burned in raids by renegade Indian bands. Located in one of the most desolate regions of the frontier, Hat Creek was surrounded by an endless terrain of bluffs and broken country called "The Breakers." Stagecoach holdups were commonplace. Desperadoes and roving Indian bands could disappear by hiding in ravines and endless sagebrush country without discovery.

Each night the family gathered their horses into a make-shift rope corral, pitched a tent near the wagon, and cooked game they found along the way. Assignments were made among the young children for night watches over the horse herd. Even the young Cunys were wary frontiersmen and sharpshooters. If anyone preyed on the caravan, they knew what to do.

Young colts in the horse herd had become a problem that slowed the journey. They considered if the troublesome colts should be shot and left behind to permit faster travel. It was decided that in future years they may become a valuable needed asset, so their travel plans were accommodated to keep them in the herd.

The Black Hills came into view when the family reached the Cheyenne River station at the entrance to Red Canyon near present-day Edgemont. The nearby cavalry post, Camp Collier, was abandoned when stage routes were changed to reach the northern hills, traveling through Buffalo Gap, rather than up the treacherous Red Canyon to Custer City. Josephine knew it well from trips Adolph Cuny made hauling provisions to the post, and even young Charles had once accompanied his father here.

Now Josephine must decide which route to follow to the reservation. She would head east along the Cheyenne River, skirting the southern edge of the Black Hills and travel to the Horse Head Junction on the Cheyenne River. It was a stage station on the newly established route from Sidney, Nebraska through Buffalo Gap and up the eastern side of the Black Hills to Deadwood. But before reaching Buffalo Gap, she left the stagecoach trail and traveled cross country, fording the Cheyenne

River. The Pine Ridge Indian Reservation was a few miles ahead.

Pine Ridge was a cultural shock to her. It reminded Josephine of the settlement at Cache La Poudre, but was dramatically different from her life of privilege at Fort Laramie. Here she had none of that. She was living in a tent alongside a wagon, and was just another Indian among thousands of others living in tipi lodges that extended as far as the eye could see. Everywhere there seemed to be a feeling of hopelessness. She could understand that. Everyone here was a displaced person. As nomads they understood that life, but they were now condemned to a place they did not choose to be; confined to a reservation. Josephine was among them as just another prisoner.

The Indian agency had recently been established here with an Indian agent in charge, and an agency building was being constructed alongside White Clay Creek. At Fort Laramie, the agency office was a place she had always been able to walk into unannounced and be accorded hospitality, but this one in Pine Ridge was closed to her. For her family's sake, Josephine fought against her own depression, the loneliness of widowhood, and the sadness of a lost past.

Survival of the family was Josephine's highest priority -- it became a tonic to her. They found a place west of the agency near a little stream with water for themselves and their horse herd. Parking their wagon, the family pitched a lean-to tent and fashioned a corral out of tree limbs and ropes for the horses. That herd must be protected at all costs, as it was now their only asset. Sons and daughters performed round-the-clock guard duty.

Beginning the semblance of a new life, the Cuny boys drove the wagon a few miles into an area of forest and cut logs to build a crude log cabin for their mother and sisters. The boys continued to live in the tent and sleep on the ground outside, except during the coldest part of the winter.

Pine Ridge in the late 1870s was in stages of transition from an empty prairie to a huge village, as thousands of Oglala arrived there from the former agency located further east at the Missouri River. They were joined by hundreds of others like the Cunys, fleeing there from the turmoil along the frontier. Nearly seven thousand Oglala were on the reservation at that time; most of them in the vicinity of the agency at Pine Ridge, as described by Charles W. Allen in his book *From Fort*

Laramie to Wounded Knee. [93] Virtually all of the Indians initially lived in canvas tipis, or in some sort of tent shelter, since buffalo hide tipis were becoming scarce. Log establishments were quickly built for the agency office and homes for government officers. Then a few log cabins were built by Indians as homes; the one built by Josephine Cuny and her sons was among the first.

When Josephine and her family arrived on the reservation, the Government Indian Agent was a Dr. Irwin, an elderly man who was about to retire. He had *"reserved a strip of land for government purposes, and designated that traffic was to follow certain specified lines designed to become streets. Otherwise people were camping wherever they chose,"* said Allen. [94] A year later, Dr. Valentine T. McGillycuddy arrived on the reservation to replace Irwin. He was no stranger to Indians. His frontier career began when he was a field surgeon assigned to General Crook's 3rd Cavalry at Fort Robinson. While there, he tended to the wife of Chief Crazy Horse, Black Shawl, who was in the infirmary being treated for tuberculosis. While she was being treated, the surgeon had arranged for visits by Crazy Horse, and in the process they became friends. Later, after Crazy Horse had been mortally wounded, it was McGillycuddy who ordered him to be moved to the agency office, dressing his wounds until his death. As a consequence of his friendship with Crazy Horse, McGillycuddy had credibility with most of the Indian population. However, it bought him little favor with Chief Red Cloud, who was an adversarial rival of Crazy Horse.

Red Cloud was the dominant Indian leader at the Pine Ridge Agency. He established his leadership of the Oglala tribe in a decisive way fifteen years before when he lead Indian forces against the U.S. Cavalry in what has been named the Red Cloud War. He was hailed as the only Indian leader who fought against the United States in a war and won by demanding closure of the Bozeman Trail through the Powder River country of the Wyoming Territory. It was a questionable victory; a battle won with a heavy ultimate cost. In the aftermath of the peace treaty signed at Fort Laramie in 1868, ending the war, the Indians became victims of subterfuge and betrayal, for their lands were gradually lost to the white man, who reneged on some of the treaty agreements. The end result was that Red Cloud and his people became confined to a small reservation in Dakota Territory. When the Oglala population arrived at

Pine Ridge, Chief Red Cloud still carried the mantle of Oglala tribal leadership.

In his book, *On the Rez*, Frazier describes Red Cloud as a big man, over six feet tall and two hundred pounds. A correspondent for Harper's Weekly who saw him in 1870 described him *"of herculean stature, six and a half feet in length and large in proportion. … He grew up in the camp of the great chief Smoke, his mother's brother. His father died of drink when Red Cloud was only a boy… In 1841, taking Smoke's part in a quarrel, Red Cloud shot and killed Smoke's rival, a powerful chief called Bull Bear. The killing added to Red Cloud's reputation but divided the Oglala for decades. Red Cloud told interviewers in later years that he had been in eighty battles… most were with other Indian tribes and occurred before many white men had arrived,"* said Frazier. [95]

And it was Red Cloud to whom Indian Agent McGillycuddy turned when he needed an Indian model to create change. One of the first initiatives of the Indian agent was to try motivating the Indians to move from their nomadic tipi existence to living into a permanent wood structure, called a house. *"McGillycuddy wanted the chief to live in a frame house in the hope it would encourage others to do the same. The four room house with a kitchen lean-to was completed late in 1879,"* said Allen.[96] But communications between Red Cloud and McGillycuddy were always strained for reasons never fully understood. Both were proud men with large egos and a tendency to pontificate while displaying a distinct deficiency in the skill of listening.

In later years, McGillycuddy was viewed as one of the better Indian agents, while Red Cloud was viewed as an able spokesman for his people, and it is unfortunate that they never seemed to communicate on the same wavelength. Red Cloud always *"continued to work for his people and had some successes under circumstances where failure seemed to be built in. The destruction of the Indian way of life in those years was such that no Indian leader really survived it; Red Cloud almost did. Crazy Horse, who died in his thirties, is a good hero for someone young. As you age and see more of life's complications, you may find sympathy, if not admiration, for Red Cloud,"* said Frazier in *On the Rez.* [97]

Unfortunately, Red Cloud is blamed by many Indians today with having caved in to the white man in a naïve quest for peace, instead of fighting as Crazy Horse did to the bitter end for his land. He died an old man in his nineties, ignored by the people he had tried to bring peace. Twelve Indian police were the only ones who attended his funeral. [98]

McGillycuddy served as Indian agent from March 1879 until May 1886. Like all agents of his time, he attempted to remake the Indian in the image of the whites. After he left the agency, McGillycuddy went on to a successful career as mayor of Rapid City, head of the Power and Light Company, and became President of the South Dakota School of Mines in Rapid City.

Life became bearable in Pine Ridge for the Cuny family. They were provided adequate food. Indian families on the reservation *"were living, not on charity as many people supposed, but on goods bought and paid for by the government through contracts which were dignified as treaties. These furnished them with the staples of subsistence in exchange for lands surrendered and vacated. Possibly it is a debatable subject, but that is the way the Indians figured it,"* said Allen [99]

The bi-weekly issue of beef to the Indians by the government became a Roman pageant orchestrated by the agency to provide beef and was done in a fashion reminiscent of the old days of the Indian buffalo hunt. A couple miles from the agency office was a corral where a large herd of cattle destined for Indian consumption was maintained. On the appointed morning, representatives of the various tribal families would be assembled outside the gate in a long line and armed with guns or bow and arrow, and a travois to carry away their prize. *"When all was ready the chief clerk, list in hand, stood just outside the corral gate… He would call out the name of an Indian. … The frightened animals would be released. … And when the hapless creature reached the open space the race was on, and the shooting began. … Thus the cattle were kept loping and jumping to a losing race with death, and soon the plain was covered with running, whirling, dodging steers, each followed by an Indian, crossing and crisscrossing each other's path, with bullets flying and arrows whizzing everywhere. Parties of the group to whom the animal had been issued rushed in with their travois and began butchering as soon as they saw their own animal drop,"* said Allen. [100]

From her days at Fort Laramie, Josephine Cuny knew the ways of the white man and the political tactics of survival within an agency environment. She knew that McGillycuddy would be hampered by his lack of knowledge of the Teton language and he lacked interpreters who could effectively communicate with the Indian population. There were few Oglala with linguistic skill in both English and the Teton language. But she knew someone who did have that skill: her son, Charles. He was still a teenager, but from his earliest days Charles had conversed fluently in both languages in his family circle and among his Indian friends at Fort Laramie. He was tall, looked mature for his age, handsome, and personable. Coming from within the Indian population, he had credibility among the Oglala and he had the "savoir faire" to gain credibility in the agency office. Josephine Cuny made a visit to the office of the Agent McGillycuddy, and Charles was hired as an interpreter to the Indian Agency.

The older Cuny children began to attend the schools that McGillycuddy built, and life took on a livable routine. Josephine still had her hands full with the younger children and maintaining a household under somewhat primitive circumstances, but the money supplied by Charles's duties as an interpreter made things easier. Then a new initiative by McGillycuddy supplied an added boost. His new program was to teach the Indians about cultivation and how to farm. He appointed what were called "boss farmers," and these were Indians who were taught the rudimentary things about farming and were then sent out on the reservation to motivate and teach other Indians how to plow and plant crops. The pay was better than that of interpreter, so Charles applied and received his appointment as boss farmer. His initial assignment was in the Pine Ridge vicinity for several years. Then he was transferred to a village further north named "Red Dog's Camp," but later re-named Manderson. After a time, his mother and her children moved there to join him. Charles was aggressive and industrious, and an opportunist who kept looking for new ways to make a better life for himself and his family.

Then his family life underwent a change, and in 1882 at the age of twenty he married Louise LaRacque. Louise's mother was Mary Pretty Hip, who was a Brul'e Indian from east of the Missouri River. It was at this time in the late 1880s that Charles began to collect a small herd of cattle, and with the help of his brothers, he established a cattle camp on a high table plateau west of Manderson.

This mesa, which is about fifteen miles long and three to four miles wide, rises three hundred feet above the surrounding landscape with sharply meandering, precipitous cliffs of pinnacles and crevices. On all sides is the rugged, desolate Badland terrain. The region was named after Charles Cuny and became known as "Cuny Table." Until Charles Cuny established cattle camps on the mesa, the spot was uninhabited, since it was extremely difficult to climb up the sandstone cliffs, and few paths led up. Charles received support from a new program to promote the raising of cattle by Indians. As his cattle herd grew in number, a few years later Charles started a new business: that of raising cattle on Cuny Table to supply the butcher shop he had started in Manderson. This butcher shop was under the auspices of the Indian agency to supply meat to Indians on the reservation. One of the supporters of his new enterprise was the Indian agent, Captain LeRoy Brown. Cuny and Brown became good friends. When Charles and Louise's fourth child, a son, was born in 1891, they named him LeRoy Brown Cuny in honor of the Indian agent. Charles also drove cattle to Scenic for shipment to Sioux City, Iowa, which was the closest livestock market at that time.

In 1887, the U.S. Congress passed the Dawes General Allotment Act. Its stated intention was to entice Indians to move away from a nomadic tribal concept to the private ownership of reservation land. This act was designed to give the head of each Oglala household 160 acres, and the Cuny family filed for allotments on the high plateau that became named for Charles Cuny.

The Allotment Act was not widely or successfully promoted on the reservation, however, and few other Indians took advantage of the opportunity. Unfortunately, the act permitted a rush by non-Indians to come into the reservation and establish homesteads, so the end result was that a substantial portion of reservation lands suddenly evaporated in the 1890s and became owned by white ranchers. *"These areas are not considered part of the reservation by the federal and state governments. Many Oglala lost their land because they did not understand the concept of land as a commodity that could be bought, sold, and taxed,"* stated Gagnon in *Pine Ridge Reservation.* [101]

What has been called the Indian Uprising of 1890 found the Cuny family living between cattle camps on Cuny Table and operating the butcher shop in Manderson. The Ghost Dance craze did not appeal to them. It was a revivalist religious philosophy that was combined with some Indian traditional customs of former years, and was taken up by many on the reservation. The religion particularly appealed to those lost in the depths of despair. However, it held little appeal to the Cuny family, who took their religious cue from the matriarch of the family, Josephine Cuny. She had long since managed to shake off the depression of a decade earlier, and led her family in adapting to their new life. While not particularly religious, their roots remained with the traditional Christian religion of her husband's European background.

As unrest grew, there was considerable turmoil throughout the reservation. The Indian agent appealed to the government for assistance, and several thousand U.S. Cavalry troopers were sent in and bivouacked at various places throughout the reservation. The Nebraska National Guard was activated and stationed along the state boundary at the southern end of the reservation to protect the citizens of Nebraska. Among the Indian population there were three elements: those who adopted the new Ghost Dance religion; ruffian renegade young males who became "hell-raisers" -- usually under the influence of liquor -- and then those in the "silent majority," such as the Cuny family, who kept a low profile and tried to lead a normal life. It was not easy to avoid the growing rebellion. One of the principal locales for the Ghost Dance ceremony was a place called the "Stronghold," located a few hundred yards north of Cuny Table in rugged badlands where the Indians felt secure from the cavalry and free to practice their dance rituals. It was indeed secure -- this isolated holdout of nearly impassible terrain could be defended against direct assault by hundreds of cavalry, and it was wisely never challenged by mounted soldiers. The Stronghold became a headache for the Cuny family during this period, because of its closeness to their cattle camps. Some of these were burned as foraging parties from the Stronghold defense camp ranged far and wide in order to find food. [102]

In the cold of winter in December 1890 -- a few days after Christmas -- the Massacre of Wounded Knee occurred a few miles east of Cuny Table. The massacre is discussed in more detail in a later chapter, but finally in the mid-1890s, a relative quiet returned to the reservation, and it was during these peaceful years when the Indian ranchers on Cuny Table and Red Shirt Table began to interrelate with the ranchers of the Cheyenne River country: Joe Norman, Bill Hudspeth, Tom and Jim Wilson, Wes Bondurant, and others. All the land was open range with no fences anywhere, so cattle roamed through endless pastureland and herds became intermixed. In early spring, the cows would give birth to calves, and in the fall a roundup would be held of all ranchers; usually under the leadership of the Cheyenne River rancher, Tom Wilson. Each calf would be identified with its mother to establish ownership, then roped and branded. Each rancher would be present or send a "rep" to oversee the sorting and branding to insure the process was honest. It was several days of hard work and a joint effort, which also led to considerable camaraderie and friendship. Joe Norman and Charles Cuny became friends, and in later years the same process would extend to their sons, Tom Norman and Pat and Chat Cuny. Tom and Pat and Chat became part of the annual roundup ritual.

Raising cattle in South Dakota's snowy winters requires hay for winter-feed. Utilizing his earlier education as a boss farmer, Charles Cuny began cultivation of grass for this purpose, but during dry hot summers it was always a marginal process, because there were few water wells on the table. Summer rainfall was unpredictable. Then the men found winter wheat -- a crop that was more suitable. It could be planted in dry fall weather, germinate under winter snows, grow quickly during spring rains, and be ready to harvest before the summer drought. Cuny Table had fields of winter wheat, and it was this farming success that brought me as a boy with my banker father from Buffalo Gap to visit with his customers on Cuny Table.

During World War II, the U.S. Government had one additional cruel blow to deliver to the reservation. They needed a bombing range where air force bombers could practice dropping their bombs and shooting 20mm guns at targets. What terrain to choose? Of course, the most expendable land of all was that which belonged to the American Indian. So in 1940, military officials designated a strip of land that ran straight down the middle of Cuny Table. The government took ownership of the land, forced everyone to move away, and razed all of the structures on the land. It was at that time that Laurence Cuny had to move, and his daughters became my classmates in Buffalo Gap. It was not until twenty-five years later that the Cuny family members were allowed to reclaim their land and move back to Cuny Table. Dave Cuny's father, Chat Cuny, remained on his place, since his ranch house was one hundred yards from the edge of the bombing range. He survived near warlike conditions as bombs and machine gun bullets whizzed past his cattle.

Charles's son (Charles Jr.), called Chat, was born in 1889 and lived on the home place on the south side of Cuny Table. He went to the Indian School in Rapid City and also rode horseback to school twelve miles away. Chat and Mabel Speck were married in 1926 and had seven children; the youngest was David, who still lives and ranches on the home place. Dave was one of the last graduates of the Buffalo Gap High School, shortly before it was permanently closed. He has assumed the role of family historian, and has researched the Wyoming State Archives in Cheyenne for early Cuny and Bissonette family history.

Recently, I visited the small Saint Joseph Cemetery on Cuny Table. It is nearly hidden beyond the pastures on what is referred to as the "old road." Traveling down the ruts of a dirt road overgrown with weeds, one sees an eight-foot-high white cross. I stopped the car and passed through the gate into a little cemetery that is lovingly cared for by the Cuny family, with cultivated natural grasses and well-tended head-stones. Charles Cuny is not buried here, because the U.S. Air Force was dropping bombs on Cuny Table, which was not accessible when he died in 1940, and so he is buried at the Rosary Mission in Pine Ridge. The headstones read like a history book: *Cuny, Swallow, Pourier, Twiss, O'Rourke, and Bissonette.*

There in the center is the headstone that reads: *Josephine Cuny 1835-1936.*

This gutsy lady lived to the age of 101. Although she traveled down many dark roads, she never looked back, always ahead to find a better life for her family. Perhaps there were few golden years, but they always had food, shelter, and safety. She was a survivor.

ABOUT PAT CUNY

American Indians were one of the largest ethnic groups to join the army during both World Wars and they made excellent soldiers, often moving into leadership roles. One of the first to volunteer after Pearl Harbor was Pat Cuny, Charles's son. Like his father, Pat was a natural leader and quickly rose to the rank of staff sergeant. He was part of the Normandy landing force that secured the Cherbourg peninsula in France, but there was to be no Paris holiday for him. Pat was wounded in action and received medals for bravery. Sixty years later, he still spends time in a veteran's hospital doctoring a marginal leg, but it has not kept him off a horse doing the hard work of ranching. Pat Cuny's family traditions go back many generations and more than a hundred years on Cuny Table. He is one of the best cowboys on the Western frontier.

Pat was not schooled as a writer, but he recently sat down and wrote something about his life to include in this book. He is now eighty four, and recently came home from the veterans hospital where he had still more surgery on his leg, the one originally injured on the battle field in France. Pat propped his leg up on a chair and wrote a dozen pages for me in longhand. These are the ramblings of an old cowboy who has finally hung up his spurs and settled for a rocking chair.

STORY OF MY LIFE: BY PAT CUNY

I guess I'm what you would call a mixed-blood. It is hard to say how much is this or that, Indian or white. We Indians used to say, "I met the boat." Then when I grew older and found I also had considerable white blood in me, I changed it to "I met the boat, and by God, I was also on the boat." I'm no different than most the rest out here. Hell, you can hardly find anybody on the reservation that isn't mixed-blood to some degree.

I was born to Charles and Alvina Cuny on the 28th day of April, 1923 on Cuny Table. We lived on the flat and our windmill is still standing. We had a real nice house. It was one big room made into two rooms with curtains. We had a very nice barn, a big corral and everything to go with it.

(Ed. note: Most of that is now gone because almost every building on Cuny Table was removed during the war when the government took it over for a bombing range. Anything you see on Cuny Table was moved in from somewhere else after the war. The home Pat lives in today was moved in from down in the flats where it was originally the Duhamel home before they moved to Rapid City.)

In 1928 I started school at the Holy Rosary Mission. I went there for a few years until they kicked me out for not shaving! After I left Holy Rosary I went to the Pine Ridge boarding school. In the summer time I would work for a couple of farmers when they would be cutting their grain.

My Pa farmed a little bit, just enough for our own use. I can remember going out and cutting hay off the lakebeds. When we got it all cut, we would haul it all in and make one big, long stack in the barnyard. We had a couple milk cows, a team of horses and one saddle horse to feed through the winter from that haystack. We also had hogs and chickens.

We had a few cows that my Pa kept on Cuny Basin, which he leased for ten cents an acre. He and Uncle Wally Twiss together leased all the land south of Cuny Table (which was Badlands area). My brothers would always sneak off so they would not have to work in the garden. I was about eight at the time and too damn dumb to leave with them, so I would have to help Ma hoe the rows in the garden, but you know, it never hurt me one damn bit, and I also learned how to cook. I learned how to do a lot of things around the house. My nephews would come up to play, and then they would ride off into the Badlands. I got to cowboy once in a while at least. When I did ride, I got to go with my Pa and ride with all of the big outfits. There were about nine different cattle outfits; two were large with big herds of cattle (several thousand head on each outfit), and then there were about seven more with small herds that were spread all over the country. (It was all open range with no fences.)

The proudest day of my life, which I can always remember, was when my Pa went to pay Joe Reed for the lease. Pa told him if I didn't do right to kick my butt. I never got my butt kicked. I asked Joe if I drove the cattle good? He never said good or bad, so I took it that I was a good hand. I was eleven years old at the time.

After that things kinda changed. I got to ride a little more and help some of the other ranchers. My brother leased a lot of land from Pargsin Creek clear over to Red Water north of Kyle. Once in a while I would get to help him, and we would ride all day. I was a teenager at the time. I don't know how many miles we would ride, but I do remember my butt would be pretty sore by the time we got home. I loved every day of it. After all of this, then we had to go into the army. That ended my cowboy life for a few years.

I worked for Uncle Sam in the army for four years. We took our basic training at a camp in Alabama, and then moved to another camp in Alabama, then from there to Camp Robinson in Arkansas, near Little Rock. We were sent to Camp Shanks in New York, where we got our shots before being sent overseas. By that time I was a staff sergeant.

It took us seventeen days at sea to get to England, and it was quite a big lake to be on. It was the month of March and the seas were rough. I was on the *George Washington*, that was a cruise ship before the war. We landed at Southampton in England. We stayed at a British base for a month and then were loaded onto another ship and headed across the English Channel toward Normandy. Our ship was hit by a submarine, but we stayed afloat. Four other ships alongside went down and one carried half our company to the bottom. It was the saddest time I ever had. Sometimes when I stand at the edge of Cuny Table and look south down into the Badlands basin that looks like a sea, I can see ships out there. It isn't so bad now, but it was real bad for a long time. I can't talk about those days at sea or when we landed in combat, and don't bring it back to my mind anymore because it brings me back to the bad parts of my young life. I got a Purple Heart and a couple other medals, which was nice, but small payment for giving what you had to do. Some friends of mine gave their life.

I had to stay over there when the war was over for another year because I only had 90 points, and you had to have 120 to come home on the first ship. During that time I got to see a lot of country in Europe.

After I got home and out of the army there was a recession and jobs were scarce. I worked at different types of jobs to make enough cash to survive until I could get another job. I worked at any job I could get. I did a lot of road work, and I even worked in the mineral mines at Rock Springs in Wyoming. That was a good winter job. Then I came home and started working as a rancher. I worked for D.H. & L.M. Witte for a time. After I left them I worked for Western Cattle Company. Then I lived in the Hermosa area for a number of years. During this time, I got to meet a lot of good people in my working around the country. I worked on four different ranches for the company of Stenger, Miller, and Hart at Battle Creek, and then went to the –N– of Midland. At that time, the company bought the Lackey ranch in Miles City, Montana. All of the men on the –N– moved to Miles City. I had a little trouble there with some Texans and lost my job. Then I came back again and worked around home for the rest of my cowboy life. I had a good time wherever I worked. There was always time for a good joke or two.

This goes back to when I was working for Western Cattle Company: I was riding a big gray horse that was everything a horse should be, but he wasn't. I rode him down to the river where the cows were. I had to get them cows off that land or pay $25 a head for each day as long as they were on that land where the lease had run out. I rode this horse for the first time and found out that he was not as good as he was supposed to be. He fell with me and I broke my neck. I laid there for a couple of hours, and David Bale and the girls went and got a chopper at the (air) base. The National Guard was not too far from the home ranch. One chopper took David home to get his pickup and the other one came up to where I was. Well, those chopper guys hurt me worse than that horse did.

Another time I broke my leg when working in the same basin on that ranch, and Larry Edoff went down to the old Bale camp and called for help. It was a long time getting to me. I remember it was eleven a.m. when this happened and almost dark when I got to the oil road. Everybody heard on their scanners that I was down somewhere out on the 505, and there was a convoy of horse trailers coming in to help find me. They didn't know if I got my leg broke from a horse fall or what, nor where I was. Most of these guys were coming home from riding for the day and they turned their outfits around and headed for the 505 that was my leased land at the time. After that experience I knew I had a couple of friends, Thank God.

I have been retired for a few years, but I help all of my friends and some other people too. All of these young kids up here are good cowboys. They all learned from being around all of the older cowboys. A couple of them turned out to be good bronco riders and just all-around cowhands. They can do anything on a horse. Sidney's oldest boy is now sixty five and still works as a cowboy. They have been long time friends and good neighbors, and there are still a few of them kind of people left.

(By way of explanation, this next paragraph describes the roundup and branding season that occurred every fall on the open range of the frontier. Frank Wilson owned the largest ranch in that region and ran several thousand head of cattle on the open range that extended from the Cheyenne River all through the reservation. His father, Tom Wilson, had been the head man of the annual roundup for many years until his death, and then Frank took over and organized and led the combined effort for all the ranches. The Cuny ranches all participated. However, at this time Pat Cuny was riding for the Bale Ranch out of Hermosa. Each

ranch supplied manpower, and sent their "rep" to insure that their own calves would be correctly sorted out and receive the correct brand of their ranch. In addition to a lot of hard work, it was also a time of considerable sociability among all the cowboys. Frank Wilson and many of the other ranchers of the area were of mixed-blood.)

Now we can start talking about the branding time over at the Wilsons. I lived across the river at this time on the Bale Ranch with the Lazy N brand, and I would start riding and rounding up cattle a month before we ever branded. After we got everything moved to the reservation side of the Cheyenne River, we would start working south to the Mule Creek branding pens. It was quite a job to get all of these cowboys in gear and going, but much of the help that worked for me knew what to do. We would leave the Ackerman corrals and cover all the ground to Mule Creek south. The men that came from the main ranch would cover to the west. We would try to get all the cattle in the holding traps before the other crew would get there, so we would not get the cattle mixed up with another herd of several hundred cattle. If the cows and calves got mixed up before we got to the holding pen, we would be in a hell of a bad deal. We did have a couple bad times.

I used to cover all of the country that everyone rode just to make sure that they never missed any cows. When we got in with everything we still had a mess, because all the cows wanted to go back north. Some of the boys would sit a gate until dark to keep them in. Come next day we would brand after we got all the cattle in the corrals or pens. I always worked the sorting pens. When we got a couple hundred of our cows ready they would start branding. By the time we got all of the cattle sorted, they would have one or two pens of calves to brand, and it took all day to sort the cattle away from the calves. One day we branded over two thousand head. Every day you had to be on the go all day long. I kept the cows coming to the alley for them and everything worked out real good. This was not an easy job. We rode long and hard, but the same people would be there year after year.

So much for me at the Wilsons.

After Frank Wilson passed, everyone asked me if I missed the big branding. I would tell them "…what do you think?" I'm like everybody else. I just miss a real good thing that is for the good of all the ranchers. More than anything else, I miss the good times we cowboys had together with people like Frank and Blutch Wilson and Joe and Tommy Norman. I think I helped the days along with a good joke now and then.

Frank Wilson's oldest girl (Lois Wilson Rapp) is the (ranch) boss now. Her son, Frank Rapp, is the right-hand man. Now they run big -- but not as big as their Grandpa Frank Wilson did -- but close.

I've helped different people at other times, but I'm getting pretty slow now, so I'm going to say good bye to the hard days of cowboying.

Frank Wilson had a catering outfit come out of Rapid City to provide food for the roundup crew. I happened to be on the road when we were going to Mule creek and walked into the kitchen. I asked him what we had for supper, and he responded chicken. I blowed up. I said a man with twenty five hundred head of cattle should not feed chicken to his crew. Well, next day he got steak for his crew and he fed over one hundred fifty places. We never ate chicken again. We had sixty sets of calves to wrestle, and six men a-dragging. We worked two weeks in the south and two weeks working the east. That was the end of the big, big branding operations back about thirty years or so ago. They still have an annual roundup and Frank's grandson, Frank Rapp, is the head man. I still go to sit beside the chow wagon and swap a few stories, but they aren't like the old days.

I spent a lot of summer days on horseback as the announcer at a lot of rodeos in the region. I guess you'd call it a hobby because it didn't pay much per hour, considering all the time I spent thinking about it. I guess I must have done the job all right because they kept coming back after me to do it again, year-after-year. Of course, I knew all the cowboys that ever entered the rodeo arena either as pick-up men, on the gates, or riding broncos. I had always spent a lot of my time in the saddle with cowboys telling a joke or two, so the job came naturally to me. I never did ride any broncos or bucking horses on purpose though, because of the gimpy leg I brought back from France. On my wall I've got hanging a real fancy-looking plaque that I was recently presented at a rodeo in Rapid City for my years as a rodeo announcer. I guess they figured it was safe to give me a trophy now that I was too old and crippled to ride into the arena and tell any more bad jokes.

I want to go back and talk about when I first got in the army. We were sent to Fort Leavenworth in Kansas. When we were new there, I was jumping over the beds and a sergeant called out for Cuny to quit jumping over those beds. I said "I am not jumping the beds, I am standing in the staircase watching you," and he said "Which bed is yours?" I showed him. He told me to tie a towel at the foot of my bed, and a corporal will be around at 3 a.m. to wake me for K.P. duty. After he left and everybody went to sleep, I tied the towel on the next bunk. That guy was woke up at 3 a.m. and got up to do the K.P. instead of me, and that was one of my best breaks in the army.

P.S.

I'm about to come to a close of my B.S. Some of it is the truth, you know.

Bernie, I've had a good time in my life -- some of it was real good, and some was bad.

I'm going to end this story by telling everybody where I'm going to be buried when I leave this old world. It will be at the Saint Joseph Catholic Cemetery right here on Cuny Table, not far from where Grandma Cuny is resting.

So long.

I've had a good time most of my life, thank God.

Patrick Cuny

THE CUNY FAMILY

Adolph Cuny,
Pat Cuny's grandfather

Josephine (Bissonette) Cuny,
Pat Cuny's Grandmother

Charles Cuny,
Pat Cuny's Father

Pat Cuny,
Lifelong cowboy

CUNY TABLE

Cuny Table with Cheyenne River in foreground

"South Basin" taken from atop Cuny Table

Original Charles Cuny "Rock Spring" ranch,
located under the south edge of Cuny Table.
Ranch is now the home of Dave and Carole Cuny

"Stronghold"
This was the nearly impassable entrance to the Stronghold,
the site of Ghost Dances during the 1890s uprising.

4
THE WILSON RANCH EMPIRE

In *Big Valley*, a TV series of the 1960s, Barbara Stanwyck portrayed the fictional role of a cattle baroness who ran a cattle empire. Today, Lois (Wilson) Rapp is a cattle baroness of the Buffalo Gap frontier in a family dynasty that extends back twelve decades. Now in her eighties, Lois divides her time between her home in Buffalo Gap and the ranch on the reservation. She and I attended the Buffalo Gap School at the same time. I was sweet on her back then, but since she was a sophomore in high school and I was only in the sixth grade, she didn't even know I existed.

The extended Wilson family dominated the cattle range of the Cheyenne River country and Pine Ridge Indian Reservation through all of the frontier years. This began with the great grandfather of Lois, Bill Hudspeth, who came up from Texas, married an Oglala Lakota, and raised a mixed-blood family. This original patriarch of the family, if such a distinguished title could be bestowed on a character such as Hudspeth, arrived on the Buffalo Gap scene sometime after the Civil War, when he was chased out of Texas one step ahead of the Texas Rangers. [103] He never acknowledged why he was on the run, but it probably had something to do with the several notches carved on the handles of the two Colts he always wore tied down on his hips. His arrival came during the time the reservation extended down into the Nebraska Territory. Bill Hudspeth knew that survival in Indian country was safer with a passport afforded by marriage to an Indian, and he married Nellie Goodwin, who had family ties to Chief Red Cloud. They settled on the reservation in the Nebraska Territory. Rather than living Indian style in a tipi, he moved with his wife into a cave dugout. When the Indian agency was moved to White Clay Creek, the reservation boundary moved to the Dakota Territory line because the new state of Nebraska did not want any part of an Indian reservation within its boundaries. At that time,

Hudspeth and his wife moved into the Dakota Territory -- just inside the newly-created Pine Ridge Indian Reservation boundary.

The early years of Bill Hudspeth on the reservation have not been documented, but by some means he became a rancher. Since all of that country was open range, to become a rancher required only that a cowboy have a horse and slap his brand on a few head of cattle he could claim as his own. So Bill Hudspeth became a rancher. I'm sure the ownership of his new herd of cattle was never challenged by any Indian or white cowboy, because Hudspeth was one of the most dangerous cowboys who ever rode the Western frontier. The colts he wore on his hips spoke for him, and his reputation said that he would not hesitate to pull a gun on any challenger.

While I knew Bill Hudspeth when I was a little boy, I cannot personally attest to all the stories about him, but his rugged reputation lives today, seventy years after his death. My Dad would have vouched for the stories, because as the local banker he had several run-ins with this Cheyenne River rancher. Hudspeth's great-granddaughter, Lois Rapp, described him as an ornery codger and she could confirm some of the stories. But people have different memories. His grand-daughter, Freda Yeager, told me that as a little girl who saw a lot of "Grandpa," she always found him kind and gentle with her, and she thought he was honest as the day was long and he never cheated anyone. "Shortie" Gallentine, who also knew Hudspeth, thought he was a tough hombre, but okay. Those are certainly at odds with my own impression as a little boy and son of the local banker. As he grew into old age, he did mellow somewhat: perhaps his reputation and even the old man himself softened during his eighties and nineties.

Bill and his Lakota wife, Nellie, had three daughters and two sons. The daughters were all beautiful girls who grew into fine adults. The two sons, Mike and Bill Jr., unfortunately emulated their father. Mike Hudspeth was perhaps the most ornery cowboy that ever rode the Buffalo Gap frontier. Pat Cuny and Tom Norman knew Mike Hudspeth well, and would probably tell you my description of him is on the money.

Let me jump ahead in time and relate several incidents that characterize Mike Hudspeth.

Like many Cheyenne River cowboys, Mike often came to town on Saturday afternoon with his first stop at Frenchie's saloon, where he would throw down shots of whiskey, join in the boisterous horseplay with fellow cowboys, and get roaring drunk. Then the cowboys would stagger out of the saloon, untie their horses from the hitching post, pull themselves into the saddle, and oftentimes they'd trot down the street to engage in their brand of fun by terrorizing the local townsfolk.

Gene Griffis was a part-time deputy sheriff, but he was not about to intervene in what some considered harmless horseplay, and it was not something the townspeople wanted to challenge.

Our family lived in abject poverty because Dad was unemployed for two years prior to coming to Buffalo Gap. Our house was a three-room unpainted bungalow, where our family of seven lived. One evening we heard a commotion outside and Dad looked through the window to see Mike Hudspeth and several cowboys on their horses who apparently had decided to pay a social call on the new banker.

"Keating, come out!" One shouted as he moved his horse up on the front step of our porch.

Dad was not about to set foot out that door to face a crowd of drunken cowboys packing iron.

"Come out you lousy banker bastard!" Then pulling out a pistol and pointing it to the sky he pulled off three quick shots. "Come out you bastard!" He shouted again. Then they started circling our house on their horses and shooting into the air. Dad pulled his twelve gauge shotgun from under the bed and loaded it. Ordering us kids to lie on the floor, he stationed himself facing the door in case they came charging into the house.

Mother was a frontier woman who could rise to any occasion, and timing her exit when the cowboys were in front of the house, she crawled out a back window and ran down the alley to our neighbor, Gene Griffis. Gene heard the shots and already had on his holster. By the time Gene and mother returned, however, the cowboys had vamoosed; no doubt back to Frenchie's saloon for another round of whiskey and more braggadocio.

Shortly thereafter, another incident involved Mike Hudspeth when my Dad had to go to the reservation to discuss a mortgage that was in default. Dad drove out to the reservation and found where he lived, made his way past three snarling dogs and was met at the door by Hudspeth who motioned him to a chair at a table. They sat down, and then

Hudspeth pulled the gun from his holster and sat it on the table with the barrel pointing at my Dad.

"Okay, Keating," he said. "Now what do you want to talk about?"

Negotiating a mortgage in those days was hazardous work for a frontier banker. A couple months later, Dad was playing cards in the evening with some of his friends in Frenchie's Saloon. Hudspeth arrived, proceeded to get drunk, and then in boisterous language challenged Dad to a fight. Dad was no fighter, and would probably have been seriously injured or killed by Hudspeth, who packed iron. Three of the saloon patrons pinned the drunken Hudspeth against the bar while Wes Dalbey pushed Dad out a side door and down a back alley.

My friend, Freda Yeager, now in her eighties, recently told me the following story about Mike Hudspeth, who was her uncle. She knew him well, as they were living in the same ranch complex on the reservation. Mike laughingly told her about one of his escapades, because he was proud of his ability to pull off that sort of thing. A train with two rail cars full of cattle pulled onto the railroad siding at Buffalo Gap and was parked there to spend the night, while the crew walked across to the Alexander Hotel to get rooms. Mike Hudspeth and several of his cowboy confederates joined them in the bar and proceeded to buy the train crew whiskey and get them drunk. Then in the darkness of night, Hudspeth and his gang unloaded the cattle from the train and drove them at top speed eastward through Cheyenne River country and onto the reservation. To complete the maneuver, he drove them to the ranch of a friend and sold the cattle to him. Everyone was happy except for the railroad crew, who awoke with a bad hangover and empty railcars. Hudspeth was happy with a nice cash payment. The rancher was happy because he got a good herd of white-face Hereford cattle at bargain prices, and he cared little that they were stolen, because soon they would be mixed with his herd on the Indian reservation where no railroad person would dare to venture.

Was this story Hudspeth told to Freda Yeager true? There is no doubt in either of our minds, because we knew Mike Hudspeth. He would steal cattle if he thought he could get away with it and some ranchers would be happy to buy stolen cattle if they could claim the role of an innocent victim. But I am ahead of my story, and let's go back in time to the father, Bill Hudspeth, and his wife, Nellie Goodwin, and look at their other children.

One of their daughters was named Thetna, who married a mixed-blood cowboy named "Creepy" Yeager (so named because of a decided limp). They raised a large family who all became very fine people. Two daughters, Freda Yeager and Nellie Cuny, now also in her eighties, operate the Cuny Table Café on the reservation.

Bill and Nellie Hudspeth also had a son named Bill Junior. He was a clone of his brother, Mike. At an early age, he was killed by a rifle in some sort of incident at a Fourth of July celebration, and there are various accounts of what happened. Some say it was an accident that occurred when a group of guys got together for target practice. Tom Norman says his father was present at the event and told him that all the participants were drinking, and that some nursed hard feelings toward Bill. Regardless of how it happened, young Bill Hudspeth was shot and killed.

TOM WILSON

Two other daughters of Bill and Nellie Hudspeth were Zona and Edna. When they were teenagers, they met and married two Wilson brothers, Tom and Jim, who were immigrants from England. Tom Wilson was to become the rancher on the Buffalo Gap frontier who ruled the open range of the Cheyenne River and Indian reservation for the next four decades. After his death, other members of the Wilson family took over, and they continue to impact the local ranching scene today.

This towering figure, Tom Wilson, did not start as a cowboy, and in fact never did look the part of a western cowboy. [104] He was born in Yorkshire, England in 1866, and came to America with his brothers, Jim and Abel, when he was seventeen. They initially settled in Missouri, and then came to the Buffalo Gap area in 1886 as members of a railroad work gang. [105] They laid track for the Chicago and Northwestern railroad when the rail line was extended north as far as the town of Buffalo Gap.

There were usually rumors associated with the prior lives of pioneers who came to the frontier, and some were true, while others were only myth. The Wilson boys from England garnered their share of these bunkhouse stories. For example, it was often claimed they came from some sort of English royalty. In a family history provided to me by Lois Rapp, the only royalty I could find was an older brother of Tom Wilson who became a Member of Parliament and was in the House of Lords. [106] I don't know if that qualifies as royalty, but I suppose it might in a cowboy bunkhouse. Another rumor that circulated among the cowboys was passed on to me by Tom Norman, and it suggested that the Wilson boys fled England as a result of some undefined "trouble" they encountered there. Whether this is true is pure speculation, but it would probably not be documented in a family history. Lois Rapp was not familiar with this bunkhouse gossip, and I am inclined to discount it as "cowboy B.S." However, it does illustrate a point: few immigrants left a happy and prosperous homeland in Europe to head into the unknown without some major incentive. There is a familiar pattern. Usually they were glad to escape a cruel or meaningless life in the hopes of finding something better. Many found only a worse life than the one they left, but not the Wilson boys. They began with the hard life of a railroad section crew, but their fortunes improved as they became successful ranchers.

Tom's older brother, Abel, was the first in the cattle business with a small spread on the Cheyenne River, just outside the reservation boundary. When his marriage went sour and he wanted to move on, he sold his spread to his brother, Tom. Tom also acquired Abel's cattle brand, so Tom suddenly found himself a small-time rancher.

A neighboring rancher had a large ranch outside the reservation boundary. He died and left it to his daughter, who was married to a man named Mackey. Her husband was struck by lightning and killed, leaving her a widow who was not equipped to run a huge ranch, and so she turned to Tom Wilson for help. He agreed to care for her, take over the herd, acquired the brand showing ownership of the cattle, and ran the ranch, which he gradually acquired. [107] This land was on the north side of the Cheyenne River and just outside the reservation. As Tom's children were born, they were each allotted land on the Pine Ridge Indian Reservation, since they were mixed-blood Lakota from their mother's side of the family. Tom used this and additional leased land from other Indian owners to form the core of the largest cattle outfit on the reservation. His cattle brand, originally registered to his brother, Abel, was called the *Half-Circle Z*. So almost overnight, Tom Wilson found himself the biggest rancher on the Buffalo Gap frontier, running a herd of beef cattle which roamed over seven sections of the Dakota Territory and hundreds of unfenced square miles on the open range. His grazing land extended on the west along the Cheyenne River, south into Nebraska and a hundred miles east half-way to the Missouri River. The northern region was the White River Badlands, and his grazing land included all of the Pine Ridge Indian Reservation. [108]

Even though Tom Wilson was the predominating rancher of this Cheyenne River country, he never shed his English traditions of dress code to fit the image of a Western cowboy. Whether in town to transact business at my Dad's bank, or when riding a horse on the range, he wore an English derby hat with a rolled up brim, always wore street shoes -- even on horseback --and was never without a well-tailored blazer coat, except in town where he always donned a full dress suit. He seldom wore side arms. Tom's was not the bawdy cowboy talk, but a conversational tone delivered with a clipped English accent.

Despite his appearance on horseback as that of an English dandy, every cowboy on the open range -- white, Indian, and mixed-blood -- knew Tom Wilson was the boss, not a person to tangle with, and no one ever did. Lois Rapp described the deference accorded him by others as somewhere between respect and fear. He had few friends and no one ever crossed him, she said.

In his heyday, Tom Wilson had more cattle than anyone else in South Dakota. Tom's brother, Jim, ranched alongside him, and was perhaps the only true friend he had. They worked together. Tom ran things and Jim became the expert on cattle and on the horseflesh of the large herd of horses they raised for sale to the U.S. Cavalry.

Now let's go back to Bill Hudspeth and his two daughters, Zona and Edna. When the Wilson boys were still small-time ranchers, they began to call at the nearby Hudspeth ranch and spark with the beautiful Hudspeth girls. Tom married Zona when she was seventeen and he was twenty-four, and Jim married Edna. Tom and Jim drove the two girls by wagon to Smithwick, where they got married.

Tom and Zona first lived in a dugout near the edge of the reservation and it was there they started to raise a family. [109] Bad luck arrived when all white men were ordered off the reservation. Tom and Jim were no exception, even though their wives were part Indian and were related to Chief Red Cloud. So they simply set up camp a quarter-mile outside of the reservation boundary, and continued to run their cattle on the open range that included the entire reservation.

Tom and Zona had four sons and one daughter: Jack, Blutch, Frank, Owen, and Maybelle. The mother, Zona, was a warm and wonderful parent, but the same cannot be said about Tom. He was often described as a cold and unaffectionate father, and his domineering demeanor on the open range extended inside the home. During his lifetime it was rumored he never gave his children anything. His sons worked as cowboys for the same wages he paid the hired hands. After Tom Wilson's sudden death from an automobile accident, his inheritance was divided up by the court. [110]

Zona died in the flu epidemic that swept through the nation during World War I, leaving the family without a mother. Maybelle was only fourteen at the time, but she was suddenly shackled with the job of cooking for the family and the bunkhouse crew, and with maintaining the ranch house. When she was old enough and able to leave the ranch, she moved away and became a beauty operator in several Black Hills towns over the years. [111]

Lois Rapp remembers that the parlor in that ranch house had a hole in the wall up near the ceiling. Every morning, Tom Wilson would reach in, pull out a bottle of whiskey and take a big swig to start the day. But she said that was the only time he drank, and she cannot remember ever seeing him drunk.

When Tom Wilson hired a new cowhand, his interview consisted of walking him to the horse corral where he kept a retinue of wild broncos for just such occasions. If they made a fair ride, they had a job. Tom would assign the day's work to his boys and the other hired hands, and on most occasions would then ride somewhere else for the remainder of the day. The boys would hurry up and get the work out of the way, then bring in the wild horses and have a home rodeo in his absence. They didn't care for gentlemen games like baseball -- a rodeo was their favorite sport and idea of fun. [112]

In addition to running several thousand head of cattle, Tom and his brother Jim also bought and sold a large number of horses. Jim's knowledge of horseflesh was the better of the two brothers, so he was the buyer, while Tom handled the finances and carried the checkbook. On one deal when the U.S. Cavalry was picking up horse stock in preparation for World War I, they loaded fifty-six railcars full of horses that shipped out to the cavalry. [113]

The annual roundup was a major event. As previously mentioned, there were no fences throughout the territory; cattle ran intermixed over the entire reservation and on every side from the Cheyenne River to the White River country. For the rancher, this was a critical time because it determined what calf belonged to which rancher, and then the calf was branded to establish ownership. Also, those male calves destined to become steers for beef were castrated. It was done on the open range by cowboys who roped the struggling and unwilling calves, brought them to ground, and then placed hot branding irons to their hide, finally using a knife to accomplish the castration. It was work that required a strong and tough cowboy. The days were long, and hundreds of calves were handled each day.

With the largest herd and his overbearing personality, Tom Wilson was always appointed as roundup boss. He would schedule the time and place for each part of the roundup and was the conciliator to settle any differences among the cowboys or ranchers. Tom Wilson ran this annual event from the 1890s until the job passed on to his son, Frank, in the early 1930s. [114] No rancher in the Cheyenne River country or on the Indian reservation ever challenged Tom Wilson's authority as roundup boss, or his son, Frank, when he took over the reins.

An early cowboy on the frontier, John Bye provides some sketches of a roundup at that time, and it is an accurate description of how round-ups were done on the Wilson range in the 1890s and past the turn of the century. In actual fact, the roundup today is little changed, except more of it is now accomplished on pastured ranges and in holding pens with chutes. Bye writes in his book *Back Trailing in the Heart of the Short Grass Country*: [115]

> *From fifteen to twenty cowboys accompanied a roundup wagon, each having about ten saddle horses in his string making from 150-200 horses for the horse wrangler to herd.... A roundup boss looked over the entire picture determining where each wagon was to work, and then each wagon had its own boss whose function was to plan the route for the wagon to take, where water was to be had and where camp was to be made. ... Each cowboy roped his mount for the day, and*

one can imagine the plunging, rearing and kicking broncos as the saddles were slapped on, cinches tightened and the rider finally atop. ... This was all incidental to driving a herd of hundreds of cattle, sorting the brands and seeing that the proper ones were left at the right places -- a complex operation, requiring skill and knowledge on the part of the men in charge.

Roundup crews worked hard and had to be fed well. The chuck wagon was a vital part of the operation, and there were established traditions for what gets fed, when, and how. Here is another sketch from Bye: [116]

Meals were at first cooked in a Dutch oven but later a cooking range was carried on a two-wheeled cart that carried the range and cooking utensils. The riders helped themselves cafeteria style and sat on the ground to eat.

Before the branding started, herds had to be gathered and held together in groups of a size that could be handled. Since the territory stretched over miles of country, every plateau and draw had to be ridden to search for the cattle that roamed nearly everywhere. Herding them together was not always easy, because some cow with a mind of its own often did not want to leave her watering hole or draw, and challenged the cowboys. Stories from cowboys about such incidents are endless. Here is one as told by A.B Snyder in his book *Pinnacle Jake*: [117]

I went on a circle drive one morning, led by Jim Lee. Jim was boss of our Ogallala wagon, and had been with that outfit for years. We got back to the roundup ground with our drive before any of the other drives showed up, so Jim told a fellow by the name of Cole to watch our herd of some three or four hundred head, and said to the rest of us, "Come on boys," and rode up on a little pinnacle. We got off our horses and set there on the hill in a cool breeze to watch the other drives come in.

Down below on the prairie Cole got off his horse and sat in the shade and watched the herd. All of a sudden a steer took out for the brakes. Cole was riding "Swede" a good little bay cow horse that had been in Bud Chamber's string when I was with his wagon in '87. I don't know why Cole was using him for a circle horse, but he was, that morning.

Cole jumped on Swede and took off after the steer. He was about up with it, and going fast, when the horse stuck both front feet in a badger hole and turned over twice. Cole was thrown but got up and jumped in the saddle again, just as the horse was getting up. He was on the horse when it got up and they went right on, almost as if they'd never stopped, and caught the steer and brought it back.

I said, "There's a man Bud Chambers must've trained," and old Jim said, "Yes, but I've got a hell of a lot of 'em Bud didn't train." He had a bunch of kids in his outfit that year, and only two or three good riders in his crew.

Snyder wrote this scenario in 1889, but it could have been written a hundred years later. Pat Cuny has told us very similar stories about his roundup days.

It was during this era of the annual roundup that considerable social intermixing occurred among the white pioneer ranchers on the Cheyenne River, the full-blood Indians on the reservation, and the mixed-blood ranchers such as the Wilson's, who lived throughout the area. It was at this time that Joe Norman, Charles Cuny, Wes Bondurant, Bill Hudspeth, the Wilsons, and their hired cowboys all rode side-by-side. They worked together to round up cattle from all the draws and buttes throughout the ranges and Badlands, roped, branded, and castrated the herd, and then enjoyed the fellowship of an evening together at the chow wagon and around a campfire.

Tom Wilson's granddaughter, Lois (Wilson) Rapp, and her son, Frank Rapp, are still owners of a ranch in the southwestern region of the reservation that continues to play a role in the annual roundup. When I visited Lois recently, she stated that several years ago they had three hundred fifty people at the roundup, and last year they had one hundred fifty at the annual event. I'm not sure how many of these are working cowboys, and others just old-timers back purely for the social time. Pat Cuny and Tom Norman do not ride a horse anymore, but they will never miss a chance to stand alongside the chow wagon at the annual roundup.

Tom Wilson retired in the 1930s at the age of sixty-five and moved to Colorado. After facing all the dangers of a cowboy and rancher on the open range of the Buffalo Gap frontier, he met his death in an automobile accident. He is buried in the Buffalo Gap cemetery. [118]

FRANK WILSON

Frank Wilson, Tom's son, was to become the preeminent cattle rancher on the Buffalo Gap frontier over the next several decades, from the 1930s until the 1980s. Frank perhaps became even a more commanding ranch boss than his father, for at the time of his death at the age of eighty, Frank Wilson's obituary called him the largest rancher in South Dakota with five thousand head of cattle. [119]

Here is his obituary:

HOT SPRINGS: Mass of Christian burial was held Saturday, May 1, at St Anthony's Catholic Church in Hot Springs for Frank Wilson, 80.

Wilson, who owned 5,000 head of cattle near buffalo Gap, was described as the largest rancher in the State of South Dakota before his death last Wednesday, April 28.

He was born January 19, 1902, on a ranch in Custer County to Tom and Zona Wilson. He attended Nettleton College of Business in Sioux Falls. He married Julia Callahan December 24, 1923, in Sturgis. He had ranched east of Buffalo Gap until his death.

Wilson was a fourth degree Knights of Columbus member and a member of the South Dakota Stockgrowers and the National Indian Cattlemen's Association.

Survivors include his wife, Julia of Hot Springs; three daughters, Lois Rapp of Buffalo Gap, Thomasetta Kuhl of Hot Springs and Colleen Suppa of Fargo, N.D.; 11 grandchildren; six great-grandchildren; one brother, Owens of Buffalo Gap, and one sister, Mabel Fischer of Sheboygan, Wisconsin. He was preceded in death by two brothers.

A Christian wake service was held Friday at St. Anthony's Church. Burial was in the evergreen Cemetery in Hot Springs.

Frank was born on the Wilson ranch in 1902 and lived there his entire life. While growing up and living the life of a cowboy, he also was able to attend college and this gave him a solid foundation in business that was to serve him well later in life. [120]

At the age of 22, he met and married Julia Callahan, a schoolteacher living at that time with the Thurston family in Buffalo Gap. After their marriage, she moved to the ranch and when their three daughters became of school age, they purchased a home in Hot Springs so Julia could attend to their school needs. At the time of Frank's death, they had been married for 57 years. [121]

When we moved to Buffalo Gap in 1932, Tom Wilson still ran the ranch and my father did considerable banking business with him. At that time, Tom was in the process of turning the ranching operations over to Frank, and then Tom moved to Colorado. After his father's death, Frank bought out his brothers' and his one sister's interest in the ranch. [122] My father took over the bank in Buffalo Gap during the time that Frank Wilson was beginning to run the Wilson ranch, and so they learned the business of frontier banking and ranching in the same era of the Great Depression and severe drought of the 1930s. Those were tough times for both ranching and banking. My mother and father became personal friends of Frank and Julia. The Wilson family frequently came to Buffalo Gap to shop and for banking. They also came in from their Cheyenne River ranch to attend our little Catholic Church in Buffalo Gap. In addition to the Keating and Wilson families, the few parishioners included the Norman, Foss, and Johnson families, and Grandma Hackel, with a congregation seldom exceeding a dozen souls. The Wilson's oldest daughter, Lois, lived next door to us with the Bill Sewright family while attending high school.

Frank Wilson was a working cowboy, and one of the best. He liked to rodeo and won the state championship one year in saddle bronc riding at the Belle Fourche Roundup rodeo. [123] He lived most of his life in the saddle on the open range, spending days at a time riding pastures, day and night, summer and winter, then often throwing a bedroll on the ground beside a campfire. Frank's cattle roamed all through the reservation and the Cheyenne River and White River country while wolves and other predators were still prevalent. They roamed the countryside in packs, crippling and killing horses and cattle. [124] Men spent days at a time hunting and killing them. From his earliest childhood, Frank Wilson led a hard life.

In those days, it was customary for ranchers to do much of their buying and selling of cattle and land in an informal way with a hand-shake and an IOU. These transactions usually took place when they met at some stockman's function, at a cattle auction, in a bar, or even on horseback at a roundup. Many of them had large land holdings or herds, but little tangible cash in a checking account, so there was often an in-adequate balance in the account to cover the IOU, or even a carefully written check. The procedure was for the rancher to come into town to the bank and take out a loan to be deposited in the checking account to cover all the outstanding debts. Then those with IOUs or over-drawn checks would come to the bank and get their money. This practice was well understood by all the parties, including my Dad the banker, and a rancher's credit was as good as his reputation. Dad cashed many a check written by a rancher on a bar napkin in Frenchie's saloon where the transaction was completed with a handshake. While a bar napkin may not be "legal tender" in many places, it was honored as such at the Buffalo Gap State Bank.

Frank often expanded his herd with an IOU. A hand shake and IOU from Frank Wilson was considered as good as cash. It was only a cash-flow situation. His land represented a capital investment far beyond any financial commitment, but Frank was never going to sell any part of his ranch. So he would travel in from the Cheyenne River to the bank, take out a loan and redeem all the IOUs. My classmate, "Shortie" (Anita) Gallentine, who ran a saloon in Buffalo Gap, received some of these across the bar when Frank was negotiating with some rancher for cat-tle.

Frank and Julia often came to our dances in the Buffalo Gap audi-torium which were held on all the holiday occasions. One of the social customs at these dances occurred during intermission, when ranchers would invite each other out to their car to pull out a bottle to share with each other. Dad tells about the time that he was invited out by Adolph Sanson, along with Frank and several other ranchers. Sanson reached in his front compartment, pulled out a bottle and handed it to Dad, who took a swig. Dad was surprised that Sanson was drinking wine, but said nothing and handed the bottle to another rancher. It went around the circle of ranchers and the bottle finally got back to Adolph, who as host was the last to drink. He took a swig, and then spit it out.

"Wine!" He exclaimed. "Hell, this isn't my car."

In about 1960, when Frank reached the age of sixty, he began to expand his land holdings and herd size and his ranch became huge. He bought out a number of ranchers in the area, and by the 1970s, the Wilson empire had pastures that started west in the Cheyenne River country, ran north to Badlands National Monument, east across Cuny Table, and south through the reservation past Oglala and down into Nebraska. They contained the herd that numbered the five thousand cattle reported in his obituary.

A counterpart to the Wilson ranch was the Temple ranch on the reservation that lay to the east. In 1960, rancher Alan Temple died, leaving the ranch to his eighteen-year-old son and widowed mother, who was a school teacher. Wilson went to the Temple ranch, befriended young Doug Temple, offered his help, and the two became close friends. Their ranches joined at the eastern edge of Cuny Table, and the Temple ranch then covered most of the entire eastern portion of the reservation, through the White River country, and all the way to the town of Interior.

My best memories of Frank Wilson are from the annual Buffalo Gap rodeo where he was always the rodeo arena boss, and he and his brother, Blutch, were always the pickup men. While Frank was on horseback running the rodeo, My Dad as the rodeo secretary and treasurer, was on the platform over the bucking chutes handing out prize money. Frank Wilson fit the romantic image of the ultimate cowboy who became a cattle baron. He was one of the best working cowboys on the frontier, rode tall in the saddle, and he continued as roundup boss of that region for several decades. After his death at the age of eighty in 1982, a roundup in his memory was held with his many friends from across the reservation invited. Over five hundred were there – the largest roundup ever held on the Buffalo Gap frontier. It was a fitting tribute.

BLUTCH WILSON

Perhaps the most colorful cowboy that ever rode the Buffalo Gap Frontier was Blutch Wilson. He was the ultimate cowboy on the open range, and a consummate fighter in a good saloon brawl. His late daughter, Alice, identified him this way in the history she provided for the book, *Our Yesterdays.*

> *Seventy years ago my Dad was born (1899), the sec-*

ond son of Tom and Zona Wilson. Charles William, he was named, but few people knew him by that. He was nicknamed "Blutch". Dad has told several different versions of how he got his name, but I think I'll use the one my mother knows. Dad's only sister, Maybelle, who was younger than he, thought "Blutch" sounded better than Charles.

Dad's home was east and north of Buffalo Gap where Grandpa Wilson had a large ranch. He spent most of his young years here, going to Omaha, Nebraska, to a boarding school where he was quite rebellious. Knowing Dad, it was probably the lack of freedom, the open range, and the fresh air; he was never one to enjoy tight places.

When World War came, Dad enlisted in the navy by lying about his age, being only 17 years old, this was in 1917. In the year 1918 his mother passed away. He was given an honorable discharge from the navy that year, receiving a disability in his left arm, being injured while cranking an airplane. After several surgeries on the arm, he still could not turn it correctly, but this didn't stop him from going on with the life he loved. [125]

My first encounter with Blutch was in Bert's Barber Shop. As a little boy I spent a lot of time there, just visiting with Bert when the shop was empty and I had nothing else to do. The shop had two swivel barber chairs -- one was up front by the window available to anyone who wanted to sit there, passing the time of day and visiting with Bert. The other one was back in the rear in front of the mirror, where the barber did his work on a customer. Bert Doughty was a fat, jolly old man who was treated with respect by everyone, including the rough cowboy crowd in from the Cheyenne River for a Saturday night in town. Bert's shop was on the way in, so they'd stop there first, tie their horse to the hitching post in front under the tree, and drop into the shop for a shave and haircut. Bert always cut everyone's hair the same, and perhaps it had something to do with the fact that he was nearly blind and had to get real close to a head before going to work with comb and scissors. If the patron needed a shave, Bert extracted a steaming hot towel from the heater and before burning his hands, dropped it on the cowboy's face to loosen up the whiskers.

We Keating kids never got one of Bert's haircuts because Dad always used the clippers on us at home, but we spent a good deal of time sitting in the front swivel chair by the window when his shop was empty, and he seemed to enjoy having someone to talk to.

I had heard Dad talk at home with mother about Blutch, because Dad had several run-ins with this cowboy from the reservation, and the name carried a high threshold of fear for a little boy like me. One Saturday afternoon when I was sitting in the swivel chair, a particularly fearsome looking cowboy entered the shop, and Bert addressed him as "Blutch." You can imagine how that got my attention.

"Bert, I need a shave and haircut," he said in a no-nonsense manner. "Am I next in line?" He said it more or less as a joke, because I was the only one in the shop. Well, I quickly slid down off that swivel chair and made a hasty exit out the front door.

Blutch looked the part of a genuine cowboy, over six feet tall, rawboned, and wearing chaps and spurs from his ride into Buffalo Gap. On Saturday afternoons, several such cowboys were usually in town. Those were the days with few fences, so the herds of the ranchers were intermixed throughout the Cheyenne River country and Pine Ridge Indian Reservation. A rancher wanted a hired hand that was not only a skilled cowboy, but also could not be intimidated by anyone. Blutch fit that description, and he always had a job. On Saturday noon after a week of hard work, many of the cowboys would saddle up and ride into town. Their first stop would be at Bert's for a shave and haircut, then over to Frenchie's saloon to throw down a couple shots of whiskey and join in the boisterous horseplay with fellow cowboys. Much of it was around the pool table or in the alcove where a card game was always in progress. Oft times, a few of them may leave the saloon, climb on their horse, and ride down the street to raise hell with the locals. The part-time deputy sheriff, Gene Griffis, wanted no part of the action and normally found other things to do on Saturday afternoons and evenings. The town folks generally ignored what they saw as harmless cowboy saloon horseplay. Although some of the cowboys carried iron, I don't recall anyone ever getting killed with a gun during those years; at least not in Buffalo Gap.

Virtually born in the saddle, Blutch could do the total job of cowboy better than anyone else on the range. He could cut a herd apart, sorting out what belonged to whom, rope a calf and place a brand on it faster than anyone else, castrate a male calf, and when required, he could spring over the pommel of his saddle from his horse onto the horns of a steer and wrestle it to the ground. His younger brother, Owen, in the book *Our Yesterdays*, related the following:

> *"He loved to rodeo being a bronc rider, calf roper, and bulldogger. His bulldogging record of 3 seconds stood for many years. I am told that he was one of the best pickup men who ever worked in an arena."* [126]

Blutch and his brother Frank were always the pick-up men at the local rodeo. Their job was to move alongside the cowboy riding a bucking bronc and assist him off the horse when the time requirement for the ride was met. One pickup man would grab the halter rope of the bronc and snake it around his saddle horn, pulling the bronc alongside him. The cowboy, if he had managed to stay in the saddle for that long, would then swing behind the back of the pickup man and fall safely to the ground. The other pick-up man would then grab and release the strap that had been tightened against the flanks which had caused the horse to buck. This activity required the skill of an excellent horseman and the strength to manhandle a wild horse traveling at full speed. Frank and Blutch were the only two pickup men, I recall, who ever worked a Buffalo Gap rodeo, and that was probably at the urging of the cowboys, because a good pickup man was often their ticket to a safe landing. The only exception was when another cowboy had to substitute for Blutch when it came his time to ride a bronc.

Like most cowboys, Blutch thought nothing of riding his horse any place, and would seldom alight afoot. His brother, Owen, relates an incident at one Buffalo Gap Rodeo.

> *Blutch decided to ride his horse into the grandstand to see some of his friends who were there. An argument took place with the deputy sheriff who ordered him to stop. Blutch didn't heed whereupon the deputy shot him, the bullet lodging just below his heart and was never removed."* [127]

He carried that bullet with him when in military service during World War Two and it was still there until his death several decades later.

Blutch also rode his horse right out onto the dance floor during one Fourth of July dance sponsored by the Buffalo Gap Volunteer Firemen.

It was a big event for the town and everyone came and stayed until the wee hours. Wes Dalbey was always the dance chairman, and was also deputized for such events. The band consisted of local amateurs who made tolerable music. When the music started, Wes would walk around the dance floor spreading Ivory Soap flakes to make the dance floor slick enough for the cowboys to dance. Dad, being the banker and someone they could financially trust, was always appointed to stand at the little window in the entrance to sell tickets and collect the money.

The old auditorium was built in the 1880s as a multi-purpose dance hall and opera house with a stage. Ringing the floor on the three sides facing the stage, was a balcony where we kids normally spent our time during the dance. There were no babysitters in those days and everyone brought their children to the dance and left them on the balcony, which became their playpen with supervision by the dancers below.

During a dance number, into the auditorium on his horse, rode Blutch. Trotting past Dad at the entrance, he rode out onto the middle of the dance floor among the dancers, whereupon he pulled out his pistol and began shooting rounds over his head into the air.

Now that sort of thing can be very unsettling to those trying to dance, and it was also dangerous to us kids who were above him looking over the balcony rail at the scene below. Wes Dalbey and Dad sprang into action with the help of some cowboy dancers. Dad took the reins of the horse as Dalbey ordered Blutch to dismount. Dad led the horse out while Wes and some cowboys escorted Blutch out the side door. The band scarcely lost a beat, and the dancing resumed. Everyone knew it was just Buffalo Gap cowboy horseplay. [128]

Blutch finally settled down and he got married. This account is by his late daughter, Alice, written in 1970.

Dad and Mom, Julia Knueppel, were married in 1921. There were six children born to them…. For the next thirteen years Dad spent in the Hot Springs area, living on a farm and working with Granddad, Herman Knueppel….. Then the next few years I remember being very happy ones for Dad when he moved to a ranch east of the Cheyenne River that bordered the Indian Reservation. Since Dad was part Indian, he was able to lease a lot of the land. He took care of cattle for other ranchers during the summers, some of them being Phil Grif-

fin, Wes Bondurant, and John Maxon. Since I was inclined to be a "tom boy", I was soon Dad's bronc buster. I spent many hours riding with him. His love of animals, especially horses, is something that is hard to explain. The animals themselves seemed to know that Dad loved them, and they would do anything for him. I learned to respect my elders from caring for these cattle. At the end of one summer, Dad was settling up with Dave and Bill Brindley. I had received a check for the little help they thought I had done, so thinking I was pretty important, I called Bill Brindley by name, "Bill". Dad let them leave, and then I got the "belt". His respect for the aged, the little guy, etc, was probably why he had so many friends.

And the love of country: when World War Two broke out, he wanted again to defend his country, only no branch of the service would take him because of his disability (from the navy in World War One), so he joined the Seabees.

Dad and Mom were separated before he went into the service, so when he got back, he was able to devote all his time to rodeos…. In 1947 he received the all-around cowboy award at Sturgis… He was a life member of the Rodeo Cowboys Association; his number was 3626….. As I remember Dad, he loved rodeoing, ranching, and was always available to help the "under dog." [129]

Blutch passed away in 1958. The account by Alice demonstrated the great affection he had for his family, and in his later years, he became a doting grandparent.

Two of Blutch Wilson's good friends were Pat Cuny and Tom Norman. They rode many a mile with him, worked dozens of roundups together, and placed their boots alongside his on the brass rail in many a saloon. Both Pat and Tom will tell you that no finer friend ever lived than Blutch, and no wilder cowboy ever rode a horse than Blutch Wilson when he was partying.

Owen Wilson described his brother Blutch this way:

Blutch, I would say, was a man born too late for his time. He was a man of the plains and should have lived in the early days of the West as he would have fitted into that era better than the one in which he lived. [130]

THE WILSON FAMILY

Tom Wilson,
father of Frank and Blutch

Lois (Wilson) Rapp, daughter of Frank
Wilson. She continues ranching
with her son on the Pine Ridge
Indian Reservation

Frank Wilson, one of largest
ranchers in South Dakota

Blutch Wilson,
brother of Frank

ROUNDUP ON THE
BUFFALO GAP FRONTIER

This is a scene at an annual roundup. Frank Wilson, "Roundup Boss", is on the horse to the right, and Doug Temple is the roper on the left. These two mixed-blood Lakota men were among the largest cattle ranchers in South Dakota during their time.

Also working the roundup was Pat Cuny in the holding pens, and ropers included Dave Cuny, Tom Norman, and Frank Rapp. This 1968 roundup had three roping pens with four ropers in each and twelve crews doing the branding, a crew of nearly 300 cowboys. They started at daylight and branded 2058 calves by three in the afternoon when a huge storm hit the prairie. The story of this roundup is described by Frank Rapp in the chapter of New Frontier Ranchers.

5
NORMAN FAMILY OF THE CHEYENNE RIVER COUNTRY

"Dad, are you really Sioux with the name High Star?" Tom asked this for the third time that morning. He was-six-years old and had just learned that his Dad might be part Indian, which would make him part Indian, too. They were called Sioux in those days.

"Well, Tommy, yes and no. I was not born Indian." They were in the horse barn where his Dad was working on a lariat and fixing to spend another day in the saddle out on the range. He'd be riding across the Cheyenne River at the Lame Johnny ford and checking on a herd of cattle on an abandoned homestead he'd taken over the year before.

"But I guess you could call me Indian since I was taken into the tribe a few years ago when I was seventeen. They gave me the name of High Star."

"Wow." Tom never tired of the story. His Dad was taken into the tribe and became part Indian. "Does that make me part Sioux, too?"

"Don't rightly know, Tommy. Reckon maybe it might be. Do you want to be part Indian?"

"Yeah, I think I'll be about half-Indian like you, and then about half-white like mother, and then maybe about half-Irish like Granddad Rush?" His Dad smiled. On these cold mornings it wasn't easy to smile, and maybe it seldom was for his Dad, because he had a lot on his mind. Joe Norman finished his job on the lariat and threw a saddle on old Buck, the horse in the nearest stall. That mustang was his favorite horse, which is why he probably was riding it today for some rough going through the sagebrush country south across the river.

Joe had a big ranch for those unsettled years of the 1920s -- a couple sections -- and that did not include the Indian reservation east of their boundary where our cattle often grazed and pastured through the fence-less country. The Norman ranch house was a few miles from Buffalo

Gap, where Lame Johnny Creek flows into the Cheyenne. There really wasn't much flow this time of year in either the creek or the river. The river could be a raging torrent in the spring when it was swollen with the winter snow melting, but come mid-summer, it died down to barely a trickle as it meandered through the sand banks. Lame Johnny Creek flowed into the river near their ranch house was about the same, except lesser so. It completely dried up by late summer, except for a few sump holes here and there, or the quick run-off from afternoon showers. Some years those showers would come several times a week and keep every-thing green. Other summers none would come and the country would dry up and blow away. In those dry years, grass for cattle would pretty much disappear and water was scarce, except for the three springs they had on the ranch. After Tom went to bed, he'd hear his parents talking about what to do.

"Dad, when you were a little boy back in the Badlands and those Indians would come through, would you be scared?"

"Yes, Tommy, I reckon I would be. You see, there was a lot of trou-ble with the Indians in those days." He threw the saddle on old Buck and cinched it up. Then he led the horse past Tom and out the barn door.

"Tommy, you be good and help your mother and sister. I'll be back by nightfall. You start the chores, throw some hay for the horses, and I'll be back in time to help you finish them"

Tom's Dad was three-years-old when he came to Dakota Territory in 1887 with his parents and grandparents. They homesteaded east of Hermosa on Finney Flat. The boundary of the Indian reservation was directly across the Cheyenne River, and nomadic Indians were a way of life. Indians were supposed to be confined to the reservation, but since there was nothing to eat on the reservation and it was a struggle to sur-vive, they pretty much went where they needed to go. Indians who had lived all their lives as warriors on this land would forage through the rough country adjacent to the reservation. The government had prom-ised them food and provisions, but sometimes nothing showed up. It did not take long for Joe Norman's father to become dissatisfied with the hardships of the frontier and wandering Indians, so he returned to the east, deserting his wife, never to be heard from again. Joe's mother, Til-lie, became a single mother who raised Joe and his little sister by herself on a homestead across the Cheyenne from the reservation.

A year later, the "Indian Scare of '90" became a troublesome time both for the Lakota and for the pioneers who lived on the Buffalo Gap frontier. The Battle of the Little Bighorn with General Custer had just occurred a few years before. Now the Indians were bitter and frightened about what might happen to them, as well they might be. One way to cope was by taking part in those rituals called the Ghost Dance, where they would circle, sway and chant for hours or even days until they dropped from exhaustion. The cavalry tried to maintain some security for white settlers in the area, but it was a feeble effort for the most part. Many of these soldiers were European immigrants who came to America, found no work, and with no other choice, joined the cavalry. Few spoke good English, some had never ridden a horse before, and none cared for either the Indians or the settlers.

Some settlers had close calls with the Indians. Many a night, Joe's mother, Tillie, would flee with her two small children to sleep in a plowed field covered with quilts as a hiding place until daylight came. The Indians burned their home and everything they owned, but they did not give up. Taking her two children with her, Tilled moved to the protection of Hermosa until the scare was over, and then started all over again on the homestead. [131]

Then later that year providence came calling. Tillie married a fine man, Jack Daley, and moved with her family to his ranch on Battle Creek, where it flowed into the Cheyenne River, but after moving there, she again soon faced the dangers of being a pioneer woman. Jack Daley and his crew of ranch hands had been out rounding up cattle and ran short of provisions. Returning to the ranch, they surprised an Indian raiding party. The heavily-armed cowboys began shooting, but Tillie Daley had already grabbed her Sharps rifle and was prepared for trouble. She saw an Indian reaching down to open the corral gate where a remuda of horses was kept and fired. Her shot knocked the Indian from his horse and killed him. The other Indians turned back, picked up their fallen companion and fled, leaving behind his horse. She kept that pinto until the day it died. [132]

Joe was eight years of age at the time his mother remarried, and Daley became the only father he ever knew. Jack taught him how to ride horses, rope cattle, care for livestock, brand, and become an all-around cowboy. After the "Indian troubles" were over, the family made friends with the Indians. Joe learned the Indian language and could speak it fluently. This was when he was taken into the tribe and given the name of "High Star." Mary Mountain Sheep made Joe a beautiful Indian suit, complete with beaded moccasins -- buckskin suit all beaded -- and a large eagle feather war bonnet of brilliant colors for the ceremony. [133]

When he was twenty-seven, Joe married Kitty Rush, who also came from a pioneer family who had homesteaded in that Cheyenne River country. Their partnership flourished, and soon Joe and Kitty expanded their ranch holdings to include acreage on both sides of the Cheyenne River. Joe's pasture lands also included leases on the Indian reservation and his cattle roamed across a vast area.

Joe Norman's Lakota friend, Chief High Eagle, would come by the ranch every couple weeks for a friendly visit, riding his horse from the reservation on his way into Buffalo Gap. Wearing a leather vest, moccasins, and his flat-brimmed hat with an eagle feather, he'd usually arrive at the Norman ranch late in the morning. They'd hear the dogs barking to announce a visitor and look out the window to see High Eagle sitting on his horse.

"Joe! Joe!" He'd shout this several times until someone responded. If Joe Norman was home, he'd walk out and help him down from the horse, and they'd be talking in Lakota language as they walked into the house. Chief High Eagle always stayed for lunch and a long visit -- all of the talk in Lakota. On the days that Joe was out riding the range and not at home, Kitty Norman would invite High Eagle in for lunch, and on those occasions he would talk in his broken English with Kitty and young Tommy. He would finish eating, and then head toward Buffalo Gap.

Tom's father spent most days in the saddle out on the open range. With his mustang saddled and ready to ride, Joe was ready to depart for his day's work. "Okay, Tommy, I've got to be off," he said. "I'm going across the river today to check the herd over there. I'll be back for supper. You help your mother and sister with the chores." Joe led his horse out the barn door and then mounted. Tommy ran across the corral and opened the gate for them, closed it again, then climbed to the top rail.

"Goodbye, Dad. If you see Ted Peterson over there, tell him hello."

"Okay," Joe yelled back. Tommy was still waving when Joe rode out of sight. Tom was six now, and would probably be a tall cowboy someday like his father. Joe often wished something better for him, because the life of a rancher in this desolate and isolated part of South Dakota was not easy, but there were good parts to the life as well. He could ride as far as the saddle horse would carry him in a day and never reach the end of his open range. Of course, across the Cheyenne River and along the east side where it bordered with the Indian reservation, he would travel with care. Even though he was an honorary member of the Lakota tribe and most of the old warriors were his friends, one never knew when some young renegade would get ornery. That wasn't really the reason he wore a sidearm, and carried a rifle in the boot of his saddle; they were mostly for the predators -- such as wolves -- that were after his cattle, but that pistol in the holster made for a more understanding conversation when necessary.

Joe could understand Tommy's fascination with Indian things, but that was not the way he felt back at the turn-of-the-twentieth-century. The Indians were no blessing to the white settlers. They came through and would scare the hell out of people; especially women and children. Cavalry troops offered little security to settlers, for they pretty much stayed in their camp up at Fort Meade, and white settlers were left to fend for themselves. There was no means of communication between homesteads, except for someone on horseback who carried the latest news, which was mostly rumor. Someone would ride by the ranch house yelling that Indians were on the loose in the area and then chaos would break loose. The men would hide the terrified women and children in cellars, if they had one, and then would collect their posse at some pre-arranged place and head out to hunt for the Indians.

One winter, two troops of cavalry established a camp in a cottonwood grove at the mouth of Lame Johnny Creek, near the Norman place. God, it was cold, and those cavalry guys had to sleep on the ground in canvas tents. Joe's old dugout shack wasn't much better than a tent, and in some ways maybe was not even as good. While the troopers were camping there, it turned even colder. Some of the horses froze and died at their stakes. Cavalry horses were beautiful and the best that money could buy. Averaging fifteen-and-a-half-hands high, they were rugged enough to handle the tough job on the prairie, but were done in by that terrible winter. How bitter it was for those cavalry boys in tents, and how cold it was in the Norman shack alongside the iced-over Cheyenne River. Lakota families living a couple miles further east in their tipis also tried to keep warm and had virtually no food. In the old days, the Indians could warm their tipis with fires of dried buffalo chips, but there were no more chips, and there were few trees in this prairie country.

How did those Indians survive? A lot of them perhaps did not.

Joe Norman did not hold anything against Indians -- particularly now that he was part one himself, in a manner of speaking. After things settled down from the Wounded Knee affair on December 29, 1890, he got to know a few of them and learned their language. Joe could talk to Indian kids just as easily as he could with his own sister, and as he grew older, he began to ride with them when they encountered each other out on the range -- Indian boys on their little pinto ponies and Joe on his mustang. They'd sit on their horses and talk. Joe liked them, and they must have liked him, too, and that is when they made him a member of their Oglala tribe.

At the mouth of Lame Johnny Creek and just up the river a couple hundred yards was a sand bar providing a ford across the Cheyenne. Joe crossed the river there where the water was shallow. He saw no point in getting his boots wet during a river crossing in the chill of early morning, and he headed up the steep bluff on the south side of the river, turning east where he expected to find the herd. Joe's big spread on the north side of the river ran several thousand head of cattle. On the other side of the Cheyenne, Joe bought an old abandoned homestead, plus the Warren place, which had been the old Gunstock Ranch, where the owners raised horses to sell to the cavalry. A couple hundred head of Herefords were now pastured there. Ranching on both sides of a river that was impassable for part of the year wasn't convenient, but if one picked the time and place for crossing, it worked out.

Joe's horse picked his way up from a draw and at the top, Joe stopped near the only tree within sight, dismounted, and taking a canteen, went over to sit under it and rest a bit after his early morning start. No point in riding hard, he thought, because the range south of the river was a small spread with good fence-lines and a herd that was likely okay -- not like that time back nearly forty years ago, when in 1892 at eighteen he'd crossed the river at this same place and passed this same tree, but there were no fences and his parent's cattle roamed thirty miles east all throughout the Indian reservation. Joe remembered that was the time he nearly shot two Indian boys rustling cattle. Leaning back against the tree, Joe closed his eyes and his mind drifted off, thinking about those times.

What was different back then? Joe's memory led him east toward the reservation where he found small herds along the way with mixed brands -- some were their cattle -- some with the Z Bell brand, but most with the Wilson's or Hudspeth's brand. Crossing onto the reservation, the boundary was not marked, but it made no difference -- it was all grazing land. Reaching the crest of a ridge, Joe paused at the top, and down the draw a half-mile away, he saw two men working over a cow on the ground. This was not branding time; therefore, it was not the season for cowboys to have a cow on the ground. Quickly, Joe pulled back behind the ridge out of sight, working his way down a nearby draw until he was opposite them. Pulling his rifle from its boot on the saddle, he laid it across the pommel, then rode to the ridge and looked down. It wasn't cowboys, but two Indians who were butchering a cow. Any Indian caught in the act of rustling could be shot on sight. Should he shoot them? He'd never killed a man before, and wasn't anxious to develop that habit. Firing a warning shot over their heads, Joe yelled for them to stand clear of any weapons. The poachers sprang to their feet and raised their hands. Rifle at the ready, Joe slowly rode toward them, and without dismounting, he could see the Hudspeth brand on the cow. This meant trouble for these Indians, since he knew Bill Hudspeth would as soon shoot a thief as talk to one.

The two were young -- probably about Joe's same age -- but he did not recognize them. Speaking Lakota, Joe ordered them to start walking in front of him heading east. Shaken, the pair were perhaps surprised they had not been shot.

Several miles into the reservation they passed a few shacks, stopping at the one where Chief High Eagle lived. The old Sioux chief, sitting in the shade of his wickiup, stood as he saw the two Indian boys approach on foot, followed by Joe with a rifle.

"How kola", Joe said, sitting astride his horse, his rifle still pointing at the two men.

Chief High Eagle responded, "Joe Norman comes with rifle."

"Chief High Eagle, I could have shot these two. They were butchering one of Hudspeth's cows. If Hudspeth had caught them, or even heard about it, he would kill them," Joe said. High Eagle could speak a little English, but Joe preferred to keep his prisoners unaware of what was going on.

"Norman," he responded, "That is bad medicine they do. You are right, I know Hudspeth will shoot. If you will give them to me, I will see that they are punished."

"Okay," Joe said, wishing nothing further to do with the matter. He did not want to make enemies on the reservation. "I will leave them with you. I am returning to my ranch. If you go to the cow and save the meat for your people, be sure to hide the carcass and bones so Hudspeth does not find them."

Turning his horse to leave, Joe placed the rifle back in the boot of his saddle, and then stopped and turned back to speak to High Eagle. "Chief High Eagle," he said. "You are a fine Oglala chief who does not rustle the white man's cattle. If your people starve because the government gives you nothing, then before you let any of your young men rustle cattle, send them to our ranch. Maybe I can find some old cow they can trail back here."

"Norman, you are a good warrior," he said.

Joe turned and left.

That memory was from a long time ago, and awakening from his short nap under the tree, Joe felt refreshed. He would check the herd and the fence lines, head home, and get back in time to help young Tommy with the nightly ranch chores. Tom could handle most of them by himself now that he was getting older, but those jobs always came easier when a father and son do them together.

Joe Norman, the Cheyenne River rancher, and my Dad, Bernie Keating Sr., the Buffalo Gap banker, became good friends. Our families were brought together as parishioners of the little Catholic Church in town, and we spent many wintery Sunday mornings huddled around the pot belly stove next to the altar. Our families often spent Saturday nights at the Norman ranch, where our parents would play gin rummy, and Tommy and I would explore the barns and horse corrals in the eerie dark of night. Tom became a lifelong rancher on that same ranch of his parents.

1970: A COWBOY'S WIFE [134]

(Author's note: This account was written by the late Audrey Norman, Tom's wife)

Tom parked the pickup and turned to me. "Well, Sweetheart, here we are," he said and smiled.

"*Where* are we"? I asked.

"We are home. This is it. This is our home."

I sat in shock as I looked at the unpainted porch and a front door that hung askew. Walking through that door, we would begin a new life; one filled with hardship, privations, tears, poverty. But far more important, it would be a life of love, family, and purpose.

I remember the moment I first saw Tom at the high school dance -- he was standing on the other side of the dance floor looking at me. How strangely the expression in his eyes changed -- eyes that could look so humorous and amused as if he found something that brought a smile almost to his lips, yet they were eyes that could be filled with such a fire that it startled and excited me. Then he crossed the floor, walked right up to me, smiled, and asked me to dance.

Little did I know then that we would become sweethearts, and it would lead to my life as the wife of a cowboy in the remote, wild Buffalo Gap country. Now as I look back fifty years later, would I do it all again? Yes. Oh, Yes! I would make that commitment again in the flash of an eye.

And that's about how fast it all began.

I guess I'd heard that the new boy in our high school was a cowboy from a ranch somewhere, and that was about as far from my own upbringing as possible. I was a city girl, raised in Omaha with all the comforts of a plush home, and lived in the fast urban lane with upwardly mobile executive parents. I'd scarcely ever been outside the boundaries of a city, and Rapid City was about as rural as I knew; the countryside was no place I ever aspired to see, let alone live in. Yet here I was in high school -- the sweetheart -- going steady with a cowboy from a ranch in the Cheyenne River country a couple miles from the Sioux Indian reservation.

How did that happen? It must have been his smile and the look in those eyes.

We became formally engaged on graduation day and married a year later with a big wedding in the Catholic cathedral of Rapid City. There followed a honeymoon in Colorado, then the return to Rapid City where we loaded our few possessions, mostly wedding presents, in the back of his old pickup truck and headed south to the little town of Buffalo Gap. Driving east from there on a rutted dirt road that jostled us from side to side, we passed through a cattle guard and stopped at a barbed wire fence gate, which Tom held open as I drove the pickup through. Then he got behind the wheel again and drove down into a valley with a grove of cottonwood trees and parked the pickup in front of an old, unpainted house that appeared to be abandoned. That's when I first saw what was to be our home for the next fifty years.

The house was on the old John Maxon ranch, which was then owned by Tom's widowed, wealthy aunt, and she made the place available to us to live in, knowing we had no place else to go, and no money. She also knew Tom was a fine young man who needed a start in life, and she was able to help him with a lease on this little starter ranch. The house was semi-abandoned -- or more accurately stated -- had never really been occupied by anyone other than an old man and his dogs. The stone foundation had been laid thirty years before in 1918, and the old relic had become an on-again, off-again, work-in-progress ever since. It was a strange deviant for the Buffalo Gap wilderness, consisting of 4 large rooms downstairs, 5 bedrooms upstairs, maid's quarters and a 32-foot by 12-foot dance hall, also located upstairs with hardwood floors. The house had a flat "beer garden" roof which always leaked. The outside had never been completed either, having merely been covered with black tar paper and no insulation. I often wondered how it had come together in this weird fashion.

We had only the bare essentials for furniture -- no electricity, no hot water, no car except for Tom's ancient pickup, and very little money. It was indeed different for a city girl and Tom had to begin to educate his new wife to the ways of country life; like cooking on a wood-burning range, raising chickens and cutting off their heads, then watching the headless body flop and run around until dead, and listening to coyotes howling just outside our window at night.

Our first winter -- my first away from home and that familiar city life -- was one I shall never forget. The blizzard came in December -- just before Christmas -- and with little preparation, we were totally snowbound for six weeks. Tom and I saw nothing looking outside the kitchen window but the endless snow drifting across the prairie, and inside, only each other. Some people may call this togetherness, but one experience like that was enough. Then there was the cold. Fortunately, we had laid in a supply of coal, but the house was so large and hard to heat that one never got warm. It was survival time. A caterpillar driver who was there to help the ranchers clear places to feed snowbound livestock stayed with us a night or two and observed, "It's warmer outside on my caterpillar than it is in this old house," and that was probably true. With the assistance of neighbor ranchers who helped feed our cattle, our losses of livestock were light; so we stayed solvent, if just barely. Then a year later with the help of a cowboy family friend of Tom's, we were able to buy the ranch from Tom's aunt. So now we were officially ranchers, and I was a rancher's wife.

A year later our first child was born. She was a beautiful baby girl with rosy cheeks and a mouth the shape of a tiny heart. We named her Kathryn Mary after Tom's mother, my mother, and my grandmother. The entire families on both sides were pleased. That summer we bought our first car -- something to go with the old pickup truck that barely worked. It was a pre-war 1941 DeSoto, and I thought how lucky we were to have so much. I decided that I should become a true ranchman's wife and had Tom order 500 baby chickens to raise; also a few turkeys and geese. All went well until it was time to eat them. One Sunday I invited my parents down from Rapid City for a fried chicken dinner. Tom thought that it was "now" or "never" if his wife was to ever learn to dress poultry, and he decided it should be "now." Then came the scene of my using the axe for cutting off their heads with much crying, and headless chickens flopping around, but we did have chicken for our Sunday dinner.

The following summer the R.E.A. (Rural Electrification Act) came into our territory. It was a long-awaited event for all the ranchers who had lived a lifetime with kerosene lanterns. Now for the first time we had electricity. Because we were expecting our second child soon, Tom bought an automatic washer, a hot water heater, and a refrigerator. Those conveniences, along with electric lights made ranch life so much easier.

That summer we had our second daughter, Judith Ann. She was a very good baby, for she slept most of the time and hardly cried. Our family was getting larger, but our house was still too large. So that fall, Tom tore off the upper story and the flat roof and replaced it with a pitched roof and just two bedrooms upstairs. Then a year later, our home was sided and insulated and now we were real comfortable. Then our third daughter, Robin Lynn, was born. She was a fat, cuddly baby and the joy of the whole family.

A year later we bought our first sheep. We soon learned that our fences weren't good enough and began building new fences throughout the whole ranch. Those old fences were the ones built at the turn-of-the-century when the landscape was tamed, and they had deteriorated over a good many years.

A year later, we came close to losing our baby Robin with pneumonia. The same day she was released from the hospital our fourth daughter, Colleen Susan, was born. She was a very tiny baby, weighing just a little over five pounds. Now we decided that our family was complete, and although we still didn't have a son, we would be content to wait for the "son-in-laws."

About that time, the Angostura Dam started providing water for irrigation into our area; so Tom turned from rancher to "farmer," planting corn and alfalfa. Irrigation came in July, and there were many new things to learn and many long, hard hours of work. Tom continued to farm and irrigate for many years, but he always disliked farming, and consequently developed a severe case of ulcers, which led to a stomach operation. During those years, we ran a band of about 1200 ewes, rotating them on the irrigated pasture. Over the years we have raised cattle, horses, sheep, and farmed, and none of it came easy for Tom. It involved hard work, long hours, and the stress of decisions about what and when to buy or sell, which seemed like casino gambling, and for us the stakes were always high, because we started with so few resources.

We entered a new phase in our family life as the older girls joined 4-H, and we bought our first Quarter horse. In the next few years, as the girls grew older, each had to have her own horse. Because these Quarter horses purchased were mares, our Quarter horse business soon began to grow, and before long we had quite a herd. These two factors -- 4-H and the horses -- then became the center of our lives. None of the family minded working hard during nine months of the year, for we knew that during the summer months there would be much fun, recreation and companionship as we traveled with the horses to shows and to participate in 4-H events. The memories and wonderful people we met through those two projects are as "gold" to us.

Our four daughters have always been the center of our lives. From the first day they were born, each has been different from the others; each with their unique personality. All are outgoing, and I suppose they get that from their father. I have never met anyone who did not like Tom or consider him a personal friend; he had that kind of quality. I am happy that our daughters all inherited some of that. In our book, each of them is a superstar, and they have many trophies and honors to confirm that; but they are also modest about their successes and accomplishments. As they become young adults, Tom and I have provided them with the best we could do, and now they go out on their own. I learned the first day I met Tom that young people will do their own thing like we did. Parents then begin their toughest job of all, watching children grow into young adults and providing them with the love and support they need.

POSTSCRIPT BY A DAUGHTER

Mother wrote those memoirs several years ago to be included in the book *Our Yesterday's*, which was the product of the Eastern Custer County Historical Society. Mother was one of the directors of the society, and the book was a labor of love that took several years for her and her many "old timer" friends.

Sadly, mother died a couple years ago, and we dearly miss her. I am one of the daughters raised on that ranch alongside the Cheyenne River and I grew up with the horses, cattle, sheep, drought, blizzards, and the Sioux Indian reservation a couple miles east of the ranch. I lived in that wonderful home in the shade of those stately cottonwood trees, just up the hill from the horse corrals. If Mom and Dad ever wanted a son, they never complained, because they had four daughters who loved them dearly.

We girls were raised in a ranch environment in a country that some would describe as isolated and desolate, but it did not seem that way to us. We learned how to be girls and good cooks and feminine inside the house, and cowgirls and ranch hands in the outdoors. I have ridden my Quarter horse all over the many miles of the Cheyenne River country and on into the reservation, and I rode those miles because our cattle ranged there and it was a cowhand's job to be there with them. I assisted Dad with bringing calves into the world, branding calves, and shearing sheep; and I can also decorate a girl's bedroom, cook a mushroom omelet, and dance rock-and-roll. I can do all those things because of the wonderful life we girls had with Mother and Dad on that ranch.

What was growing up on a ranch like compared to something else? I can't tell you and compare it to anything else, because it was the only life I have lived. I married a cowboy rancher and my early life led naturally right into the next. Hopefully, I will have many years of this ranching life with my Quarter horses and my own family ahead, because I love it. Then someday we cowgirls will get together at round-up time with Mother and Dad in that big ranch in the sky.

6
TOWN OF BUFFALO GAP

Cuny Table on the Pine Ridge Indian Reservation borders the Cheyenne River and is twenty miles east across the river from the town of Buffalo Gap. It was a four hour horse ride; three on a good trotter. Since Cuny Table was isolated by the steep cliffs at the edge of the plateau and a badland region which separated it from the Pine Ridge Agency to the south, Indian families often traveled west to the Cheyenne River country and Buffalo Gap for their provisions and social contacts. The cultures of Reservation Indian, Cheyenne River rancher, and Buffalo Gap townspeople became intertwined.

Buffalo Gap had a general store, post office and a few other businesses, but after the railroad terminus was extended beyond the town in 1887, it pretty much died. However, it did still have the few things the ranchers in the vicinity needed, and there was no other place within traveling distance where they could shop.

Buffalo Gap became what today is popularly called a "ghost town." Only a few souls inhabited it, and a main street that had burned to the ground had little to offer. During the gold rush, the population exploded to three thousand, and then afterwards the town went from boom to bust. Only one hundred -sixty people lived there when we did in the 1930s, but the town still had these remnants from the early days:

 Livery barn run by Mel Thompson
 Blacksmith shop run by Burl Degnan
 Ferrier Ed Cole to nail shoes on horse hoofs
 Charlie Streeter's saddle shop
 Henne's Gristmill powered by water wheel
 J.B. Berry, the telegraph operator at the train depot
 Hitching post in front of Frenchie's saloon for cowboys
riding into town

We also had the white pioneers and Indian warriors from the battles of yesteryear. Hunched-over old men, hobbling on canes, spent most their days sitting on the bench in front of Frenchie's spinning tales about the good old days. In later years the saloon was renamed the Stockman's Bar, then Bill's Bar, and is now Stormin' Norman's. In truth, those times in the old days probably weren't so good. Most had spent a lifetime in a saddle out in that Cheyenne River country and when crippled-up, turned the ranch over to a son or daughter, and then moved to the comforts of town. Younger cowboys came to town on Saturday night to get drunk and raise hell in the saloon.

Indians from the reservation were living at the edge of town, in tents alongside Beaver Creek. They worked on the Sewright ranch to repay their debts from the previous winter, when their services had been bartered for meat and potatoes, so that their families could survive the winter. Perhaps Bill Sewright took advantage of their desperate situation to his benefit, but even at that, he was more charitable than the U.S. Government.

When I was a boy in Buffalo Gap, I did not realize I was living among those who would become legendary in future years. To me, they were just old folks; nice to a little boy, but they didn't seem to amount to much. Gene Griffis lived next door in a big ranch house, but he didn't do much ranching anymore, seldom rode a horse, and he left all the heavy work to a hired hand. My Dad told me that Uncle Gene -- that's what we kids called him -- came up from Kansas with a cattle drive. Years later he was appointed deputy sheriff, which was hard to believe, because now he was all hunched over and walked with a cane.

Then there was the elderly No Water, who came from the reservation in the summer with his family and lived in a canvas tipi. While his grown son -- also called No Water -- worked on the Sewright ranch, the old man sat under a cottonwood tree all day and never talked to anyone except us kids, because we were the playmates of his grandson.

I did not know much about the history of the place, and why would any kid care much about history? You can't play with it, eat it, or trade it with other kids for marbles. Then I grew older and wiser, looked back, and realized that Buffalo Gap and those old folks were a memory to be treasured. That was wasted on me as a young boy.

A little stream flowed down from the Black Hills and meandered out onto the plains and emptied into the Cheyenne River. Buffalo herds traveled along this water route, so it was a favorite hunting place for the

Lakota who lived on the plains. Pitching their tipis along the stream, they created an Indian village during the fall and spring when buffalo were on the move.

Frazier in *On the Rez* reported *"Whiteman, a Cheyenne holy man, said that the sun dance, sacred to many Plains tribes originated at Buffalo Gap, where the buffalo themselves first performed it and later taught it to the Indians."* [135]

Frazier also quoted Charlotte Black Elk, granddaughter of the famous Lakota chronicler, Nicholas Black Elk, describing the Buffalo Gap this way: *"Two low hills rise on either side of the entrance to the gap. … If you turn off onto the gravel road leading up the gap, you proceed along the creek and follow a little north-south sidle around some bluffs. In the next moment, the terrain shifts from rolling prairie to mountain canyon. In another moment, mountain landscape has enclosed you on all sides. The gap is one of the magical places of the West."* [136]

This mountain landscape also has personal memories for me as I worked here as a cowboy on the 7-11 ranch for a year in my youth.

The surrounding valley provided access for stagecoaches to enter the Black Hills. A stagecoach station was established there to provide fresh teams. [137] Passengers, who spent days riding inside the uncomfortable coaches could disembark, buy whiskey at the crude bar, get a hot meal, and sleep in a bed. They could also check for general delivery mail at the official U.S. Post Office which operated from a beer crate with slots for sorted mail.

Stagecoach stations attracted other businesses, and gradually the place became the town of Buffalo Gap with twenty saloons and two thousand people. Three livery barns were opened. In those days when everything was done by horse, the livery barn was a service station for horses. The town also had "sporting houses" according to local historians, but they never explained what sport went on in those places, where the women came from, or what they did for a living. When asked about it, most historians simply referred to it as the world's oldest "profession."

Arch Wilder Riordan was a cowboy who came from Texas to Dakota trailing a cattle herd in the 1880s, and by the time he arrived in Buffalo Gap he'd gotten tired of the lonesome life as a drover. Arch decided to give up the life of a cowboy and go into business for himself, so he started a drug store - saloon combination. He had the prerequisites for a successful businessman: handsome at six feet, Kentucky accent, friendly, and likeable. His business did well, but lawlessness in the town became an increasing problem. With all the shootings, people knew something must be done to bring law and order to the place. The businessmen held a secret meeting and asked Riordan if he would take on the job of town marshal. He accepted, so they pinned a star on his vest.

Soft spoken, Riordan tried to fade into the background. He began to bring as much law to the town as could be expected with the rough transients who were passing through, his gun was the option of last resort.

Quenna Stewart in *Our Yesterday's* reported that Riordan seemed to have a charmed life *"escaping many close calls. To relate one incident: after taking the gun from an obstreperous bad man, Arch locked him in the jail. The jails, in that day, were heavy 10 ft. by 10 ft. buildings with solid doors and small iron-barred windows. As the Marshal walked away, the prisoner called him and shot with a small revolver which had been secreted in his boot-top, but missed. Riordan returned the shot and advised the prisoner that he would carry the evidence of attempted murder the rest of his life. With that, Riordan proceeded to shoot off the lobe of Sam's left ear."* [138]

But he did kill one man, Charley Fugit, a hired gun from Wyoming who had come to Buffalo Gap, announcing his intention to kill the marshal. The gunslinger made a mistake, because Riordan was not intimidated. Riordan met him on the street in front of the saloon, drew fast, shot straight, and killed him in self-defense. Fugit was buried that evening on Boot Hill. Law had been firmly established.

Riordan married a girl who was rumored to work in a sporting house. After she died, he retired, and then moved away. Arch was eventually replaced by another cowboy who trailed a herd up from Kansas, arriving at about the same time as Riordan. That man was our next-door neighbor, Gene Griffis, whose wife was Anna.

"Good morning. My goodness, is it the three little Keating kids?" asked Aunt Anna, which is what all the kids in town called her.

"No, ma'am, we are not the Keating kids," I announced in as firm a voice as my seven years would permit. "We are hobos, and we are begging today." Our little town of Buffalo Gap got its share of hobos who lived in the box cars that traveled up and down the train tracks at the edge of town, so the migrant bums figured prominently in the minds of local children. When one hit town, all the doors were locked.

"Oh, you look just like some Keating kids that live next door, but I guess you aren't."

"No, ma'am," spoke up my little sister, Betty, age six. "We aren't them. We are bums begging for food."

"Oh, I see. Hobos are you? Well, I heard there were hobos in town. Would you like to come in the kitchen and I will look for some food?"

"No, ma'am," said my little brother, Billie, age four. "Mom said we can't bother you. If she finds out, she will be mad."

"Well, I'm sure it will be alright with your mother if three little hobos stand here on the porch while I check the cookie jar in the kitchen to see if it has anything in it." She returned with three cookies.

"Is Uncle Gene at home?" I asked. He was a favorite cowboy of mine.

"No, he's out in the pasture working with the hired hand today."

"Okay. Well, thank you for the cookies," I said as we walked away.

"Goodbye, hobos," Anna said. It was a game familiar to her played, many times during the summer, and she always kept a full cookie jar for just such occasions.

Gene Griffis had trailed a cattle drive up from Kansas, decided to settle down in Buffalo Gap, and began working on the Sprague ranch. A pretty girl, Anna, came up from Kansas on the stagecoach looking for him. She wasn't exactly a mail-order bride. She was a niece of the Sprague's, and they told her family back in Kansas that they had a good bachelor cowboy named Gene in mind for her, and when she got to Buffalo Gap, they were married. The Sprague Ranch house with its barn and corrals was located next to the house where we lived. When rancher Sprague died, his widow asked Griffis to take over the ranch, move into the big house with Anna, and run the place. Then the widow Sprague left to live in California. Many years later after Riordan had retired as town marshal, Buffalo Gap was again in need of a lawman, though it could no longer afford to pay someone on a full- time basis. Gene was asked to become deputy sheriff part-time while he kept ranching. Griffis accepted. Most of the time he ranched, but when trouble was brewing -- like on Saturday night or at rodeo time -- he'd pin the star to his vest, strap on his gun leather, and head downtown. He seldom had to draw his gun, and he never did pull the trigger. No one ever wanted to challenge him. They all knew that if they shot Gene Griffis, the townspeople would have them hanging from a rafter of Frenchie's saloon before sunset. Gene and Anna had one son, and some way or another, he attended medical school and then entered the army. During World War II, he became one of the top medical generals in the Army Air Force. It didn't seem possible that a boy from a ranch in Buffalo Gap could accomplish all of that. I attended Gene Griffis's funeral when he died in his late eighties from the ravages of rheumatism.

Another pioneer family was also our next-door neighbor, Charlie Streeter. Traveling through the town of Custer where General Custer found gold, you must visit the museum which occupies the former courthouse, and see a marvelous horse saddle with the maker's inscription, "Streeter." I spent many hours as a boy at the elbow of Charlie Streeter watching him craft cowhide into beautiful saddles, and also listening to his never ending string of stories.

"Charlie," I addressed him as I peered over his shoulder while he hammered an embossing tool into the leather. "How did you learn to make saddles?"

"Well now, it's like this. Some folks say I never did learn." Then he laughed so hard he had to stop hammering for a minute. "You see, I never had anyone to teach me, because there weren't any other saddle makers in the territory. So I just purchased some saddle trees and started making saddles." He paused as if he'd never considered the question before. "Guess, I just learned it by myself."

"Wow!" I exclaimed. "You just started making saddles on your own? But how did you know how?"

"Don't rightly know." He laid down the tool. "Well, that about does it for that flap," he said as he submerged the leather in the oil vat. "That's all for today. You'd better head for home before your mother comes looking for you." He was right. I had already been at his elbow for most the afternoon, and it was nearly supper time. Better get home before I caught the dickens from Dad for pestering Charlie Streeter too much. But Charlie didn't seem to mind.

The Streeter Hardware and Saddle Shop in Buffalo Gap never had any finished saddles on the premises, because they were all sold and out the door the instant Charlie finished one. In fact, in later years the ranchers who could afford a C.G. Streeter saddle and wouldn't ride on anything else, commissioned them all in advance.

Charlie came to Dakota Territory before the turn-of-the-last century, when his father homesteaded west of Buffalo Gap, at the headwaters of Beaver Creek that flowed down though the valley. Charlie was one of thirteen children. They all grew up and married in the local area, so virtually everyone in the vicinity of Buffalo Gap and the Cheyenne River was a Streeter "shirt tail" relative. Charlie spent years in the saddle on the ranch, but by the age of thirty he got tired of being a cowboy, and decided to move to town and open the Streeter Hardware and Saddle Shop. It was a tiny shop and only stocked a few things ranchers would need, like nails and barbed wire. Nails came in tall wooden casks that did double-duty as stools for customers and kids who wanted to sit and talk with Charlie, or more likely, listen to Charlie talk, because he was a talker.

I can hear him still. "You kids here in Buffalo Gap have got it soft," he would begin. "The only schooling I got was in a tiny shack they called a school out near the ranch. I had to ride on horseback whether sunshine or blizzard. All the grades were in the same room and sometimes it was so crowded we'd have to share a desk with two other kids. It was usually my luck that I ended up in a desk with Carl and Adolph Sanson and someone else would get to sit with the pretty Parker girls." Then Charlie would laugh, and with any encouragement would continue to tell another story.

"You'll notice I always wear a hat, even here in the shop. Well, that goes back to my school days. Seems I never knew where my hat was when it was time to go to school. Mother was disgusted with me, so one morning she took off her sunbonnet, placed it on my head, and told my two older sisters to see that I wore it to school. They obeyed her, and I wore that sunbonnet to school, and all the kids laughed at me. It was a good lesson, because there hasn't been a minute since that I did not know where my hat was." Then he laughed again. In all the years that I knew Charlie, I could have told you where his hat was, because it was always on his head. The only occasion I can recall otherwise was one Sunday when our family was invited to his place for dinner, and he removed his hat for the blessing.

The focal point of the saddle shop was the workbench at the rear where Charlie crafted his saddles. When he started the shop, his saddle experience consisted of riding a horse with one, and he had never spent a day with any other saddle maker, so he learned the craft entirely on his own. He purchased a few saddle trees -- the underlying skeleton of a saddle -- and began to fashion the leather, then carve designs with his variety of leather-embossing tools. Soon Streeter saddles became recognized by all the local cowboys as the best ones available in the Cheyenne River country, and then the word spread elsewhere. He always had a large backlog of unfinished orders, but Charlie never became rich for two reasons: his prices were always reasonable, and his output was always low because Charlie liked to stop work and visit with anyone who entered the shop, whether it was a customer or a local kid like me.

One of my prized possessions was a C.G. Streeter belt. In the early thirties during the Depression years, the town's entertainment consisted of such things as pie socials held in the Methodist church and amateur hour contests held in the old auditorium. One year at an amateur hour one of the events was "Best Cowboy Singer." Everyone knew Leo Mohler, a cowboy from the Cheyenne River country would win it, because he was a real cowboy -- handsome, and a good singer. He sang at all the local country dances and was a spitting image of today's Country-Western star, Clint Black. The prize for first place was to be a leather belt crafted by C.G. Streeter. Leo came out in his leather chaps, silver spurs that jingled, and wearing a holster like he always did. With his gut-string guitar, he sang in his usual fine voice, and received the deserved applause.

But there was to be a second mystery entry.

Then onto the stage stepped my little brother Billie, age four, and myself, age seven. We wore canvas chaps mother had sewn, toy six-shooters, hats purchased at the five-and-dime store in Rapid City, and each strumming the rubber band strings on a guitar made by my older brother from a cigar box and broom handle. And in wavering kid voices, we sang the hit song of the day, *"Empty Saddles,"* from a movie featuring the new crooner, Bing Crosby. That was seventy years ago, but I may remember some of the lyrics:

> *Empty guns, covered with rust*
> *Where do you talk tonight?*
> *Empty boots, covered with dust*
> *Where do you walk tonight?*

Refrain:

> *Empty saddles in the old corral,*
> *Where do you ride tonight?*
> *If you'll only say you love me,*
> *As you carry my old pal,*
> *Empty saddles in the old corral.*

Buffalo Gap gave us the biggest standing ovation that auditorium had ever seen, and we were awarded first place. What to do with a belt that was several times too big for us? Charlie Streeter came up with a solution. He crafted two small belts, one for Billie and one for me, and I suspect he give that other belt to Leo Mohler. When I grew older, that original belt became too small for me, so Charlie made it longer with an extension, and I continued to wear it until I left for college. I wonder what happened to it after that, and wish I still had it. Something by C.G. Streeter would be a collector's item today.

At July Fourth celebrations in Buffalo Gap, we always had a rodeo and festivities. A dozen wagons of Oglala Lakota families would ride in from the Pine Ridge reservation and pitch tipis in a vacant lot next to the main intersection in town across from my father's bank. They were lured off the reservation by the prize money they could win as rodeo riders, and they usually won. The Indian women competed in horse-drawn wagon races down Main Street; also for prize money. This was our white man's celebration of a national holiday, but it was also a celebration for the Indians who honored their Indian traditions in the shadow of *pah-HA SAH-pah*. When darkness fell, they met in the bank intersection for a night of dancing around a camp fire. Several braves pounded on drums chanting a hypnotic rhythmic beat, while a couple dozen warriors in full tribal dress danced in a circle around the fire. The Indian women stood off to one side in a long line and swayed in a heel dance to the beat of the drums. We townspeople watched this spectacle that, even then, we knew was a passing pageant on the Western scene.

Each summer of my youth, the U.S. Cavalry passed through Buffalo Gap on their annual expedition from Fort Meade, sixty miles north, to Fort Robinson, a hundred miles south in Nebraska, and the troops with their horses bivouacked in the open field west of our school. This regiment from Fort Meade was the last place, along with Fort Robinson, where a horse cavalry was still maintained with all of the old traditions unchanged until becoming mechanized during World War II.

One of the thrilling sights of my childhood during the 1930s was watching three hundred cavalry troopers riding their horses four abreast through Buffalo Gap and up the school hill to their bivouac in the field behind our school house. While they normally wore khaki, for this annual event they wore the cavalry blue, now seen mostly in Hollywood movies. Leading the contingent and wearing a sword was the commander, followed by the colors and bugler. The troopers carried rifles in the boot of their saddles. There were six companies, fifty mounted troopers in each, and all the horses in each company were the same color: A Company, coal black; B Company, bays; C Company, sorrels; D Company, blood bays; E Company, grays; F Company, horses of mixed colors; and the two flag bearers rode white stallions. My memory may be blurred about some of the horse colors, but that is how I remember them. [139] My favorite was A Company, leading the regiment with their beautiful black steeds. After the troopers had watered, rubbed down, and picketed their horses, they pitched their tents in long rows, and then permitted us to enter the camp. George No Water and I were the first into camp and the last to leave. It never occurred to me until years later that this was much like the U.S. Cavalry that his grandfather had defeated at the Little Bighorn, and that had been involved in the Massacre of Wounded Knee. In those days, we kids never thought in those historical terms.

In our era of the 1930s, we saw the Fourth Cavalry which was then stationed at Fort Meade, but the idea for matched horses was started with Custer's troopers in the Seventh Cavalry who earlier participated in the Battle of the Little Bighorn. [140]

If I could relive my youth, I would spend more time searching the roots of the Indian culture. I would ask No Water to tell me more about his nomadic life on the prairie.

What was it like to camp here at Buffalo Gap with the Lakota tribes and join in the hunt?

What about the spirits, his Gods, and the vision of the White Buffalo?

I would love to have the chance to visit again with Chief High Eagle, and perhaps he would share with me again the events of that day at the Little Bighorn. I would spend time again with Black Elk and talk about his anguish at Wounded Knee. John Sitting Bull was a deaf mute, but he spoke sign language, and perhaps he could convey to me what it was like to live with his father, that great chieftain.

In her book, *Bury My Heart at Wounded Knee*, Dee Brown provides this song:

SONG OF SITTING BULL [141]

I-ki-di-ze wa-on-kon
He wa-na he-na-la-ye-lo
He i-yo-ti-ye ki-ya-wa-on

A warrior
I have been.
Now
It is all over.
A hard time
I have.

7
GUS HAASER

When I see some of the old cowboy movies, Gus Haaser comes to mind, because this eccentric type is often portrayed by Hollywood. A rugged, cantankerous, gun-toting, extraordinary cowboy of the Old West, Gus may have been the one in mind when they scripted many of those old cowboy flicks. He was once a scout for the U.S. Cavalry and I can see him riding alongside John Wayne as they parlayed with Indian warriors.

I first saw Gus in the early 1930s when I was sitting on the sidewalk outside my Dad's bank in Buffalo Gap. Up the dirt street on a horse rode this old cowboy in a cloud of dust. He stopped alongside the bank, dismounted, dropping the reins over the hitching post. Gus had a tall, ramrod figure, wore a huge ten gallon hat adorning the top of a craggy face like a king's crown, and owned a handle-bar mustache that drooped down at the ends to add accent to a mouth indicating he'd take no truck from anyone. Pant legs tucked inside high-top boots that reached nearly to his knees, no doubt replaced the need for chaps when riding in sagebrush and cactus terrain. Finally, Spurs jingled as his boots hit the ground: working spurs meant to draw attention in the ribs of a cutting horse in the middle of a longhorn herd.

I thought I'd seen all of Gus, but then there was that pistol -- the one with the fancy handle tied down in a holster on his left hip -- not needed for a quick draw, perhaps, but rather as a statement he took no nonsense from any man. Without looking right or left, Gus slapped the side of his trousers to relieve them of twenty miles of trail dust, and strode into the bank.

Gus would be sober. Unlike most other cowboys riding into town whose first stop was always Frenchie's saloon for a couple shots of whiskey or to Bert's barber shop for a shave and haircut, Gus was different. He never frequented the barber shop and seldom entered the saloon.

When he did go there, it was for some poker hands back in the corner, or maybe just to lean on the bar with his boot on the brass rail, sip a beer, and stand beside some cowboy doing all the talking. Gus would listen to the chatter; but he seldom said anything. He had little to say and no inclination to do much talking. I guess that was why the saloon crowd thought him odd. My Dad did not consider him strange though, because Gus always stopped by the bank to politely say hello, and then with much flourish, he'd transact what business he had to handle. In the 1930s when Dad was the banker in Buffalo Gap, Gus was already in his mid-seventies and slowing down with only a token amount of business to conduct.

How did this old cowboy become so peculiar, or even survive through the times and trails he traveled?

Gus was born in Sandusky County, Ohio, the same place as my Dad, and I'll bet that may be one reason they got along. I expect they used to talk about it, but maybe only to recall they were both glad Ohio was in their past. Gus did not start life as a cowboy. He left home early in his teen years and worked on steamboats on the Mississippi River until he was sixteen. He got a taste of the cowboy experience back in Kansas on his sister's place. They raised hogs. Gus's first experience with a "cattle drive" was helping his sister's husband shepherd a herd of fifty hogs through thirty miles of Kansas countryside to a railhead for shipment east. [142]

Did you ever hear of a "hog drive"?

In 1874, gold was discovered in the Black Hills and Gus joined the gold rush to seek his fortune along with everyone else. Riding the train as far west as Sidney, Nebraska, the jumping off point for people traveling north into Indian country, Gus boarded the stagecoach, and after paying the full fare, the men found they had to spend most of the trip walking beside the stage during the rainy season, keeping the clay gumbo out of the wheels. [143] The stage traveled up prairie through Nebraska into Sioux-infested Dakota Territory until it reached the stage station located along Beaver Creek at the edge of the Black Hills. The stage station, called Buffalo Gap, consisted of a couple log buildings and a horse corral. Gus spent the night in that rip-roaring town, and then continued his journey on toward Deadwood where he'd find the gold fields and rowdy crowds of prospectors.

But he never got there. Instead, he got off the stage at another log cabin settlement called Rapid City situated on Rapid Creek. Gus decided to forget about finding a fortune in gold, and hired out to a cattle outfit.

With a natural flare for the job of cowboy, Gus Haaser was quickly recognized as one of the best, and so was hired as a trail boss to travel to Oregon and bring a herd of thirty-five hundred cattle, plus two-hundred fifty horses back to Dakota. Once arrived, Gus hired his crew of cowboys for the return trip -- mostly Spaniards. He bought two grub wagons, laid in supplies, and headed east with the herd in April, just after the snow melted. Two men were hired to handle the horse herd, another eight for the cattle, and two to drive the grub wagons and cook. Trailing the herd, Gus traversed the Mullen Trail across the Cascades and Rockies of Idaho and Montana and crossed several rivers. The trail crew encountered thousands of buffalo in eastern Montana bedded along the banks of the Musselshell River which prevented passage, so they had to stampede the buffalo out of the area before proceeding further.

Arriving at the final destination on the Cheyenne River east of Buffalo Gap, they completed the thousand mile trip in seven months, through Blackfoot and Sioux Indian country. Gus was paid his wages and with that money purchased two hundred-fifty head from the herd for the cost of trailing, which was $13.50 per head. They were excellent stock of quality Shorthorns that the government issued to Indian reservations. That herd could have started Gus on a ranching career, but that wasn't his style; so he sold them for a profit.

Gus Haaser's reputation as a trail boss was now established in western Dakota Territory. Three years later, when the big cattle herds started to pass through Dakota coming up from Texas on their way to Montana, Gus was hired by local ranchers and positioned at the stage station at Hermosa to monitor the herds passing through, and to cut back any cattle that belonged to the Black Hills range. More than 180,000 head of cattle from Texas passed through Hermosa during those two years.

Putting that number of cattle in perspective with some mathematical assumptions, if cattle were herded five abreast with a distance of eight linear feet from nose-to-nose, that string of cattle would extend for fifty-four miles. Of course, it was not one large herd, but many smaller ones spread though those two years, and they averaged about thirty-five hundred head per herd, or about fifty herds passing through the Hermosa station. (Imagine the cow manure and smell at that checking station.) Gus's job was to check each herd to ensure the Cheyenne River and Black Hills ranches were not losing cattle to the rowdy Texas cowboys headed north to Montana. Anytime Gus cut out some unbranded local cow from a passing herd, he'd be challenged by gun-toting cattle drive cowboys, so it took courage, moxie, and considerable diplomacy to do that job.

Cattle herds traveling up from Texas without any water or other provisions had to find everything they needed from the land traversed. Rivers or creeks with water had to be available at some place during each day of the drive. Cattle grazed as they walked along the way, leaving the landscape looking like devastation by locusts. The first water after entering Dakota Territory was at the Cheyenne River crossing southeast of Buffalo Gap. The drive would continue north along Lame Johnny Creek, cross over French Creek and arrive on Battle Creek at the Hermosa station. Then herds proceeded north to the Belle Fourche River; finally arriving at the Little Missouri River in the vicinity of Camp Crook and followed up into the northern plains grazing area.

Gus was riding alone through Cedar Pass in the Badlands one day in 1885 when his horse fell on him and his leg was broken. Unable to move, he fired his rifle three quick times, which was a universal signal for help. Some cowboys found him and carried him on a travois to the Hot Springs hospital. It wasn't long until Gus was back in the saddle again.

With the job of checking herds at the Hermosa station completed, Gus was next hired as foreman of the Gunstock Ranch on the Cheyenne River, twelve miles east of Buffalo Gap. It was a big spread, located south of the Cheyenne River opposite of where the Lame Johnny Creek flowed in, and owned by T.M. Warren from back east. The ranch had hundreds of horses that were raised for sale to the U.S. Cavalry, and the ranch was operated with a crew of dozens of cowboys. While working as foreman at the ranch in 1890, Gus got married. He met his bride, Martha, at the Buffalo Gap stagecoach station where she lived with her uncle, George Boland, who ran the station. Gus was either very lucky or had some hidden asset she saw in him. Martha was one of the few available single girls in that part of the country and a rare beauty, but what she ever saw in Gus is a mystery. Forty years later when I lived in Buffalo Gap, Martha and Gus's granddaughter, Bobby Conger, was a classmate of my brother.

Gus and Martha were living at the Gunstock Ranch when the Sioux Indian uprising of 1890-91 occurred. It was a time of unrest. Sitting Bull had been killed by Indian police working for the white man, and the Indians had been brought nearly to frenzy by the Ghost Dance. This combination led to an uprising when the Mineconjous Lakota left their reservation, alarming ranchers in the Cheyenne River country. Most ranchers moved their families to town in Buffalo Gap or Hermosa for the duration. Warren bought twenty-five Winchester rifles to arm the men remaining at his Gunstock ranch. During the two year uprising, Gus left his job at the Gunstock to become a scout for Captain A. B. Wells of the U.S. Eighth Cavalry. It was in that job as a messenger, that he witnessed the massacre at Wounded Knee from a nearby hilltop. The following is a third or fourth party story of the battle as related by Gus many years later to his daughter, Edna (Haaser) Conger, which she provided to the writer, Bert L. Hall. It deviates somewhat from other accounts of the massacre.

> One of the cavalry captains had been ordered to disarm Big Foot's Mineconjous band of Indians and take them to Pine Ridge. It would not have been safe to take these Indians into the Pine Ridge Agency armed, as there were so many Indians already there on the warpath. This captain ordered his men to surround the Indians and take their weapons. Big Foot was off to one side on a little knoll. He had a ghost shirt on which the Indians thought was bullet proof. He was making a lot of noise and dancing, when suddenly he stooped and picked up two handfuls of dirt and threw them into the air. (Author's note: Gus must have mistaken someone else for Big Foot, because the chief was ill in his tent with pneumonia.) Like a flash, the Indians started fighting and even the squaws used their war clubs. Thirty soldiers were killed and many Indians. If it had not been for the black Cavalry from Fort Robinson who arrived on the scene shortly after the fighting began, many more soldiers would have been killed. After the battle, Gus helped load the dead and wounded into wagons and they

were taken back to Pine Ridge." [144]

I will not enter into any debate as to the accuracy of the various accounts of the melee, this particular one seems rather biased by Gus; perhaps reflecting the prejudice at that time of many white people and cavalrymen toward the Indian, which they considered to be semi-savage.

After the Indian outbreaks had been put down, Gus was appointed Government Brand Inspector to check those cattle being delivered to the Indians on the reservation, and he held this job for a number of years. The government was paying good money for these cattle. It was the job of Gus to see that they were worth the money the government paid for them and that the cattle were actually delivered to the reservation. This responsibility was a tall order, and Gus was made for the job.

Gus never owned a large ranch. Most of his life was spent as a cowboy for hire, but since the family of Gus and Martha kept growing and numbered eight children, it was time to settle down. With the help of a mortgage, Gus scraped up enough money to get a small spread on Lame Johnny Creek where he raised horses, cattle, and even sheep. It was struggling with that mortgage that brought him riding on horseback the fifteen miles to Buffalo Gap and his visits with my Dad at the bank.

Gus loved to play poker with other cowboys at the table in the back corner of Frenchie's saloon. Sometimes he'd get angry as part of his bluffing strategy, but one day it back-fired on him. In the midst of a hand, Gus was shouting angrily at an opponent who kept raising the pot, so Gus drew the gun from his holster, pointed it at the floor, and pulled the trigger. Unfortunately for Gus, he shot himself in the foot. With the ribbing he got from local cowboys, that was hard for Gus to live down.

Gus seldom came to Buffalo Gap to socialize, but one year he did come to the Fourth of July Volunteer Fire Department dance in the auditorium. In his high-top boots with the pants tucked in, silver spurs, and packing leather, he cut quite a figure on the dance floor. After a few drinks he loosened up and began to dance his version of an Irish jig. Carried away by the joy of the moment (and more than a little liquor) Gus pulled his six-shooter and began firing into the air, keeping time with the music. His adult daughter, Mary Edna Conger, was mortified. How to live in a community where your father was such a colorful character? (Mary Edna had married a local rancher named Pete Conger, and it was their daughter, Bobbie, who was my brother's classmate.)

When Gus came to the bank to discuss his mortgage payments with my Dad, he joined a long parade of Cheyenne River ranchers. Almost every one of them was saddled with a large mortgage in which their ranch was held as collateral and since few of them had any money or income, they all faced foreclosure. The good times of the early 1920s, when everyone had money, was followed by the crash of 1929, when suddenly no one had money. During those good times, many ranchers extended themselves by purchasing more land, building new barns, buying bigger herds, and accomplishing all this with a bank loan covered by using their ranch as collateral. The Buffalo Gap bank had plenty of money on deposit and was happy to accommodate them. But then the bubble burst with the Wall Street crash. Fortunes were wiped out overnight, commerce came to a halt, no market existed for cattle, and the rancher had nothing with which to make payments on his mortgage.

Over the next couple years, which is when Dad became the banker of the Buffalo Gap bank, he found few deposits, a huge stack of mortgages, and every rancher in default on his payments. It was a desperate scenario.

What was the rancher to do? What was the banker to do?

With great wisdom and the backing of the bank board of directors who were ranchers, Dad decided it was better to work with the ranchers and accept small token payments to keep them afloat, rather than to take them into foreclosure. It was not a pleasant time for either the ranchers who had to go to the bank and beg for mercy, or for the banker who had to assume great financial and personal risk; so when Gus Haaser rode his horse to town and strode into the bank, it was the kind of stuff of which Western movies were made.

Gus's story had a happy ending, though. The old reprobate was not yet ready to hang up his spurs. He became lonely after his wife died, as did the widow on a nearby ranch. Gus went over to her place to help with the weekly washing and evening supper and it was not long before he just moved in. They lived together for ten years until well into their nineties, and when unable to care for themselves, they simply moved together to a local nursing home.

Wonderful, eccentric, Augustus Haaser -- a genuine cowboy -- died at the age of 99 years and 9 months. His funeral was the last formal ceremony conducted in the Buffalo Gap Catholic church, with burial in the local cemetery. After his funeral, the abandoned church was moved to a site near the town of Custer to become a tourist attraction. I do not recall having ever seen Gus in church in all the years I lived in Buffalo Gap and do not know how his funeral happened to be held in that church, but it was fitting that the old cowboy and the missionary church, both from a bygone era, should travel together into a golden sunset.

Gus Haaser was an unforgettable character of my youth.

8

GRANDMA SEWRIGHT

Perhaps few could fit the image of the pioneer woman better than Molly Sewright, one of the earliest women in the Black Hills, who arrived by stagecoach shortly after the Battle of the Little Bighorn.

"How much do you charge for splitting a rick of wood?" asked the old lady who stood in her doorway facing me.

"Twenty five cents a rick and I split it into small pieces so it will burn real good in your kitchen range, and I stack it too, nice and straight; so it's easy for you to pick up and haul into the kitchen," I replied. At eight years of age it wasn't easy for me to make a sales pitch to a total stranger. I knew she was Grandma Sewright, who lived down the street all by herself, and she was the mother of Bill Sewright, the guy who ran the ranch across the road from our home, and he was a good guy, but I'd never talked to her before, and anyway I was shy around strangers.

"That sounds like a fair price. Are you sure you can chop it so it burns good?"

"Yes, Ma'am," I replied with as much enthusiasm as I could muster for a total stranger, and an old lady at that. "And if you've got some blocks with knots and a lot of pitch in them, I'll cut it extra fine and keep it stacked separate for you to use when you've got meat to fry that needs high heat from that old range. And I'll cut up a few blocks into really small stuff for you to use in the mornings to start a fire."

"That's good."

"And if I find some pithy blocks of wood, I'll stack that wood aside so you can save it for when you're baking bread in the range oven and need a slow heat."

"Good. I see you've split wood before, and know how to do it right."

"Yes, Ma'am, I split wood for Grandma Dalbey all the time. You can ask her. She'll tell you I do a good job, and I charge her the same twenty-five cents a rick." In truth, that wasn't much pay for splitting a rick of wood and placing it in a stack four foot high and eight feet long, but these were the Depression times of the 1930s, and it was about the only spending money a kid could make. Twenty-five cents would buy me five Power House candy bars at Mel's Service Station; enough to last me a week -- one per day. Mel Thompson had just opened up his new station to sell gas for cars and he also sold bottles of pop and candy bars -- a new thing for him after closing his livery barn during the past year. Few ranchers or cowboys rode their horses into town anymore, and those that did just hitch them under a shade tree somewhere. Sometimes I'd help my big brother deliver the weekly *Chicago Sunday Tribune* on Wednesdays after the train arrived and we could keep three cents out of every dime the paper cost. With twenty customers, that was sixty cents my brother split with me. So I was able to keep myself supplied with candy bars and an occasional bottle of pop and still save some money for the future. Those Power House candy bars were about the only big luxury I had in Buffalo Gap.

It was hard times. Even though Dad ran the bank and everyone in town thought we were rich, he only made fifty dollars a month, and that was only a dollar more than most other fathers in town made from working on the WPA -- only they also got crates of oranges and their kids got warm snow suits for the winter, while I got nothing -- only the patched hand-me-downs from my big brother.

"And I supply my own axe," I said as a final clincher. "My big brother keeps it nice and sharp."

"Okay," she said. "You are the little Keating boy, aren't you?"

"Yes, Ma'am, I'm Bernard. I'd rather be called Bernie, but that's what Mother calls Dad, so that name is already used up."

"Okay, Bernard," she said as she smiled. "Twenty-five cents per rick, and I think one rick is about all I will need done. When you finish, knock on my back door for your pay. Maybe I'll even have a glass of cold milk and a piece of angel food cake for you."

The deal was closed, and it was a good deal with some income for me and a fair price for the old lady.

That was the occasion when I first met Molly Sewright, who I always knew as Grandma Sewright. Little did I realize at the time, nor even care, that she was one of the first white pioneer rancher women in the Black Hills. Everyone in Buffalo Gap seemed to be a pioneer of something, so no big deal.

In 1878, her family arrived by stagecoach in Rapid City. Her father was General Warren Shedd of the U.S. Union Army. He served during the Civil War under General Grant, and was with General Sherman on his "March to the Sea." He became a brevetted Brigadier General of the U.S. Volunteers for "meritorious service" during the war, and when it ended he was honorably discharged. [145]

Three years after arriving in the Black Hills, the General died of a heart attack, leaving a widow with three sons and five daughters. After her husband's death, she became postmistress in a small settlement in the local area.

Mollie was seventeen at the time of her father's death. She was being courted by William Sewright, who was thirty-five, and she married him that same year. Sewright had arrived in Deadwood as one of the earliest gold seekers. He bought some land in Lead for five hundred dollars. Later he sold it for a thousand dollars, which was a bad decision, because it later became the Homestake Gold Mine.

After marriage they lived as ranchers in the Buffalo Gap area by Lame Johnny Creek. Their initial ranch included the Lame Johnny "hanging tree" where the horse thief was lynched by a local posse. The creek near the tree was later given his name. A cave behind the Sewright ranch house surrounded by trees and shrubs, served as a hiding place where Mollie would flee with her children during Indian scares, while her husband mounted his horse and joined fellow ranchers in a band of home-guard militia riding hard after the Indians. During the uprising of 1890, all the men throughout the area were issued fifty-caliber Sharps guns by the Army corps stationed in Buffalo Gap. They were the best that money could buy. During the uncertainty of those uprising days, there were many panics.

However, the Indians never did attack homes north of Buffalo Gap where the Sewrights lived, but fighting east of town in the Cheyenne River country led to the death of several whites and some Indians. The Sioux finally went back to their reservations after the Wounded Knee Massacre and caused no more trouble in the vicinity of Buffalo Gap. Over the years they become friends with the Sewrights, rather than enemies, and "buried the tomahawk." Sewrights later moved to another ranch situated along Beaver Creek where it passed through the gap into the valley.

Bill Sewright was Mollie Sewright's son. His ranch house, barn, and horse corrals were across the road from where we lived, and we looked out our front door at his barnyard. I spent most days of the summer across the road over there playing with his grandson, and we shadowed "Pop Bill" everywhere he went. The previous year, his only son had drowned in a flash flood, so he seemed to welcome the constant companionship of we two young boys. Or at least, if he did mind, I never heard about it. During the summer, I would saddle up a horse and drive his herd of milk cows to and from their pasture which was several miles east of town.

In July, he'd take his mother, Grandma Sewright, and us kids camping. He'd load the back of his pickup with a tent and camping stuff. Grandma Sewright would sit in the cab in front, and we kids would sit in back on the gear while Pop Bill would drive us to the old Sewright ranch. He helped set up the tent, then he'd leave, and we'd spend a couple nights camping. There were four of us kids: Dick and Geraldine Sewright, her two grandchildren from Hot Springs, and my sister and I. Grandma Sewright did the cooking over a camp fire in an old iron skillet that she said came with her mother to the Dakota Territory in the stagecoach. Those camping trips are some of my fondest memories of childhood. Around the campfire at night, Grandma Sewright told us how it was to be a bride living in the Dakota wilderness, and how scared she got when the Indians came though during the uprising. Grandma Sewright was in her seventies when we went camping and seemed awful old to be doing that sort of thing.

Funny thing; now that doesn't seem so old anymore. Grandma Sewright died at the age of 92.

Bill Sewright exposed us to the Indian culture. Each winter he'd kill some old milk cow that stopped producing and butcher it in the barn with us kids watching the process. Some winters he would also kill a couple of hogs and some sheep. Then he'd take them out to the reservation. He didn't actually sell anything, because the Indians were destitute. It was a bartering process: he would trade in return for their agreement to come to his ranch during the summer to work off their debts. Besides the No Water family who took up residence in tents by Beaver Creek, Francis and Sylvia Stands and their two children lived across the street from us in an abandoned rail boxcar Sewright had moved onto his property. Some of the men who came without their families slept in a hay barn.

John Sitting Bull was there; a deaf mute in his seventies when I knew him in Buffalo Gap. He was a teenager at the Battle of the Little Bighorn. His father was the famous Chief Sitting Bull. John was a tall, austere-appearing man who projected great presence -- even with his silence -- but he was kind to us kids and let us ride with him when his team of horses and wagon moved out into the hay fields. Comes Again and Pursey Kills-A-Warrior were others I knew who had fought against Custer, and Sally Spotted-Bottom was a teenage girl in the Little Big-horn encampment at the time of the battle.

Chief High Eagle was a friend of my father and always dropped in to visit with him at the bank. He usually wore a flat-brimmed hat with a feather when he came from the reservation for business, but sometimes on ceremonial occasions he wore his feathered headdress. The wooden statue of an Indian chief we associate with the old five-cent cigar may have been patterned after Chief High Eagle. Other frequent visitors to Buffalo Gap were Nicholas Black Elk and Iron Hail (whose name was changed to Dewey Beard), who were both at the Wounded Knee Massacre and later became famous as Indian historians of that conflict. Dewey Beard was a good friend of my Dad and often came into the bank just to visit. I knew Black Elk only slightly, because he never did work on the Sewright ranch.

Bill sometimes took his grandson, Billy, and I along on these barter-ing trips. I suspect it made for a more respectful image and safe journey with a couple of kids in tow, rather than traveling alone. The meetings always began with *HOW-ko-dah*, [146] which was a respectful hello. Later in the bartering, process the definitive phrase was when the Indian asked *mah-zah-SKA E-cha-zo*, -- how much do I owe you? I was never sure Bill was a fair trader -- an old cow that died of old age and some pota-toes given to a starving Indian family in mid-winter in return for a full summer's work on his ranch, but even at that I now feel he may have been more charitable than the U.S. Government.

Children of the Lakota who came to Buffalo Gap became my play-mates. I was *pah- HA SAH-pah* a *hok-SHE-lah*, a Black Hills boy. I've never been sure how these Indian phrases were spelled, because I learned

Sioux only as a speaking language, and never saw them written before.

George No Water and I rode our stick horses around the neighborhood and through the ranch. Sometimes we were permitted to saddle up and ride real ponies. In a boyhood custom of that day, we made small cuts on our wrists and held them together in a symbolic exchange to become blood brothers. He became part white and I became part Lakota.

When I delivered the *Chicago Sunday Tribune* in Buffalo Gap during the 1930s, there was a comic strip named "Alley Oop," which had a professor character who invented a time machine that could transport you back to some unique time and place. If I can find that professor in real life and his time machine, I will ask him to send me back for a visit to the Bill Sewright ranch in Buffalo Gap, so I could have another conversation with those elderly Indian friends of mine.

THE EARLY PIONEERS

Gus Haaser, one of earliest cowboys on
the Buffalo Gap Frontier

Charlie Streeter, rancher who
became famous saddle maker
with a shop in Buffalo Gap.

Mollie (Grandma) Sewright, one of the
earliest pioneer women on the Buffalo
Gap Frontier. She was grandmother of
my boyhood friend, Dr. Dick Sewright,
dentist in Hot Springs.

Joe Norman, Tom Norman's father. Joe
was made an honorary member
of the Oglala Tribe and given the name
of "High Star".

9
THE BONDURANT RANCH

The first time I saw Hazel Bondurant, I thought she was Shirley Temple. It was in 1935. Hazel was six, my same age, and so was Shirley Temple, who was the sweetheart of every little boy in America, including me. Hazel was Shirley's look-alike. She bounded from the Model A Ford and raced to the Streeter porch to embrace her grandfather. Her parents were Wes and Nellie Bondurant, and they had driven in from their Cheyenne River ranch to visit the patriarch of the family, Nellie's father, Norman Streeter.

"Hello Grandpa," she exclaimed as she flung her arms around her grandfather's fat belly.

I peered from my yard next door, too shy to make my presence known, so I did not meet her until a year later when her father bought the house on the other side of Streeter's, where Nellie Bondurant could come in from the ranch with her children during the school year to avoid the twenty-three mile commute over dirt roads that were nearly impassable during the wintertime. Hazel became the best friend of my sister, and I usually tagged along. While she was one year ahead of me in school, grades one through four and five through eight shared the same classroom and teacher, so in effect, she and I were classmates sitting in different rows.

Hazel's two grandfathers were early frontier pioneers. Her mother's father, Norman Streeter, homesteaded in 1889 on a ranch northwest of Buffalo Gap, and it is still the Streeter ranch operated by grandchildren. Norman Streeter hung up his spurs and became the Buffalo Gap banker in 1914, a position he held until he retired in 1932, when he was replaced by my father. You will hear more about Streeter in the chapter on banking, and the key role he played in keeping the bank solvent during the financial crash of 1928.

Her other grandfather, Joseph Bondurant, was a Baptist Minister who moved from Missouri to Harrison Flat, east of Buffalo Gap, in 1890. Two years later he moved his family across the Cheyenne River adjacent to the Indian reservation and started the ranch that remains today as the Bondurant ranch, operated by the sixth generation.

Hazel's father, Wes (Wesley) was thirteen when he arrived with his father in South Dakota. [147] Those were perilous times to be living adjacent to the reservation with the frontier in upheaval during the Indian Uprising of 1890. Hazel recalls her father talking about huddling with his mother and sisters in the Harrison Flat School House while the men folks were out on patrol. The Wounded Knee Massacre occurred in December of that year. Wes told me he accompanied his Dad with a group of Cheyenne River ranchers, riding to the site of the disaster to help bury the dead in the frozen turf. Hazel does not recall her father ever telling her that story, and such are the fragments of history, recalled differently seven decades later. I have a very good memory, and I am sticking to my version of the story.

Wes, Joe's oldest son, was raised on the ranch and also worked for other ranchers in the Dakota Territory. At the age of twenty-three, he married Mabel Streeter of Buffalo Gap. [148] Then a few years later after Mabel died, he married her younger sister, Nellie.

When you married a Streeter, you became part of an extended family that populated much of the frontier. The patriarch was Norman Streeter, the rancher who eventually became the cashier of the Buffalo Gap State Bank, and who had numerous children. A couple sons remained on the Streeter ranch, which was located west of the gap in the foothills that led into the Black Hills. Another son, Charlie Streeter, grew tired of ranching and became a saddle maker in Buffalo Gap. Several daughters, in addition to Mabel and Nellie, married local ranchers. Edith Streeter married Lloyd Thurston, who ran various enterprises in the town of Buffalo Gap, including a garage, and maintained the county roads with a grader. He ran the Buffalo Gap water system after the town well was drilled. Each of the extended Streeter family offspring had numerous children and many grandchildren, so when someone married a Streeter, they became related to nearly half the local population.

Wes and Nellie Bondurant raised six children on their ranch alongside the Cheyenne River. All attended a nearby one-room country school, then later the Buffalo Gap schools after they moved to town, and several attended college, which was a big accomplishment in those Depression years.

The Bondurant family had three children in uniform during World War II. Joe fought in the army in Germany. Helen became a WAC (Women's Army Corp.) Norman, who was nicknamed "Tubby", became a Seabee, and was sent to the Pacific. He was killed in action while fighting on Iwo Jima. He was in my oldest brother's class during high school and his death was felt very deeply by our family. During the war, the front window in the Bondurant home held two silver stars for Joe and Helen and one gold star for Norman.

The war years were an emotional time for all of us in Buffalo Gap. Virtually all the young men and several women were in the military service in battle theatres all over the world. Just from our little street alone, we had Vic Streeter in the army, Ed Streeter in the navy, Edith Sewright an army nurse, the three Bondurant's in the service, and my two brothers in the navy: eight men and women in combat, with Norman Bondurant killed on Iwo Jima. The war news was very personal.

Joe, the oldest Bondurant son, normally would have become a rancher, but he had no interest in ranching. After being discharged from the army, he moved away to Denver. Ranching duties then fell to Wes's second-oldest son, Charles. He lived his entire forty-nine years on the ranch where he was born, with the exception of the four years of high school in Buffalo Gap. He married Viola Williams, who was raised on a nearby ranch, and they were sweethearts from their earliest years. They became parents of a little girl, Marian Faye. Wes and Nellie retired from the ranch and moved into Buffalo Gap in their house near us.

In 1949, Charles and Viola purchased the ranch from his parents.[149] He was a very progressive rancher and in the vanguard of many advances to come about during those years. Charles spent a good deal of time and energy on conservation and irrigation practices, performance testing of Hereford cattle and promoting electricity and telephone services for his community through the local Grange, of which he was a charter member. He was a 4-H leader for eight years while his daughter, Marian, was growing up, and he was a finalist for South Dakota Stockman of the year honors.

Frenchie Gerber, who later became owner of the well-known Frenchie's saloon in Buffalo Gap, had originally settled on 160 acres in the Cheyenne River country which adjoined the Bondurant and Wilson ranches. During the Depression, he had moved into Buffalo Gap, took over the saloon and stopped paying taxes on his Cheyenne River spread. Howard Gallentine (Anita Gallentine's husband) took ownership of it in a tax sale, and eventually sold it to Charles Bondurant.

Charles and Viola's daughter, Marian, graduated from Chadron State College and then taught for many years in Fairburn and Buffalo Gap schools. She met Bob Trew while in college, and they married after graduation. Daughter, Mary Alice was born in 1965. After Charles died a year later, Marian and Bob returned to the ranch and joined Viola in running it. Both her mother, Viola, and husband, Bob, have since died, and Marian continues ranching with the help of her daughter and son-in-law Kelly Kritenbrink. Supplementing their income, Mary Alice works as a beautician in Hot Springs, and Kelly as a trucker. Their two daughters, Ashlee and Addison, represent the sixth generation of the family living on the Bondurant ranch.

Emulating her father, Marian Trew always been active in community affairs in addition to teaching school, and she was one of the principal leaders in organizing the Buffalo Gap Centennial celebration in 1986.

My classmate, Hazel Bondurant moved to Hot Springs to live with an older, married sister, and finished high school there. After graduation she married a classmate, Harlan Krutsch, and his career took them out of state. Like so many South Dakota people who move elsewhere, when it comes time to retire, the Black Hills look very nice, and Hazel and Harlan have moved back to Rapid City.

I recently visited the Bondurant ranch and enjoyed the beauty of that Cheyenne River country nestled up against the Badlands. The rugged pioneer scene has been filmed as backdrop for such Hollywood movies as Hildago, but it continues to be a tough place for ranching. Six generations of Bondurant's can vouch for that.

THE BONDURANT FAMILY

Wes and Nellie Bondurant. Wes's father was one of earliest pioneer ranchers in the Cheyenne River Country.

Norman and Helen Bondurant, children of Wes and Nellie. Helen was a WAC and Norman was killed in action on Iwo Jima

Charles Bondurant, son of Wes and Nellie. He was one of most progressive ranchers of the new generation.

Bondurant family in from their Cheyenne River ranch for
a day of shopping in Buffalo Gap. My classmate,
Hazel (Bondurant) Krutsch is second from left.

10
MY DAD AND FRONTIER BANKING

Running a bank in Buffalo Gap during the Depression of the 1930s was the sort of financial and social challenge that few men should have to face. My Dad was a champion to the town's people who needed his banking skill, to the ranchers he kept financially afloat through rough waters and most of all, to his family. At the depth of the Depression, he and Mother always found a way to keep us five kids fed, clothed, in a respectable home, going to church, and enjoying life. We had few luxuries, but all the essentials. That was a tall order for a hillbilly who never graduated from the sixth grade and raised as a semi-orphan by a gold miner father. Even with those humble accomplishments, Dad had reached the high point of a family tree of Irish immigrants who had nothing. He referred to his ancestry as "shanty Irish."

My great-grandfather, Bernard Keating number-one, was born in County Wexford, Ireland in 1825. While he considered himself pure Irish -- like all good Irishmen do -- that analysis is somewhat fiction, because most of their ancestors arrived on the Irish Isle from someplace else. The Celtics originated in the Caucasus Region of Central Europe and migrated westward during the early centuries. These fierce warriors conquered and populated much of Europe with their bloodline; including France, England, and the Irish Isle. In France, after some cross-breeding, they gradually assumed the identity of Normans. Later, during the twelfth century, the warlike Normans conquered their Celtic cousins in England and the Irish Isle. The Irish Isle Celtics gradually tamed and absorbed the Normans into their culture, who then adopted the Gaelic language. One of these Norman warrior immigrants in Ireland took a beautiful Celtic lass as his wife, and his Norman name was gaelicized by her as "Ceitinn." A few centuries later when the Gaelic language gradually became corrupted with the barbaric English language, the name "Ceitinn" became "Keating."

That is enough information about early Irish history.

Now to Bernard Keating the first, my great-grandfather from County Wexford. Like everyone else in Ireland during the 19th century, he was a potato farmer. Unfortunately, a potato blight came along that turned all potatoes black and made them poisonous, so that many of the Irish population died from starvation. Those who could, fled the island to live elsewhere by whatever means possible; the most common means being by cattle boats normally utilized to transport cattle across the sea to far away places.

Bernard the first climbed aboard a cattle boat destined for America, along with hundreds of others who huddled in the darkened bottoms of ships where cows were normally kept. Impoverished and starving people came aboard with no food or water for the long voyage, and many died on the trip. Crowded in the bilge of that same ship with Bernard were Mister and Mistress O'Rork and their two small sons, Tom and Frank. Mister O'Rork did not make it and died at sea. His body was thrown overboard. Mistress O'Rork arrived on the pier in New York, a beautiful widow, penniless and with two small sons.

What was she to do?

There on that same pier stood the thirty-year old bachelor, Bernard number one. What could he do? Of course, he did the only thing a decent guy could do. He proposed marriage on the spot. She accepted. Finding their way to Sandusky, Ohio, Bernard began his life's profession by working in a cigar factory. Tobacco leaves arrived from Cuba, and he became probably the best cigar roller-upper of his day. There was a huge market for good Cuban cigars. Everyone smoked, and his were the best.

Now to this union of Keating and O'Rork: in addition to sons Tom and Frank O'Rork, there were added three other children with the last name of Keating: Bernard number two, my grandfather; Julia, who married Frank A. Gira and moved to Custer in the Black Hills during the gold rush; and Ellen, of whom there is no record. As Bernard number two grew to manhood, he got a job as driver of a horse-drawn wagon and delivered milk around the neighborhoods in Sandusky. This fact I verified by reading the Sandusky telephone book of 1888 in their museum, which listed the address and occupation of everyone in town.

When Granddad was about the age of thirty, he met and married a beautiful Irish lassie. Oops, I'm wrong. She was beautiful, but her father came from Wurtenberg, a region in what is now Germany in the area between Baden and Bavaria. For anyone to leave that beautiful area and move to Sandusky, they must have been desperate. Perhaps he was a horse thief who fled, but let's assumes some better alternative. Anyway, the lady that Granddad married "tarnished" the Keating pure Irish bloodline with German blood. There is only one photo that remains of her, and she was indeed beautiful, and even looks somewhat Irish. From this marriage came two sons: Bernard number three, my father; and Elmer, his younger brother, who was more-or-less the black sheep of the family.

At an early age, my grandmother died from what was diagnosed in those days as "consumption." I don't know what that was, and since they were too poor to see a doctor, I suspect they did not know, either. She was buried in a grave in Sandusky that remained unmarked until my father at the age of sixty-five returned to Sandusky, found her grave, and had an engraved tombstone placed there. After the death of his wife, Bernard number two took his two sons to the Black Hills of South Dakota where he went to work in a gold mine owned by a rich old geezer named Gira whom his sister had married. With a touch of nostalgia, Gira named his mine Cuyahogo, after the county in Ohio where his home in Sandusky was located. The gold mine was a few miles from Custer City on Iron Mountain and located adjacent to the Rushmore ranch, from which huge granite formations carved with the faces of four presidents could later be seen. In his youth Dad hunted deer on the Rushmore ranch.

My Dad, Bernard number three, was seven years old in 1899 when he arrived with his father at the Cuyahogo mine. He became a hillbilly and roamed the mountains with his rifle to bring food for the family table. School was done on the fly. Sometimes he attended school by horseback in Keystone. Other times he stayed at the Gira home in Custer and attended school there. My Dad's classroom education ended at the sixth grade. Then as a teenager he knocked around the hills and worked in several gold mines: the Cuyahogo, the Clara Belle, the Holy Terror Mine in Keystone, and the Spokane Mine. Only the Clara Belle and Holy Terror mines ever prospered or amounted to much. The Holy Terror in its heyday was one of the best producing mines in the hills.

At the outbreak of World War I, Bernard number three tried to join the army in Rapid City and was turned down because one of his thumbs was shot off in a hunting accident. Since he was already in Rapid City, he attended a business college, learned something about accounting, and then returned to Custer. Everyone always liked Dad, including the banker in Custer, Tom Delicate. The banker had no job for Dad, but one Friday afternoon he told him he heard there was an opening at the bank in Belle Fourche, and he'd give Dad a recommendation. Dad had neither horse nor other means of transportation and no money; so he begged a sandwich and walked the eighty miles through the Black Hills from Custer City to Belle Fourche. At seven o'clock on Monday morning, the bank president arrived to find Dad at the front door waiting. The president hired him on the spot and gave him his first assignment, which was to sweep the front sidewalk. That started Dad on a banking career that was to extend for forty-six years.

Several years later as assistant teller at the bank in Newell, a lovely young lady named Ethel, who was cashier at the Bratton General Store, went to the bank to make daily deposits at the teller window of the bachelor named Keating. They were married, and had four sons and one daughter. Bernard number four, that's me, had a happy childhood, and at the age of twenty-nine he married a beautiful lady also. I am happy to report that Bernard number four and his wife did not stick any of their sons with the name Bernard, so there will be no Bernard number five. Our sons thank us for that.

But, back to my Dad. He had some rocky times in banking. In 1931, after working at the bank in Camp Crook for ten years, it closed in the aftermath of the nation's financial crash, Dad found himself unemployed, while living in one of the most desolate, isolated regions in America with a wife and five small children. Leaving Mother and us kids with her parents in Newell, he went to school again in Rapid City to learn how to sell insurance. One day at lunch, Art Dahl, who had been a bank examiner, told him about an opening at the bank in Buffalo Gap. Dad went down, was hired, had a banking job again, and the family happily moved to Buffalo Gap.

Most of the able-bodied men in town were unemployed until Roosevelt's W.P.A. and C.C.C. programs came along. Nobody had any money beyond that needed for food and shelter. It was the same in every other town in western South Dakota. [150]

In his autobiography, Art Dahl, chairman of the Rapid City National Bank, quoted a list he got from Dad of banks for the year 1918 when he started his career in banking. The list included the forty-eight banks in the six counties of the Black Hills for that year. By the time of World War II, thirty-three of them, or sixty-eight percent had been liquidated.[151]

But let's talk about banking, which was where I was headed when I got sidetracked talking about all the family. Like the question of how a bank in a small community like Buffalo Gap gets started. As I understand it, a couple of ranchers and businessmen get together and agree the town needs a bank. They each throw in some money to buy stock, which provides the initial capital. They get a charter from the state and hire someone to run the bank. The banker invites deposits from the community and agrees to pay four percent interest on any money deposited. It's a good deal, so local folks deposit money. Then the banker loans money from this "kitty" to other people who need it and collects nine percent interest. That is an estimate, since there is no record of the actual percent interest paid. The difference of five percent is where the bank makes money. Of course, I am ignoring things like the Federal Reserve Bank, member banks, bank examiners, and a few things like that; all of which I do not fully understand.

I also neglected to mention the young janitor who climbed out of bed at five o'clock on cold winter mornings to run to the bank through snow drifts to fire up the pot-bellied stove and warm the bank for the banker and customers when they arrived.

Guess who got that job?

Buffalo Gap undoubtedly had some form of bank going back to gold rush days, but banking regulations in that era of the Dakota Territory were questionable since no government existed. The first formal bank of record in Buffalo Gap was established in 1886 at the time the railroad was extended from Nebraska up to the town and three years before statehood. Then the bank had difficulty, as the town died a year later when the railroad was extended to Belle Fourche. There is no record of a bank from 1894 until 1907 when the Buffalo Gap State Bank was opened. Mr Henne was elected president. He owned a grist mill with a water wheel powered from the old mill stream, and supplied the town with flour.

In 1907 those bank director guys included Mr. Towers, who owned one of the three local grocery stores. [152] With other ranchers and businessmen, they scraped up $5,000 to buy stock in the bank. Local folks deposited a total of $40,946.72 in the bank in 1910, and the bank made loans of $24,960.95 to the people of Buffalo Gap and ranchers of the Cheyenne River country. For a small town during that era, that was big money and reflected a now-healthy ranching community.

In 1914, Norman B. Streeter became the banker; a position he held until 1932 when he decided to retire, already in his eighties. Dad became banker. Bill Snyder, a Cheyenne River rancher, was bank president. When the financial crash came in 1930, there was a run on banks as depositors rushed to withdraw their money. Buffalo Gap's bank managed to weather the run on its deposits and the reason that has been told over the years is that Bill Snyder brought his own money into the bank and said, "This bank will not close," and it did not.

Snyder was never timid about taking the credit. Tom Norman's ranch was adjacent to Snyder's and I asked Tom where Snyder got that kind of money. Tom replied, "Hell, I don't know, but that old b------ never did spend a plugged nickel for anything, so I guess he just saved it up."

Now, seventy-five years later, let me tell you the other side of the story that related to me recently by Ed Streeter, age eighty-five, who was Norman Streeter's grandson. According to Ed, his grandfather was quite wealthy from his early years of owning a ranch, followed by many years as the banker. At the time of the financial crash, Snyder came to Streeter and suggested that Streeter loan all his money to Snyder, who would give him an IOU, and then put that money in the bank available to depositors, thereby stopping the run on bank deposits. All the money Streeter loaned Snyder went out the door to depositors, but then, according to Ed, Snyder never did honor his IOU and pay the money back, leaving Streeter broke.

So it was Streeter's money and not Snyder's that saved the bank.

Why was this story never told? Ed Streeter said the only two people other than Snyder and Norman Streeter who knew about it were Charlie Streeter, the banker's son, and himself. The old man pledged them to secrecy and never told another living soul because of his anger against Snyder and his embarrassment at having been played for a fool. Norman Streeter retired from the bank penniless and moved in with his son's family, being forced to live off their charity until his death a couple years later. As Charlie Streeter was our neighbor, I would often see the lonely old man sitting hunched over under an apple tree in their back yard.

Is this new account by Ed Streeter correct? I don't know, and I guess it will remain one of those mysteries of history. However, since I personally knew all the people who were involved, I am inclined to accept this recent clarification by Ed Streeter. Norman Streeter was a kindly, naïve old man, and Ed Streeter a straight-shooter with no reason to rewrite history. This is the kind of stuff that gives historians something new to write about.

In 1937, the bank of Buffalo Gap became a branch of the Southern Hills Bank in Edgemont. In 1941 my Dad began working in the Edgemont bank to support Leo Seppala, the bank president, because of a huge increase in activity due to the boom that came with the nearby Black Hills Ordnance Depot. My mother ran the Buffalo Gap branch for a year, and a year later our family moved to Edgemont. Buffalo Gap's bank was then operated by a number of people over the next few years as activity declined and the town died once more during the war. Bankers were Carp Carpenter, Bob Emery, Lloyd Soske, and finally Bob Nolan. By the 1970s, activity declined further and the bank operated only a couple days a week. The branch was finally closed in the 1980s, and the red sandstone bank building, a beautiful relic of the frontier days, was sold to the town of Buffalo Gap for one dollar. Like many other business buildings of yesterday, it now sits abandoned.

Dad was absolutely, totally honest when it came to money and financial transactions. That is why he was asked to handle the money and finances for public organizations and events for forty years. But there was one exception -- a sideline business of the bank was selling various kinds of crop insurance to people who wanted a loan for their crop. Hail insurance was expensive, but a wheat farmer could not afford to take the gamble that his entire crop could be wiped out without insurance. One Wednesday afternoon, Bill Engelbrecht came to the bank to purchase hail insurance. Returning to his ranch that evening, he found that a hail storm had destroyed his entire crop during the time he was in town at the bank. That night, we got a knock on our door at home and there stood Engelbrecht in tears. Dad returned to the bank and predated the insurance application to the previous day. It was nearly midnight when he went to the home of the postmaster, Jack Nolan, and got him out of bed.

Together they went to the post office and Nolan placed a Tuesday post-mark on the sealed envelope. Bill Engelbrecht got his insurance payment and continued to successfully raise wheat for many more years. This story was told to me many years later by Jack Nolan after Dad had died. Dad, Jack Nolan, and Bill Engelbrecht have been dead now for many years and the statute of limitations has expired, so I feel it is safe now to relate the story.

After talking about "My Dad and Frontier Banking," let me add a tribute to my mother. On those days in Buffalo Gap when Dad was too ill to open the doors of the bank, Mother was there to do it, and she did it well. Later, when Dad had to move to Edgemont during the boom years of World War II, Mother ran the Buffalo Gap bank for a year until they found a replacement. After the family moved to Edgemont, her services were needed in the bank there because other help was not available. Mother worked as a cashier during the war years. Perhaps a more appropriate title for this chapter should have been "My Dad and Mother, the Frontier Bankers."

Many years later after the local history book, *Our Yesterday's*, was published, I asked Mother why she and Dad had not contributed anything to the book about the bank and that era. She told me that she and Dad had talked it over, reminisced about all those hard times during the Depression Years of the 1930s when they ran the bank, saw all the hardships their friends endured and they could not bring themselves to relive those years again on paper.

As I drive east of Buffalo Gap through the Cheyenne River country and see the fallen-down homesteads of seventy years ago lying on their sides covered with weeds, I can still name the rancher who lived on each and his children who were my classmates in Buffalo Gap. Yes, I can empathize with my parent's reluctance to revive those memories. They were tough times then, and are yet today for the few remaining survivors who still ranch in that Cheyenne River country.

FRONTIER BANKING

Norman Streeter,
Banker 1914 – 1932

My Dad, B.W. Keating,
Banker 1932 - 1942

Buffalo Gap State Bank

Cabin at the Cuyahogo Mine in 1899 where my Dad,
B.W. Keating, spent his childhood

11
THE WOUNDED KNEE MASSACRE

The valley of Wounded Knee on the Pine Ridge Indian Reservation has a special place in American history for several reasons; not the least of which is because it was where the last pitched battle between Indians and soldiers took place on American soil.

In 1890, the frontier was a boiling pot of intertwined, dysfunctional cultures, which included the townspeople of Buffalo Gap, settlers in the Cheyenne River country, the Lakota Indians and cavalry troops. There were the Sixth, Seventh, Eighth, and Ninth U.S. Cavalry companies within a two day ride, plus some infantry. They were the only law of consequence on the frontier, but their credentials were tarnished by the defeat of General Custer a dozen years before.

In 1889, South Dakota officially became a state. Its political base existed on the other side of the Missouri River in the eastern half of the new state. The western frontier of gold-seeking ruffians in the Black Hills and uncivilized nomadic tribes of Indians was an embarrassment that the state chose to ignore. The Federal Government also wiped its hands of this situation by designating six areas of western South Dakota as Indian reservations where the problem could be confined.

Unfortunately, ignoring the frontier issue would not be that simple.[153]

While the Pine Ridge Indian Reservation had been officially created by Congress in 1889, the concept of a reservation was still in flux. In 1868, a treaty was signed by the government with Red Cloud in which *"the United States recognized the western half of South Dakota as Indian land, and eastern Wyoming and Nebraska north of the Platte River, as unceded Indian Territory. It guaranteed that no Americans would ever be allowed into this region except under specific provisions such as trade and government business."* [154] White men rushed in during the next few years, openly violating the treaty and corrupting the original concept of the reservation. The Indian agency of Pine Ridge was originally established as the Red Cloud Agency in Nebraska, but the location was moved five times as the Indian lands dwindled away. Finally in 1899, Pine Ridge was designated as the permanent agency after shrinking to its present boundaries.

The second culture on this frontier was the town of Buffalo Gap, but by 1889 the town had essentially died. A population of three thousand suddenly evaporated, leaving less than four hundred people with little economic enterprise.

The third culture involved the ranchers in the Cheyenne River country. Many of them struggled to survive in dugouts alongside whatever wagon brought their possessions, living day-to-day on scant produce from their own land, plus what little they could afford to buy in Buffalo Gap. Theirs was an infertile landscape that perhaps no one should have attempted to farm.

The homesteaders' plight, nevertheless, seemed better than that of the Indian. In 1890, there were over ten thousand Lakota living on the Pine Ridge Reservation. They waited for subsistence promised them by the government, but these supplies were minimal and sometimes failed to show up. Indian families lived in tipis, dugouts, wagons, caves, shacks, under corrugated tin and tar paper -- wherever they could. To the writer's mind, describing them as depressed is an understatement. They lived at the absolute edge of despair.

Then into this climate came a new element called the "Ghost Dance" -- a revivalist kind of religion imported from Nevada and introduced onto the reservations of South Dakota. By 1890, the Lakota and several other Plains Indian tribes were Ghost Dancing by the hundreds to drive the white men away -- not by war -- but by divine intervention. [155] When it first came to his attention, Chief Red Cloud, principal leader of the Oglala, sent a committee to Nevada to investigate. They returned with a mixed report. The religion had vaguely defined beliefs that white people would be eliminated, the buffalo would return, and dead Indians would be brought back to life. It was a promise of better times ahead for Indians and was rooted in disaster for the whites. Centerpiece of the Ghost Dance was a ritualistic swaying and circling around a fire, which was to continue for four days. On the last night, the dance was to continue until the morning of the fifth day, after which all were to bathe, go home and sleep. The custom of sweathouse for purification was part of the ritual. The desperate Indians latched onto the craze that was to cause the frontier to erupt.

Other events caused great unrest among the Indians. Provisions promised by the U.S. Government were all too often siphoned off by political appointees, so with no buffalo to hunt, many Indians were on the edge of starvation. Chief Crazy Horse had come in to Fort Robinson under a flag of truce, and was killed by U.S. Army soldiers. Sitting Bull was assassinated by Indian police in the employ of the Standing Rock agency. Both were reportedly betrayed by some of their own people.

The Ghost Dances of the Indians feared by whites to be an indication of an uprising, so they asked the government for protection. The Gunstock Ranch bought forty of the best Sharps fifty-caliber rifles for their crew. The cavalry issued rifles to settlers in and around Buffalo Gap. Stories created by both real and imaginary raids led to panic among ranchers, and posses were organized. Many stalwart men sent their families to Buffalo Gap or Hermosa for protection and all these events combined to create what became known as the "Indian scare of 1890."

Indian agents soon became concerned and asked Washington for help. Cavalry were stationed at the Pine Ridge, Rosebud, and Cheyenne agencies, and the presence of troopers added to the excitement. [156] Five thousand soldiers were placed in bivouac throughout the area; the Nebraska National Guard was called to active duty and placed along the Nebraska border.

As these elements built to a crescendo, there came the inevitable clash between Indians and the Seventh U.S. Cavalry, sent from Fort Riley, Kansas, and who were reported to be still bitter about being defeated at the Little Bighorn a dozen years before. [157] After Sitting Bull's assassination on the Standing Rock Reservation, some of his Hunkpapa tribe fled south seeking refuge on the Pine Ridge reservation. They reached Chief Big Foot's Mineconjous tribal camp near Cherry Creek -- a hilly area some distance north of the Pine Ridge agency. But that same day the War Department issued orders for the arrest and imprisonment of Big Foot, since he was on their list of "fomenters of disturbances."[158] Other accounts say Big Foot was to be intercepted and taken to Fort Meade by the Eighth U.S. Cavalry for his own protection. Regardless, as soon as Chief Big Foot learned that Sitting Bull had been killed, he started his people toward the Pine Ridge agency, hoping that Red Cloud could protect them from the soldiers. Big Foot was ill with pneumonia, and unable to walk or ride a horse, so he was carried in a wagon. As they arrived at Porcupine Creek, they saw cavalry troops approaching. Big Foot ordered a white flag raised over his wagon, and he greeted Major Whiteside, who told Big Foot he had orders to take him to a cavalry camp on Wounded Knee Creek. Big Foot replied he was going in that direction already, because he was taking his people there for safety.

Two troops of cavalry took the lead and the Indians were herded into a compact group behind them with two other cavalry troops and a battery of Hotchkiss guns on wagons bringing up the rear. Twilight was falling as the column began descending into the valley of Wounded Knee. At the camp, the Indians were halted and counted. There were one hundred-twenty men, and two hundred-thirty women and children. Later in the darkness, the remainder of the Seventh Cavalry regiment marched in under the command of Colonel Sandy Forsyth, who now commanded Custer's old regiment.

Colonel Forsyth informed the Indians the next morning that they were now to be disarmed. Here, some details of what happened remain unclear and others are controversial. The Indians, it was said, stacked their guns in the center of the camp. Not satisfied, Forsyth ordered the soldiers to search the tipis. He then ordered the Indians to remove their blankets for more searching, even though it was bitter cold. The soldiers found two more rifles.

Almost immediately there began a deafening thunder of rifle shots which choked and filled the air with powder smoke. Among the dying sprawled on the frozen ground was Chief Big Foot. Indians and soldiers grappled at close quarters, using knives, clubs, and pistols, and then as the Indians fled through the valley, the big Hotchkiss guns of the army on the hill, opened up, raking the Indian camp. Tipis were shredded with flying shrapnel. Killed were men, women, and children, and soldiers caught in their own crossfire. [159]

When the madness ended, twenty-five soldiers lied dead. Chief Big Foot and more than half of his people were dead or seriously wounded; one hundred fifty three were found dead, and many others crawled away to die afterwards. One estimate placed the final total of dead Indians at nearly three hundred men, women, and children.

A blizzard arose that evening of December 29, 1890 as soldiers loaded survivors onto wagons for the trip to Pine Ridge. The dead were left to become covered with snow. Wounded Indians were unloaded at an Episcopal mission church where benches were removed and hay scattered over the crude floor to accommodate them. Those still conscious could see the Christmas greenery hanging from open rafters.

Above the pulpit was strung a crudely lettered banner: PEACE ON EARTH, GOOD WILL TO MEN. [160]

BLACK ELK'S LAMENT
(From *Bury My Heart at Wounded Knee*, by Dee Brown) [161]

I did not know then how much was ended.
When I look back now from this high hill
Of my old age, I can still see the butchered
Women and children lying heaped and scattered
All along the crooked gulch as plain
As when I saw them with eyes still young.

And I can see that something else died
There in the bloody mud, and was buried in
The blizzard. A people's dream died there.
It was a beautiful dream . . .
The nation's hoop is broken and scattered.
There is no center any longer,
And the sacred tree is dead.

- BLACK ELK

After Wounded Knee, the Oglala Lakota knew they must accommodate to domination by the United States.

Efforts to undermine the validity of Oglala culture and language have been resisted by many; so the culture has survived. However, great damage was done. Many Oglala lost their language, and accepted the message that theirs was an inferior culture," said Gregory Gagnon and Karen White Eyes in *Pine Ridge Reservation – Yesterday and Today.* [162]

It would be eight decades before anything of great social consequence occurred on the Pine Ridge Indian Reservation.

In the American Black community, the 1960s ushered in the civil rights movement as the Black population challenged the norms of intolerance, and the nation began to take slow steps toward racial equality of that minority group. On the heels of this, in the 1970s, a similar movement began within the Indian community. Similar to historical patterns elsewhere, this one began when a new generation would no longer accept the status quo. It began in fits-and-spurts of conflict involving confrontations within both Indian and white communities and spawned a group called the American Indian Movement (AIM). In February, 1972, a protest of several hundred reservation people in Gordon, Nebraska, occurred concerning the beating and killing of an Indian. That October, a nationwide caravan reminded Americans of the many treaties made with Indians which remained unfilled. That same year in November, there was a take-over of the Bureau of Indian Affairs headquarters in Washington D.C. by the group and with other such happenings, the pot was brewing.

Finally, the spark igniting the fire occurred on a dirt street in front of a saloon in Buffalo Gap. It was a brawl between a reservation Indian and a white -- one wielding a log chain and the other a knife. In the fracas, the Indian was stabbed and killed. On the Buffalo Gap frontier, the stabbing death of an Indian from the reservation in the old days would scarcely have made the local paper.

Not this time. It became national headlines with climactic events to follow.

Facts involving the fight are still controversial and a full discussion is beyond the scope of this book. However, there were protests, sit-ins, and occupations by Indians at such places as Mount Rushmore and Alcatraz Island that received support by white celebrities, such as Marlon Brando at the Hollywood Academy Awards ceremony. Then in 1975, two F.B.I. agents were killed on the Pine Ridge Indian Reservation, leading to a seventy-one-day standoff between armed Indian activists and police in the valley of Wounded Knee. This conflict is now referred to locally as Wounded Knee II.

The Wounded Knee II situation is difficult to place in perspective. Bruised feelings remain among white and Indian people now over three decades later, but some historians think of it as a "turning point." Out of this standoff, more tolerance and acceptance of the Indian among the white community seemed to emerge. And perhaps even more important, a new feeling of pride within the Indian community about their own ancestral roots and traditions has come to the fore. As just one example of an improved climate, the superintendents of the nearby Mount Rushmore National Memorial and the Badlands National Monument were both American Indians, the first ever appointed to those posts.

Conflict is the price that sometimes must occur as a spark to ignite social progress. Wounded Knee II, which started on a dirt street in Buffalo Gap, may well have been a turning point for the American Indian.

12

NEW FRONTIER RANCHERS

More than a century after the Wounded Knee Massacre, this region remains unchanged in many ways. Extended families of early mixed-blood Lakota ranchers have evolved to form the nucleus of a new frontier. While this is still an impoverished area, its latest generations have produced some of the most successful present-day ranchers in South Dakota. Family names include as examples, Doug Temple of the White River country, Frank Rapp of the Cheyenne River country, and Dave Cuny of Cuny Table. Tracing their ancestries to Lakota people forced to the reservation, this trio was born and raised on the Pine Ridge reservation in the mid-twentieth century, and they have operated prosperous ranches here now for many years.

Another rancher fits a different pattern. She is Anita (Shortie) Gallentine, a classmate of mine from our school days in Buffalo Gap during the 1930s. Shortie runs a cattle herd on her ranch at the headwaters of Lame Johnny Creek, adjacent to Custer State Park. Her husband, Howard, died a few years ago, but Shortie continues to operate the ranch they purchased with money they earned when operating a saloon in Buffalo Gap.

Recently I visited with these four ranchers to get their stories. It was difficult finding a time convenient for them, because they are so busy. They love their life and would not trade it for anything, but it is not an easy existence. Ranching is hard work requiring long hours, year around, in all kinds of weather.

Doug Temple is one of the largest ranchers in South Dakota today. He could probably afford to kick back and take it easy, but he is one of the hardest working and most dedicated ranchers I know of. Six o'clock in the morning finds him with a cup of coffee, bracing for the day which begins on a horse or in a pick-up truck off to check on some remote portion of his ranch, perhaps twenty miles away. He finishes his workday after dark. Asking if he would meet with me on a weekend, Doug responded, "Fine. A weekend is like every other day to a rancher." His herd will require attention in some place or other nearly every day of the week.

Nothing about this ranching scenario has changed. Lois Rapp told me that her father, Frank Wilson, would climb on a horse and be riding for days and nights, summer and winter, as he had thousands of head of cattle spread over many sections, dozens of miles in every direction -- and he took nothing for granted. As it was a hundred years ago; ranchers still spend a good part of every day in the pasture with their cattle.

Ask a cowman about the size of his ranch and how many cattle he has, will get you vague answers. It was the same when I worked as a cowboy in my youth. For one thing, most ranchers are conservative and not boastful or expansive. Then there is also gamesmanship: ranchers are continually negotiating to buy and sell resources, so they are reluctant to lay their cards open-face on the table and hold them close to their vest.

Here are four ranchers who grew up during the final years of the Buffalo Gap frontier, and continue to ranch these same lands today.

DOUG TEMPLE

I was somewhat intimidated as I waited in the parlor of the ranch house to spend an evening with Doug Temple. He is already a legend on the reservation. A mutual friend suggested I talk with him about Frank Wilson, because they were neighboring ranchers forty years ago before Wilson's death, and perhaps Temple could provide some insight into certain aspects of the complex life of Wilson. These, more than any others, were two men who ruled the range in South Dakota over a span of many decades, and Temple continued his influence long after Wilson passed on. Frank Wilson reigned as the cattle baron of the western part of the reservation and Cheyenne River country, while Doug Temple controls much of the middle range on the north part of the reservation and in the White River country.

It was not easy to find a time when Temple would be available; we finally agreed that I would come to his ranch on a Saturday evening for supper. My trip out of Rapid City to the ghost town of Scenic was mem-

orable; the abandoned buildings of the town resembled an old movie set
-- except that these were the real thing.

Then I headed south into colorful country that appeared to be straight
out of a travel magazine. The rugged region was spectacular with its
multicolored layers of sandstone buttes. A sign indicating Badlands National Park confirmed where I was. A few miles later, a second sign
indicated I was entering the Pine Ridge Indian Reservation.

I am always nervous when traveling isolated reservation roads, for
it seems somewhat like a trip through Mongolia.

The Temple ranch nestles along Spring Creek, two miles north of
the White River in a northern portion of the reservation, and is wedged
among the checker-boarded boundary lines of Badlands National Park.
The reservation and national park exchange reciprocal pasture rights,
and Doug Temple's cattle graze on the open range of both.

Then I passed through a gated fence and traveled a dirt trail for several miles along a ridge line above the White River, thanking my good
fortune there was no rain. The deeply-rutted road would be impassable
when wet for anything – except maybe a horse or four-wheel-drive vehicle.

Doug Temple indicated he had to move cattle that afternoon, so may
be back for supper on the late side. I arrived at five-thirty, and it was
now seven. Darkness had settled in, and a full moon began to rise over
the Badlands buttes to the east. In the moonlight, I saw Temple ride
into the corral, and knew he would be in shortly after he unsaddled his
horse.

In my prior life as a business executive many years before, I once
stood in an airport line alongside actor John Wayne when the airport
was fog-bound and we were counter-hopping to find a way out of town.
Wayne must have come straight from a movie set, because he still wore
broad-brimmed hat, boots, and the entire cowboy garb except for sidearm, projecting his image that was so famous world-wide. As Doug
Temple entered the parlor of his ranch house and approached me, I saw
John Wayne again. Temple looked every bit the rancher legend he has
become and could have been "the Duke's" movie double. Extending his
hand in a warm greeting, Doug wore a welcoming smile, and we began
as pleasant an evening together as I can remember.

Doug Temple was nineteen when his father died, leaving him alone with his widowed mother. Mrs. Temple was a school teacher and County Superintendent for Shannon County schools and knew a lot about ranching, but most of the burden of seeing the work was done fell immediately on the shoulders of her son. That was in 1961. Now in his sixties, Temple is no longer a young man; but he still works the twelve-to-eighteen hour days, seven days a week, which began in his youth.

Conversation quickly turned to Frank Wilson, because Doug gave credit to Frank for much of his early success. He said it was Wilson who came to the Temple ranch and offered moral support, encouragement, and fatherly advice. Doug considered Frank Wilson his closest friend; someone who was always there to help when help was needed. Over the next few years, Wilson multiplied the size of his spread from very large to an absolutely huge operation.

Our conversation began in the front room and now we moved to the kitchen table and supper. The Temple ranch house is comfortable, but not ostentatious. It and many other homes on the reservation had the misfortune of being located on a World War II bombing range, so the original ranch buildings were razed by the government and most present-day structures had been moved in from elsewhere after the war.

The conversation soon turned to Doug Temple's ancestry and family background, since he is a mixed-blood Lakota. His great-great-grandmother was a full blood by the name of Burnt Thigh, who married a white man with the last name of Terry. The story of how they met can be found in a book written by Doug Temple's aunt, Mabel Lange Swanson. Samuel R Terry was a corporal in the Second Cavalry sent to Dakota Territory during the Indian troubles. One day while he was a scout, Terry was riding a horse through brush and tall grass, when *an Indian girl hiding in the brush jumped up, ran to him and grabbed the stirrup of his saddle. She begged him not to kill her, because that is what she thought he would do. She later became his wife.* [163]

Temple's other great-grandfather, August Lange, arrived as an immigrant from Germany in 1850 and settled in Iowa. His son, who was Doug's grandfather, J. H. (Henry) Lange, left home at eighteen years of age and ended up in Chadron, Nebraska at the edge of the Pine Ridge Indian Reservation. A few years later, he moved onto the reservation near Imlay, lived in a dug-out and raised cattle. He and Anne O'Rourke, daughter of a shopkeeper in Kyle on the reservation, were married in

1896. Henry Lange was a successful rancher who continued to expand his ranch and eventually owned a lot of land with good water all the way eastward to the town of Interior. He had twelve children, eight of which lived to adulthood: four girls and four boys. Losing children to flu and other sicknesses convinced him to move the family off the reservation to Rapid City, where doctors were more readily available.

A daughter of Henry Lange, named Georgiana, married Allen E. Temple from Lead, and they became the parents of Doug Temple. In the Lange ancestral line, all male offspring had white family names and all married Lakota women. None of the older brothers or sisters had any interest in moving from Rapid City back onto the reservation to take over the ranch, except for Georgiana and her husband, Allen Temple. So in 1930, they moved back to the home ranch – formerly called the Cook Ranch -- and now named the Pitchfork Ranch.

Doug Temple was born on the Pitchfork Ranch in 1942, and within a month, everyone in the path of the bombing range was forced off their land by the U.S. Government. The bombing range was a rectangle thirteen miles-wide and forty-three miles-long, extending across Cuny Table and eastward, nearly to Interior. Landowners were given eight days to abandon their homes and ranches, remove their cattle herds, and move elsewhere. It was an unbelievably harsh treatment by the government as the Indian people scattered. Doug was still a baby in diapers, and after a frantic search for other suitable land, his parents eventually settled southwest of Rocky Ford, where they remained. Twenty-eight years later, they reclaimed title to their former ranch lands lost to the bombing range.

As our talk turned to ranching, Doug admitted it requires someone such as himself with considerable dedication, stating that there are few easy-going ranchers these days because they all went broke and are long gone. Ranching, he said, requires a full day's work from before dawn until after dusk, and through good years when they make money and bad years when they don't.

Most of Doug Temple's pasture-land can be traversed only on horseback, and when trailing cattle there is no alternative. In winter, he uses a four-wheel-drive pickup to feed cake to his cattle and spring finds him with several roundups on different portions of his ranch, or else helping neighboring ranchers with their roundup. In the fall, he is driving trucks loaded with cattle the hundred and fifty miles to the sale barn in Presho. Doug takes Christmas day off as a holiday and manages to escape for two or three days to attend an annual livestock show. Other than that, it is all ranching time. With one son and a son-in-law who operate outlying spreads miles away, between they share the assistance of only one hired hand who lives on the next creek east.

In actual fact, Doug Temple is his own hired hand.

I told Temple I was not going to pin him down about the size of his spread or how many cattle he had, but I had heard rumors from people who should know that he was one of the largest ranchers in South Dakota. Doug laughed, and took another sip from his cup of tea. "Well, you said one of the largest? That leaves plenty of wiggle room, so I guess that is probably true." He paused, and then continued, "I don't rightly know. Ted Turner, the billionaire, has a huge ranch in the center part of the state and it is probably bigger, but that is an absentee corporate thing that employs dozens of hired hands, and I'm not sure it qualifies as a ranch."

Then I told him that the obituary of Frank Wilson stated he was the largest rancher of his era in South Dakota and had a herd of five thousand head of cattle. Some friends of mine, I told him, questioned the size of Wilson's herd, and felt he had only half this number of cattle. Doug thought about this and responded slowly as he recalled numbers from fifty years before. "Oh, that might be a slight exaggeration. I believe in 1950, Frank was only half the size he got to during the late 1950s and 1960s. My recollection is that in the 1950s, portions of that range still belonged to Witte, Barta, and the Ackermans. Frank later bought those spreads and expanded. Then he moved south buying or leasing more land with his daughter and son-in-law, Lois and Freeman Rapp, and their spread bordered the Curtis Coomes spread east of Oglala. When Frank was at his biggest, he had the western and southern sides of the reservation, north into the Badlands, and west through the Cheyenne River country."

"How far east did he come?" I asked.

"He never did come any further east than Cedar Creek there under Cuny Table on the north side. His and our pastures never did touch. I have some pasture up on Cuny Table. Sid Cuny's spread was always a buffer between us."

"What about the herd size that was reputed to be five thousand head of cattle?"

Beginning a long, rambling analysis, Doug was adding figures in his head, calculating as he went along to get a total. "Well, if you take cows and calves, maybe. I know we branded eighteen hundred and fifty head of calves and two hundred-fifty cows on one day during that time. So you have to have two thousand to two thousand three-hundred head of cows to have that many calves because you've always got some dry ones. So there are nearly four thousand head of cattle right there, plus he had a pure blood herd up at the ranch and probably some yearling heifers, maybe five or six hundred head of those, and then there were one hundred-twenty to one hundred-fifty head of bulls. Let's see; yes, all this could add up to somewhere around five thousand."

As Doug Temple provided this description of the Wilson Cattle Empire, their pastures and herd size, I had the impression he could look in the mirror and see something of the same order of magnitude as his own. It is almost certainly true that the biggest cattle baron of the 1950s and 1960s was Frank Wilson, that and he was replaced by Doug Temple.

"Do you still run horses?" I asked.

"I raise all my own horses. I get twenty-five to thirty colts per year -- more than I need. I used to get them all handled, give some to neighbors, sell some for saddle horses, bucking horses and such things, but I don't seem to get as much done as I used to."

"How about beef for your table, do you butcher your own?"

"We used to, but now we take it to a meat locker. We eat our own beef; no point in paying taxes on something you don't have to."

"Doug," I said, "I've read different accounts about how large a ranch has to be in this day and age to be self-sustaining and economically stable. What is your take on that?" I asked. Doug replied that the average rancher probably needs somewhere around five hundred head of cattle to be successful in meeting the variables of economic times and still have enough income to raise a family. With a smaller herd, it would probably take some secondary source of income, he said. Today, most small ranchers hold down some other job, and if herd gets larger than five hundred head of cattle, problems multiply.

Contrary to myth, it is no longer economically feasible to employ the number of hired hands necessary to do the work. Instead, most successful ranchers have become their own hired hands, so Temple is fortunate to have his son and a son-in-law who help run things.

Doug married during his twenties and raised a family of six children, losing two sons at an early age. His first wife died and he married again for a short period of time, then divorced -- living most of his adult life as a single parent. One son and a daughter are now a part of the ranch operation and a second daughter works in a nursing home in Chadron, Nebraska. With four grandchildren close by, there is a lot of support. Doug spends time with some of the family nearly every day, and some of the grandchildren often are on horseback alongside of him.

As mentioned before, the Temple home ranch resembles something out of a coffee table book of colorful photographs. It lies along Spring Creek, which meanders among the buttes of the Badlands, interspersed with green pastures that slowly fade into white desolation. In actual fact, this region has often been the subject of photo sessions and art works that line the walls of museums and tourist bookstores in the West and some of those photos of cattle herds against their Badlands could have been taken today or a hundred years earlier, there have been few changes to the basics of ranching since then.

FRANK RAPP

The profile of Frank Rapp is certainly different from the norm for a "reservation" Indian. A mixed-blood Lakota who was born and raised on the Pine Ridge reservation, Frank is highly-educated with several college degrees. He was engaged in social work during his early professional life, spent many years as director of a reservation school, and is now a full-time rancher.

His Indian name is *Tuwikiya Wawo'kiye Itancan*: "A Leader that Helps Everyone." That name is certainly appropriate, readers will find as they learn about the middle years of Frank's life as a leader in social work and education on the Pine Ridge Indian Reservation

Frank is the son of Lois and Freeman Rapp, and grandson and namesake of the legendary Frank Wilson. Lois and Freeman Rapp ran the Wilson spread, located in the southern part of the reservation ten miles north of Oglala on the White River, where Frank was born in 1954. He learned to ride a horse before he was old enough to reach the stirrups, and was cowboying before he was a teenager. During the school year, Frank stayed in town, but returned to the ranch many week nights, weekends and summers.

I asked him how it was growing up on a ranch and being a part-time cowboy.

"It was great," he said. "I wouldn't trade it for anything."

"You were the grandson of the legendary Frank Wilson. What was he like?"

"I didn't see a lot of Grandpa when I was little. He lived up at the home ranch along the Cheyenne River that was thirty miles north, so it wasn't an everyday thing. The spread that my father and mother ran was down here in the southern part of the reservation closer to Oglala. But later when I was cowboying as a teenager, I'd see a lot more of him in the spring and fall when we'd be gathering cattle for roundup and during the summer haying season on Mule Creek and Cheyenne River spreads. Grandpa Frank Wilson was roundup boss, and a good one," Frank said.

"I guess the roundup was an exciting time on the range?" I asked.

"Yes, the highlight of the year. I have never seen a western movie that did it justice. I remember the biggest one ever held, because I was one of the cowboys doing the roping. I was just a teenager, but we boys on the ranch always did the work of a man. Frank Wilson was roundup boss and my Dad, Freeman Rapp, was his right-hand man, and my mother, Lois, took care of the chuck wagon operations to feed the crew."

"You said it was a big one. How big?"

"We had three hundred cowboys at that one," Frank replied. "On the final day after the cattle and calves had been gathered and cut into different groups, the fun began on branding day. The cowboys were all busy doing the different jobs required: gathering, moving cattle, cutting out the calves, roping, branding, castrating, inoculating, and keeping things organized. This was one of the first roundups where Frank Wilson asked my Dad to help as his right-hand man, and Dad did a great job. Of course in later years, my Dad replaced Frank as roundup boss."

"Wow," I said, "Three hundred cowboys. Where did they all come from?"

"Everywhere," Frank answered. "All the other ranchers came over with their hired hands, because all the ranchers helped each other during the roundup season -- even after much of the range became fenced and the herds isolated. Then Granddad had many personal friends all over the reservation he invited, so we had Indians from Oglala, Pine Ridge, Kyle, Porcupine and other reservation towns -- in addition to all the Cheyenne River ranchers."

"I suppose it was also somewhat of an annual pageant or celebration that attracted cowboys?"

"Absolutely, like a dog attracts fleas," Frank responded. "Any cowboy in that part of the range wanted to be a part of the big annual event -- and of course, Frank Wilson wanted to put on a good show and get people to attend, because he needed manpower -- lots of it."

"How many cattle were involved?" I asked.

"An unbelievable number. That one day during the 1968 roundup, we branded over two thousand calves: two thousand and fifty-eight calves, to be exact," Frank stated.

"Wow. That is unbelievable. How is it possible to brand that many calves in one day?" I continued.

Frank answered ... "It takes organization. We had three roping pens going on simultaneously and four ropers in each pen, so at any time during the day there were twelve cowboys on horses roping calves -- and of course -- twelve crews were working with them to do the branding and so forth. I was one of the ropers. You can't imagine the noise, movement, dragging, scramble, and shuffling with over a thousand calves blatting, another thousand nervous mother cows creating havoc -- with horses, branding fires, cowboys everywhere. But it was all organized and went off like clockwork."

"What a spectacle. I would liked to have been there to see that scene," I said.

"But the story is not over. Talk about a closing ceremony -- the one we had that day was a perfect ending," Frank added.

"Tell me about it," I urged.

Frank went on ... "We finished branding the last calf on the early side about two in the afternoon, so we cowboys rode our horses out of the arena up to a grassy area where we kept all the horses -- and every cowboy had two or three -- so there were probably five or six hundred head of horses, and dozens of horse trailers off to the side. We took off the saddles, picketed the horses, and headed to some trees by the ranch house where my mother and the caterer had all the meals prepared. As I walked there, I noticed a dark, threatening, greenish cloud -- suggesting hail -- moving in from the horizon. A breeze came up, and then midway through the meal, the storm hit ... and *I mean a storm hit* ... it was the most violent storm I had ever seen or have seen since. It was sheets of drenching rain interspersed with hail and gale-force winds, lightning rocketing off nearby trees and thunder that shook the ground. Food-laden tables were upturned ... chairs blown over ... food flying everywhere in the wind ... and people scrambling for cover where no cover was available -- except for one shed and the vehicles. There was no protection ... and it continued on and on. After a while, three hundred cowboys had to rescue their nervous horses in a driving rain storm -- either load them into a horse trailer or saddle them and ride away; the ground was being covered in a white bog of frozen hail and rivulets of water. It was an absolute mess, and no one bothered with any goodbyes."

"In future years," Frank concluded ... "that round-up and the storm made for a lot of great storytelling. It is still referred to as the 'roundup and storm of 1968,' and I've always been proud to have been a part of it."

Frank went to Chadron State College and earned a bachelor's degree in social work; then he went another couple years and obtained a master's degree in mental health therapy. After receiving his masters degree in 1987, he became an outpatient and service coordinator for the Pine Ridge Mental Health Clinic, expanding their services from one to seven therapists. As District Supervisor for an area that comprised the reservation and took in four adjacent counties of South Dakota, Frank Rapp developed clinical services for the O'Kola Alternative School and Guardian Mountain Group Home, which provided outdoor therapeutic encounters for abused and neglected children and those with conduct disorders at the ranch. The highly-acclaimed Wilderness Experience program provided services to hundreds of children from western South Dakota and the Pine Ridge Indian Reservation. All of this was undertaken while Frank continued to spend weekends and vacation times at the ranch of his parents.

After five years, he left social work activities to become director of the Loneman School located near Oglala. Frank was founder and past-president of the American Indian Livestock Association. He was president and executive director of the Dakota Area Consortium of Treaty Schools, and in this capacity, worked extensively in Washington, D.C. with Congress to improve the education of Indian children and to unify the sixteen Bureau of Indian Affairs (BIA) funded grant schools of North Dakota and South Dakota.

Early in adult life, a marriage ended in divorce, and Frank now lives with his second wife, Mary. The two met when she was a speech therapist at the Loneman School. They have two sons, Zachary, who lives in Oregon, and Ryley, who is a "Screaming Eagle" of the 101st Airborne stationed in Iraq. Both sons own cattle at the ranch, and Frank expects them both to be returning to become the sixth-generation of the Wilson Ranch dynasty.

In 1998, Frank's father, Freeman Rapp, became ill, so he resigned at the school and began his "new profession" -- taking over his father's ranch as a full-time rancher. These most recent years have involved the hardest work of his life, according to Frank, but also the most enjoyable.

Let me relate a recent conversation between Frank Rapp and myself:

"Frank, it is no secret that the Pine Ridge Indian Reservation is one of the most impoverished regions in America, and it has its share of social problems. With your extensive formal education in social work, followed by many years as an educator on the reservation -- and now a rancher, I am interested to hear your perspective about life on the reservation -- particularly as it relates to young people. I've been told the young adult man or woman feels they live in a ghetto with no way out?"

"You are pretty close," Frank responded. "It is a simple fact that the reservation is impoverished and there are no jobs. So what is a young guy or girl to do? Many of them join a gang. What can they do for a living? Or what else can they do during the day? There is nothing to do. That is the crux of the social problem on the reservation. Yes, there may be other inter-related problems that flow from that, but the heart of the matter is there are no jobs."

"Well, that certainly places the problem in focus," I replied. "What is the solution? How do we get at that problem?"

"That is the one hundred dollar question," replied Frank. "There are no easy answers, and few are forthcoming. The government can play a bigger role than it has in the past and make a difference, but that is not the whole answer."

"Unfortunately," Frank stated, "There are few resources on the reservation that lend themselves to the kind of economic opportunity seen elsewhere. Companies do not come to the reservation for a variety of reasons -- and one reason is its geographic isolation. There is insufficient water and good soil for farming; the landscape for ranching is marginal, and supports only small herds at best. There are no minerals to support mining. -- The reservation was located where it is in a backwater of the nation where no one else wanted to live," he explained to me.

"Is there any way out from this morass?" I asked.

"Well," Frank went on ... "one faint ray of hope involves education. A higher percentage of Indian youth are now completing high school, and a substantial number now go on to further their education in one of the several Lakota colleges we now have. So at least they are becoming qualified for many different kinds of jobs -- even though those jobs do not yet exist. So one valuable resource we are developing is the human resource of an educated population. But that is only a start, and there has to be some sort of economic development that can provide employment. After a work ethic has been established, it can become generational," Frank emphasized.

"What role can the federal government perform?" I asked.

"The answer is not clear ...because its performance in the past has been checkered, and there is no success story to build on. They have done a few things in support of education (on the reservation) and that is perhaps the only improvement trend-line, but their programs always seem to stop short."

"For example," Frank stated, "they have done a great job of establishing colleges in several communities, yet leave them with fragmented programs, so a student is required to drive from town to town: to Oglala, to attend one class -- Porcupine for another -- and so on. Other than its assistance in education, there are no government programs of consequence that address our biggest problem -- *something that will bring jobs to the reservation.*"

"Frank, there are nine Indian reservations in South Dakota, and a sizeable Indian population which would seem to be the potential for considerable political clout, but I don't hear much about that. What is going on with political organization?" I asked next.

"Not much," Frank responded. "Political action by the Indian is a weakness. In fact, it became a giant negative in the aftermath of the uprising and violence of the 1970s. That was thirty years ago, and we are still paying a heavy price. Yes, we do have nine reservations, but their political activities are fragmented, and there is no unifying organization."

"There was a quasi-confederacy Tribal Chairman's Council that attempted to pull together a few things," Frank continued, "but it has not been effective. In actual fact, there is no coordination among the tribes on the various reservations -- so the potential we have for political clout has never been developed. Unfortunately, the Indian continues to stand on the sideline of the political process."

"Frank, now we come back to you," I said. "You seem to have the Indian social problems in good focus and some ideas for what is needed and how to go about getting there. You have a strong academic background with several college degrees, and much experience in the field of education. Now you are a full time rancher. At some point in the future, are you planning to get back into that social and education arena?"

"No, Bernie, I don't have any plans for that," Frank answered. "In 1998, when the opportunity came for me to go full-time into ranching, it became the absolute love of my life. I am a rancher now, and I don't want to live any other lifestyle. I do feel a sense of responsibility to my Indian roots and community, and will help where and how I can -- but I am first and foremost a rancher. The job of ranching is a full-time job if you want to be successful, and that is where I am going to spend my time."

"Yes, Frank, and you continue the unbroken six-generation dynasty of the Wilson Cattle Empire. You are walking in the boots of frontier legends. Good luck to you, and keep those doggies moving."

DAVE CUNY

With the ancestry of Dave Cuny, we can look back more than three centuries through the Cuny and Bissonette intertwined family trees from the 1700s -- when this part of North America belonged to France prior to the Louisiana Purchase. Dave Cuny's earliest ancestors of record were French fur trappers who married Indian women and lived on the frontier with mixed-blood families.

Dave's great-grandfather, Adolph Cuny, was one of the earliest pioneers in Wyoming Territory at Fort Laramie and married into the Bissonette family. His grandfather, Charles Cuny, came to the Pine Ridge agency in the 1870s, following an epic journey with his Oglala mother. Dave's father was Chat Cuny. Chat and Pat Cuny were half brothers.

Dave and Carole Cuny live on the historic Rock Spring Ranch established by his grandfather, Charles Cuny, as a cattle camp in the 1890s. For more than a century, this ranch has been a magnet for visitors crossing the high plateau to stop and water their horses at the fresh flowing spring that gushes from the side of the table. Chat took over the ranch from his father and Dave did the same. Chat was in his fifties when Dave was born. As the youngest of seven children, Dave was taught to ride horses by his father and older brothers before he can even remember, and he was roping cattle and breaking horses before he was a teenager.

Every time I visit Dave and his wife, Carole, I hold my breath during the last two hundred yards of road into their ranch. One must drive to the edge of Cuny Table where cliffs tumble straight down several hundred feet to the floor of Cuny Basin to the south, and then, just before falling over the edge, the road takes a blind turn onto a steep down grade, and with courage and a good pickup, one can drive down to the ranch house which sits on a notch below the lip of the table. The historic house looks over the barn and corrals and beyond to the Cuny Basin -- a stretch of Badlands stretching thirty miles to the southern horizon. It could be described as pasture land, but that is a misnomer, since cattle must hustle to find water and grass even in a good year. On top of the cliff on the plateau there is pasture land with good grass, but water is available only from windmills.

Dave was born on the ranch in 1941, shortly before World War II began. His family was one of the only Cunys who did not have to move off Cuny Table when the bombing range was established there in 1942, because the Chat Cuny ranch house was one hundred yards outside the range boundary over the side of the perimeter cliffs. While the family remained living there during the war, they had many noisy times when U. S. Air Force bombers dropped practice bombs and shot tracer-bullets at targets just across the fence from their property.

Dave Cuny has the unique distinction of being one of the few graduates of Buffalo Gap High School in 1959, during its short life. It was closed in 1941 and during World War II, then reopened in 1947 after the war, and closed again permanently in 1964. If one were to check the records, I suspect they would find Dave Cuny had fewer than a dozen classmates in the entire high school. Then even the elementary school was closed and students were bused to Hot Springs. The old school house on the hill above Buffalo Gap was sold, and has now been refashioned into a private residence. Even though that seems odd, at least it makes for one less abandoned building in a near ghost town.

Survival and success on the Dave Cuny ranch has never been a given. From earliest days, it has been a struggle to maintain economic stability on such a marginal landscape in the rugged Badlands, but Dave has always been ingenious and aggressive in developing whatever opportunities were available. He engineered and then built a gravity aqueduct system that fed water from the spring at the ranch, twelve miles out into the Cuny Basin, to supply water to his cattle with the run-off going into sumps; turning the Badlands landscape into viable pasture land.

Despite economic hardships, Dave and Carole raised seven children to adulthood on the ranch. Their oldest son, Scott, now has an adjoining ranch to the south on Cuny Basin. Their youngest son, Ross, recently graduated from the University of Wyoming with a degree in Rangeland Ecology, Management, and Land Restoration, and he has returned to the ranch in a partnership with his father. Dave runs a herd of several hundred cattle pastured on the table, in the basin, and elsewhere. He also maintains a herd of horses, which provides colts to break and use for working with cattle on the ranch. This herd no doubt includes descendants from that epic journey of Grandma Cuny from Fort Laramie to Pine Ridge after Adolph Cuny was killed.

I asked Dave about the problems he faces as an Indian rancher on the reservation: are these improving or becoming more difficult? His assessment was somewhat neutral, indicating there have been good years and some very rough ones. The most recent ones have been the most difficult.

Let me place these in the perspective he and Carole related.

A recent visitor to the reservation was Gale Norton, the forty-eight

Secretary of the U.S. Department of Interior, which includes under it the Bureau of Indian Affairs (BIA). The BIA was established in 1824 and has the responsibility for government relationships between the federal government and the tribes. Their mission statement is:

> *To enhance the quality of life and to provide economic opportunities in Indian Country, and to protect and improve the trust resources and assets of Indian tribes and individuals.*

That mission statement is somewhat like the traditional "pledge of good motherhood." What kind of job is the Department of Interior and the Bureau of Indian Affairs doing in carrying out their mission? Probably a good job in some activities, such as progress in encouraging Indian youth to further their education through high school, with an increasing number now attending the several branches of Lakota Colleges located in reservation communities, but progress has been too slow in some other areas.

Dave Cuny provided me with one example that impacted the viability of his own ranch, and this refers to the problem of prairie dog control. Dave first brought the problem to the attention of government officials and reservation tribal leaders thirty-five years ago, but it has been met mostly with deaf ears for three decades and prairie dog infestation remains a major problem.

It would seem that the control of prairie dogs would be a simple problem, but the opposite is true. It has had a profound effect throughout the ranching country of western South Dakota. These little animals have few predators and they multiply quickly. When they invade an area with their network of underground burrows, they eat all the plant roots, rob the area of its vegetation and in a few years the grass is gone and the land becomes worthless for farming or pasture. This infestation has brought Dave Cuny to his knees two different times, when his pastures were devastated. He had to sell his herd, get a long-term lease on land elsewhere, start over with a new herd, and then face the same problem again elsewhere. The Cunys survived with a great economic penalty, but some of neighboring ranchers were driven into bankruptcy by the prairie dog infestation.

A drive through western South Dakota indicates it is more than an Indian problem, and other large areas are affected.

So why has it taken so long to recognize and control this major infestation? The problem for many years was that initial attempts at eradication by strychnine and such chemicals gave secondary problems to other animals in the environment, so ranchers soon found themselves in confrontation with environmentalists. The U.S. Department of Agriculture should have carried the ball, but did not. The U.S. Department of Interior was in a weaker position to do anything and its sub-department, the Bureau of Indian Affairs, was helpless to do anything other than commiserate with those Indians who suffered the same fate as white ranchers. People such as Dave Cuny could do little about it other than shake their heads and try to survive. In the 1970s, Dave first brought the seriousness of the situation to the attention of neighbors, the BIA, the Governor, U.S. Senators, and tribal leadership, but his was a lone voice. Dave received occasional token letters of support from politicians in response, but generally his efforts fell on deaf ears.

Dave Cuny is now able to tackle the problem on his own ranch with poisons he must pay for himself, but it remains a major problem elsewhere.

Carole sat in the comfortable front room and visited with us. She seemed knowledgeable about ranch life and did not hesitate to chime in. She is a blonde Scots-Irish lass. I found out she was originally from back East, and I asked, "Carole, how does a city girl from New Jersey end up marrying a Lakota and living on the reservation?"

She laughed, and then responded "This city girl had a job as a secretary, but wanted something more meaningful and fulfilling, so she decided to volunteer for the Peace Corps and asked the assistance of a nun in the Catholic school she had attended to help her fill out an application." The nun said it would be a few weeks before she'd learn if the application was approved. In the meantime while waiting, she asked if Carole would be interested in "a two-week assignment with a Catholic mission school on an Indian reservation in South Dakota where they needed some temporary secretarial help?" Carole laughed again. "So my Peace Corps assignment got scrubbed, and my two week temporary assignment in South Dakota lasted for a full year, and then later it got extended for thirty-nine years."

"Those temporary assignments, you have to be careful of them," I said. "Also be careful of nuns who offer assistance. How did you meet

Dave?"

"Well," Carole began, "I was at the Holy Rosary Indian Mission in Pine Ridge, and I suppose that God, a nun, and a mission priest had a lot to do with it. During that stint at the mission, Dave's cousin -- who was a nun -- was being transferred and I was asked to drive her and the missionary priest out to Cuny Table, so she could say goodbye to her relatives there. It was roundup time and this handsome, rugged cowboy, Dave Cuny, emerged from the roping pen to say goodbye to his cousin. We were invited that night to dinner at the Chat Cuny ranch, and as the nun and priest talked to the parents, Dave and I sat across the table from each other."

"And you made eye contact?"

"Yes, we made eye contact, and we talked. I guess neither of us normally found it easy to talk to strangers, but somehow we seemed to be doing a lot of talking that night."

"So you came out to a South Dakota Catholic mission to help with secretarial work on a temporary two week assignment ... and you got trapped by the conspiracy of a nun and a priest?"

"Something like that, I suppose. Then as things will happen, that particular night, a heifer was giving birth in the barn to a calf. Dave said he had to go out and help the heifer and asked if I wanted to come along, so we walked together to the barnyard. I'd never seen anything remotely like that birthing process before. It grew late, so I drove the nun and priest back to the mission. It was a full year before I flew back to New Jersey."

"Carole, that is obviously not the end of the story."

"No. I returned to the mission to help again. I ran into Dave at a couple funerals and other events. One day the missionary priest asked me if I'd like to use my car and drive him to the Chat Cuny ranch where we were invited to spend a few days."

"So Carole, did you trap Dave, or did his family trap you in a conspiracy with a missionary priest?"

"I don't know, I think it was mutual. But we did have some help from circumstances -- just as I was getting ready to leave the Cuny ranch to return to the mission, the engine on my car blew up."

"Yes," interjected Dave laughing, "and she also got a speeding ticket. So I had to drive the priest and her back to the mission that night, and then meet her the next day to drive to Hot Springs so she could pay her fine."

Carole took up the story. "We went to the court house and Dave stood beside me in front of the judge. The judge said, 'What a wonderful couple. I'll bet you are here to get married.' We both turned red. I responded, 'Oh no, I'm here because I got a speeding ticket.' The judge scolded me, and then said, 'The next time I see you two, I want you here to get a marriage license.'"

I laughed. "So the judge joined in this tangled conspiracy with a priest and nun and it was the judge who did the actual marriage proposal?"

"Well, Dave and I spent the afternoon driving around Hot Springs and walking in the park along the river, and then he drove me back to the mission and returned to his ranch."

"After I got back to the ranch," said Dave, "I did a lot of heavy thinking and worked up my nerve to return to the mission. When I got there it was dark and very late, but I made a lot of noise and got Carole down to the front door. Right then and there, I proposed."

"Wow!" I said. "A romantic cowboy. Just like something out of a western novel, except in those books the cowboy sometimes rides off into the sunset. This was one time when the cowboy got his foot caught in the stirrup and stayed around to look at the stars with his sweetheart."

Dave and Carole were smiling, and I thought Dave may have been blushing a bit.

"Those were happy times," Carole said. "That night when Dave came back to the mission, it was very late and an excited nun came to my quarters to announce that a tall, very handsome cowboy was at the door asking for me. Dave was very cute, blustering out a marriage proposal, and I immediately accepted."

"So you were married." Then I asked, "Carole, here you were a New Jersey city girl, ... so what sort of cultural shock did you experience when finding yourself married to a mixed-blood Lakota and living on a ranch on the Indian reservation?"

"I don't recall much shock, because I always thought I seemed to fit right in okay. At least, we've been married now for nearly forty years and I'm still here. Now we have seven children and fourteen grandchildren," she replied. Dave told how Carole's sister-in-law came from New

Jersey to visit them on the reservation soon after the wedding and on her return, reported to her parents, "I don't know what in hell that girl is doing in that country out there."

"For me, it has been an exciting life," said Carole. "I tried to go out in the fields and pastures with Dave every day and become a rancher's wife. One of the early challenges came that first winter. We had three blizzards in a row, and those things out here on Cuny Table are an experience, even now. During the spring snows, I'd go out in the drifts to rescue little baby calves who were struggling for survival. There have been ups and downs, but ranching is a wonderful life. At least it has been for me with Dave and our family, and I couldn't wish for a happier time. Thank God for that two week temporary assignment."

Thanking Cunys for their hospitality, I said goodbye, climbed into my rental car and said a short prayer to help me get up that treacherous road to the lip of Cuny Table, down the long and lonely dirt road, and back to Rapid City.

The Rock Spring Ranch is a busy place on most weekends. Dave and Carole are joined by their children and grandchildren for home cooking and help with the ranch work, so the colorful Cuny legacy is being passed on to the next generations.

SHORTIE (ANITA) GALLENTINE

Perhaps you remember the TV series of Gunsmoke: It ran from 1955 until 1975, and was the longest running dramatic series in the history of television. Miss Kitty was the alluring barmaid and owner of the Long Branch Saloon and Matt Dillon was the town marshal who was making time with her, among his other adventures. During this same era, Buffalo Gap had its Kitty and Matt in the names of Shortie and Howard. They may not have been as glamorous as their TV counterparts, but they were real-life people. One difference was that Matt never caught Kitty, while Howard did woo and win his barmaid.

Their story though is much more than just about saloon-keeping; it is about two kids from a small town who started with virtually nothing and ended up owning one of the most beautiful and legendary ranches in western South Dakota. But Shortie and Howard are also a bridge from the past, because they knew nearly every old-timer of the late 1800s from that part of the country; many being the Lakota from the Indian reservation. Entering the twenty-first century, their thriving ranch continues to prosper.

Shortie (Her real name is Anita, and no one can remember where the nickname came from) was raised in Buffalo Gap in a house across from the livery barn. Her great-uncle was William Coad, the first sheriff in Custer City during the gold rush, when Fly-Speck Billy was taken from the jail and hanged on Main Street. It has sometimes been referred to as a lynching and that job of sheriff may not be a strong recommendation for a law enforcement officer, but there was little actual law in Custer City at the time. An unsavory and necessary job was completed and the town moved on.

Shortie was a classmate of my oldest brother, which would place her in the mid-eighties, not particularly old for a ranch lady in these parts. She graduated from high school just as World War II started, and like other young adults, she quickly left town -- all the men were being drafted into the army, and the girls seemingly all fled to California. Shortie worked in several aircraft factories as a "Rosie the Riveter."

Upon returning to Buffalo Gap at the war's end, Shortie found only two businesses still in operation and they were both saloons. Her brother owned one of them with a partner named Howard Gallentine. Shortie became a barmaid in the saloon. I asked her for the name of the establishment, hoping for something like the "Long Branch Saloon," but she said it didn't have a name and was never referred to by anyone other than as the "bar."

This distinguished it from the other saloon establishment in town though, which was known as "Frenchie's."

Howard Gallentine also came from pioneer stock and was raised on the Pine Ridge Indian Reservation. His parents ranched and had a store at Potato Creek and most of their friends and customers were Native Americans. The family lived there until the four boys were ready for high school, and then they moved to Newcastle, Wyoming. After high school, Howard left for California at the start of the war and worked in a shipyard until he joined the army. He was assigned to the Tenth Mountain Division, serving in the Italian Alps. Upon discharge, he returned to Buffalo Gap where his parents had a ranch, and he entered the saloon business.

As such things will happen, this saloon owner, Howard, fell in love with the barmaid and he proposed. Shortie was very popular with local patrons who frequented the bar -- which consisted mostly of ranchers or their hired hands -- and migrant combiners during the harvest season. Shortie's brother, Bill, bought Frenchie's saloon a few years later and renamed it "Bill's Bar."

The Indian uprising on the reservation in the 1970s began with a confrontation between an Indian and a white in Bill's bar, which ended with a killing in the dirt street out in front of the saloon. Fortunately for the "bar" of Shortie and Howard, they escaped that kind of trouble, having already sold the establishment. They had begun their new career of ranching.

Upon being asked if she ever had any brawls or trouble with patrons during all the years she and Howard operated the saloon. Shortie replied, "No," she said, "but if I did, I would have called the law."

"What in hell law would you have called?" I asked. "The closest thing to law was a part-time deputy sheriff in Custer, and he would not have driven to Buffalo Gap to intervene in a saloon brawl if his life depended on it. Anyway, I don't recall that your saloon even had a phone" I reminded her.

Shortie laughed, "I guess that was true, but we never thought about those things back then."

However, Shortie related the one time she did have trouble, and it was not with a bar patron but with her own husband, Howard. Shortie tells the story:

> One evening Howard left me alone in the bar with some excuse that he had to go to Hot Springs. It was the busy harvest season with all the combiners coming up the highway. There were hundreds of them parked in Buffalo Gap on their way north to the wheat fields. They had just left the dry states (at that time) of Kansas, Oklahoma and Texas, and so they were ready for a drink. The bar was jam-packed, and I was tiffed. I closed up at midnight. We had no phone at the bar, so I went home and called the Vets Club in Hot Springs and asked if Howard was there. Yes, they'd go get him. I said never mind, but tell him to get home. Finally he arrived, and he was drunk and feeling no pain. He said he'd been playing

poker. I was mad as hell and got right on his case. He got mad and said, "By God, if that's the way you feel, then I'll sleep on the floor." I said that was the way I feel, and he could damn well just sleep on the floor. So he got his army sleeping bag, crawled in, and in no time was out. So I zipped it up and pulled the draw strings tight so he was bound like in a straight jacket. Then I bounced him around, drug him bouncing down the stairs into the yard and around and bounced him back up the stairs. He begged to be let out and threatened if he ever did get out he'd kill me. So I said if that's the way you feel, you'll never get out. So finally he begged and promised he'd never do it again, so I let him out. He crawled on his hands and knees to the bed and got in. And he never did do it again, and never did leave me alone in the bar.

"Once a week in a back room at the saloon, Howard ran a poker game," Shortie said. "As a rule the same players always showed up and they included Frank Wilson, Bill Sewright, Wes Dalbey, Herman Hanson, Slim Marak, and Carl Dow. Some of the pots got pretty big. One day, Carl Dow told Howard he might sell his ranch and move to Arizona. Howard told him to let him know if he decided to do that, because he would like to buy it. We sold the saloon and with that money and a mortgage we bought the 7K ranch east of Buffalo Gap, which had been owned in the early days by Frank Stewart; then we gradually expanded with other property.

Carl came to Howard a couple years later announcing he was going to sell his Lame Johnny ranch. He gave Howard first chance to buy it, and the deal was made with the help of a mortgage. So they also found themselves owners of the historic Dow ranch. Both of their families came to the frontier as ranchers in 1894; returning to the land must also have been their destiny.

From Shortie:

Howard loved this ranch as it fulfilled his dreams. A year before he died we were debt -free, which he had worked so hard to achieve. It was left for me and my two sons to keep the ranch going and we have. I have my four-wheeler instead of a horse to check the cows and fences. I do some feeding and love every minute of it. Where else can you sit on your front porch and see the Black Hills, view two parks, Mount Coolidge, Harney Peak, and watch buffalo, elk, and deer in the wild? At eighty-five years young, I still keep busy and enjoy my life, and know that I have two sons who will be good stewards of the land.

That final statement by Shortie Gallentine seems appropriate, too, for the other New Frontier ranchers profiled: Doug Temple, Frank Rapp, and Dave Cuny: "Good stewards of the Land."

THE NEW FRONTIER RANCHERS

Doug Temple

Anita (Degnan) Gallentine

Dave and Carole Cuny

Frank Rapp, grandson of Frank Wilson

13
A REVISIT

It had been a long time since I'd been back. Visiting the landscape of my youth, the cultural differences of yesteryear -- Indian, cowboy, townspeople -- seemed about the same. Conditions on the reservation remained poverty-stricken. Wounded Knee was still an empty valley with little evidence of former tragedy. Driving into the Badlands terrain, I climbed up the steep cliffs to the top of Cuny Table and found it had mostly reverted to grassland.

I pulled into Pat Cuny's place where he and Tom Norman were awaiting my arrival. We boyhood friends exchanged handshakes, but we were never much for sentimentality. Then we climbed into my car and headed west, down the cliffs of Cuny Table into the Cheyenne River bottoms. Driving along the dirt road toward Buffalo Gap, Tom Norman nodded to empty spaces where the homesteads of our friends of yesterday used to be. We crossed Lame Johnny Creek and he pointed down the ravine to where he had ranched for seventy-five years, until he became crippled and moved to town. Tom's wife died the following year.

Entering Buffalo Gap, I drove past my Dad's vacant bank building and down the street of tumble-down reminders of yesterday. The little post office still had its doors open, but all the other buildings were abandoned. The roof had caved in on my old home and the ranch house next door fared little better. The Sewright barn and corral was now an empty, weed-covered field. To my mind, Buffalo Gap had truly become a ghost town.

Stopping briefly at the cemetery to pay our respects at the grave of Tom's late wife, we walked among the headstones of our old friends. Then we headed out of town, driving up through the Buffalo Gap that had seen thousands of migrating buffalo in better days. North of Custer City the mountain carving of Chief Crazy Horse came into view. We parked the car and found a granite ledge to sit on.

"Why Crazy Horse?" I asked.

"Yeah, hell, why him?" asked Tom. "It could have been Sitting Bull or Red Cloud, or many others. Why, if they only wanted a symbol, they could have used our old friend High Eagle. Why Crazy Horse?"

Pat did not respond for a while. Then he began slowly. "That man up there riding a horse across PAH-ha SAP-ha is made of stone. He represents our culture, the emblem of a brave people who struggled here. They may have lost, but they fought for their land. Maybe someday they will see their White Buffalo. Why Crazy Horse? Because he is our promise of hope for better times to come."

ABOUT THE AUTHORS

Top: Bernie Keating: born in 1929, he was raised in Buffalo Gap. His grandfather came to the Black Hills in the 1890s to work in the Cuyahogo Gold Mine.

Bottom left: Tom Norman: born in 1927, he ranches in the Cheyenne River Country. His grandmother was an early pioneer on the frontier.

Bottom right: Pat Cuny: born in 1922, he is a mixed-blood Lakota who ranches in the Pine Ridge Indian Reservation. His ancestors include French-Indian fur traders on the western frontier.

ENDNOTES

Chapter 1: MY LAKOTA FRIEND, NO WATER

The initial scene is an account from my childhood in Buffalo Gap in the mid-1930s when I lived adjacent to the Sewright ranch as depicted. The following scene with No Water takes place seven decades earlier at the same locale, and is a story that is based on the author's knowledge of the life of Indians and his later friendship with No Water when he was an elderly man.

[1] The encyclopedia in our bookcase when I was a kid living in Buffalo Gap referred to my hometown as a "ghost town", and we took great delight in living in a place with such a distinction.

[2] Paul WarCloud, *Dakotah Sioux Indian Dictionary*, Tekakwitha Fine Arts Center, Sisseton, SD, 1971, p. 181. Since this chapter deals with a personal account from an Indian's point of view, it utilizes the Teton dialect for parts of the vocabulary. *"Pronunciation of the Dakotah words and expressions is indicated in the simplified phonetic system, so that an English-speaking person can easily approximate the correct sound without having to learn an additional system of complicated symbols."*

[3] Charles W. Allen, *From Fort Laramie To Wounded Knee*, University of Nebraska Press, Lincoln, NE, 1997, p. 40. Fort William was subsequently named Fort John and each time the fort was moved to new ground. In 1849 the fort was purchased by the United States Government and a troop garrisoned there for the protection of Oregon Trail travel. It was re-christened Fort Laramie.

[4] Mari Sandoz, *Crazy Horse – Strange Man of the Oglalas*, University of Nebraska Press, Lincoln, NE, 1942, p. 178. Marie Sandoz wrote this book over sixty years ago, after interviewing many persons who had a first-person acquaintance with Crazy Horse and knowledge of the events of that time. She is generally recognized by many historians as one of the most authentic authorities of that era.

[5] Ibid., p. 191.

[6] Ibid., p. 232.

[7] Ibid., p. 247.

[8] Ibid., p. 255.

[9] Ibid., p. 428.

[10] Ian Frazier, *Great Plains*, Farrar, Straus, Giroux, NY, 1987, p. 80-81.

[11] The Little Bighorn is spelled in two different ways. In this book we will use this spelling, which is the official name the U.S. Government has used for the Little Bighorn National Monument.

[12] Benjamin Capps, *The Great Chiefs*, Time Life Books, New York, 1975, p. 207.

[13] Mari Sandoz, *The Battle of the Little*, University of Nebraska Press, Lincoln, NE, 1966, p. 225.

[14] Ibid., p. 170.

[15] Capps, op. cit., p. 408.

[16] Sandoz, op. cit., *Crazy Horse – Strange Man of the Oglalas*, p. 408.

[17] Ibid., p. 413.

[18] Freedman, *Life and Death of Crazy Horse*, Holiday House, 1996, p. 32.

[19] Capps, op. cit., p. 211.

Chapter 2: THE EARLY FRONTIER

[20] Paul WarCloud, op. cit., p. X. When I grew up, the standard name for our local Indians was Sioux, and although we did not have any Black people living in our vicinity, we referred to them as Negro. Today, we should make reference to ethnic people in the way they now prefer. So the name Sioux is out, except in a certain historical context; they want to be referred to as Lakota or Native American, and the name Negro is out; they want to be referred to as Black or African-American.

[21] Gregory Gagnon and Karen White Eyes, *Pine Ridge Reservation Yesterday and To-day*, Badlands Natural History Association, Interior, SD, 1992, p. 6.

[22] *Buffalo Gap Centennial*, Buffalo Gap Centennial Committee, Buffalo Gap, SD, 1986.

[23] Ian Frazier, *On The Rez*, Farrar, Straus, Giroux, NY, 2000, p. 91.

[24] Gagnon, op. cit., p. 9. When I was young, my grandparents lived on a farm near Newell, South Dakota, and their dining room window looked out at Bear Butte ten miles to the south. In those days of the 1930s, Bear Butte represented only an interesting mountain to the local people, and no one seemed aware of any Indian tradition concerning it. My mother climbed it as a teenager in 1915, and she was one of the few who ever did since there was no good trail up it at that time. In recent years I have followed a well-worn trail to the observation platform on top a number of times, and it is now a South Dakota state park, in recognition that it does have a unique history in the Indian tradition. When I recently climbed it, I met at the top three Southern Cheyenne/Arapaho Indians from Oklahoma who had carried various cloth artifacts from their elders in Oklahoma and were attaching them to trees. Then on the way down, I encountered a Hunkpapa lady from North Dakota who was collecting sage from the mountain to take back to her family for use in religious rituals and for medical purposes. Adjacent to the parking lot, sitting in the shade of a simulated "squaw cooler," was a bus-load of elderly Indians from Oklahoma who were unable to climb the mountain, but had made it to this symbolic spot part-way up. It became obvious to me that for many Indian tribes of the West, Bear Butte has become their "Mecca," and a place they must, if possible, visit sometime during their lifetime.

[25] Frazier, op. cit., *On The Rez*, p. 185. No other Indian leader compares in physical or historical stature with Chief Red Cloud. He was a huge physical specimen, six-and-a-half feet tall and well over two hundred pounds. With that presence he was successful in over eighty fights during his lifetime; mostly with other Indian tribes. It was Chief Red Cloud who negotiated with various U.S. generals and Indian agents over several decades, and he signed peace treaties in good faith. That good faith was seldom reciprocated by the U.S. Government which repeatedly broke the terms of the documents they had signed. Red Cloud pledged to remain in peace and his word was never broken, despite the actions of his adversaries. In retrospect, many Indians blamed him for caving under to the United States and allowing their lands to be taken from them. He lived to be an old man of nearly ninety. Feeble, blind, forgotten, he died in his government-built frame house on the Pine Ridge Indian Reservation. Long before he died, he had fallen into disrepute among many Lakota living there. He died in obscurity, and only twelve Indian police were in attendance at his funeral -- a chieftain who had presided over some of the most climatic events in Lakota, and indeed, Indian history.

[26] Hoig, *Indians of North America-Cheyenne*, C. State of Oklahoma, Enid, OK, 1989.

[27] Gagnon, op. cit., p. 9.

[28] Gagnon, op. cit., p. 9.

[29] Gagnon, op. cit., p. 10. The movie, *Dances with Wolves*, has been one of the most-watched Hollywood movies about Indians, and it may even be somewhat accurate in its portrayal. Whenever I visit South Dakota, someone will indicate some locale where it was filmed. The small creek a few miles north east of Bear Butte has been pointed out as a place where the river scenes were filmed. Friends have indicated two different locations where the buffalo scenes were filmed. I think it is fairly accurate that the final winter mountain scene was filmed in Spearfish Canyon. It is a mark of a good movie that various people and places want to be remembered in the credits.

[30] Merrill J. Mattres, *The Great Platte River Road*, Nebraska Historical Society, Lincoln, NE, 1969. Fort Laramie was well preserved and is now the Fort Laramie National historic Site. In a recent visit, Librarian Sandra Lowry was quite helpful in making their voluminous historical archives available to me for use in my book.

[31] Gagnon, op. cit., p. 9.

[32] Charles Rambow, *Bear Butte*, Pine Hill Press, Sioux Falls, SD, 2004, p. 24.

[33] "South Dakota," *Collier's Encyclopedia*, P.F. Colliers and son, 1960, Vol. 17, p. 519.

[34] Frazier, op. cit., *On The Rez*, p. 211.

[35] Sandoz, op. cit., *The Battle of the Little Bighorn*, p. 173. This is an interesting observation, because it makes a connection that is often historically overlooked between the economic "special interest forces" at work within the nation and the political pressures that led up to various events. The great depression of the 1870s came at a time when the railroad czars who were trying to get financing for their projects did create great economic pressure to find gold in the western

lands that had long been rumored. It partly led to the hysteria that followed the reported finding of a minor gold strike at Custer's park in the Black Hills.

[36] Ibid., p. 176. This is another interesting observation by Mari Sandoz: that after the Civil War was ended, career army officers who wanted to advance their careers had to go to the Western Frontier and fight Indians and engage in bloody and "heroic" tactics. It was the "only game in town."

[37] Ibid., p. 175.

[38] Frazier, op. cit., *On The Rez*, p. 9. Iroquois Indians attended the meeting of the colonists in the years before the American Revolution and advised them to unite in a scheme for self-government based on the confederacy that ruled the six Iroquois nations. Benjamin Franklin said at a gathering of delegates from the colonies in Albany in 1754, "It would be a strange thing if six nations of ignorant savages should be capable of forming a scheme for such a union and able to execute it in such a manner that it has subsisted for ages and appears indissoluble, and yet that a like union should be impracticable for ten or a dozen English colonies." Two hundred years later, I often heard the same description of Indians among some townspeople of Buffalo Gap.

[39] Rezatto, *Tales of the Black Hills*, Fenwyn Press, Rapid City, SD, 1989, p. 79. This was certainly subterfuge by a general that six years before had affixed his signature in the treaty with Chief Red Cloud granting the Indians the ownership rights to the Black Hills.

[40] Jessie Sundstrom, Editor, *Custer County History to 1776*, self published, Custer, SD, 2002, p. 72.

[41] Agnes Wright Spring, *The Cheyenne and Black Hills Stage and Express Routes*, University of Nebraska Press, Lincoln, NE, 1948, p. 71.

[42] "Hickok," *Collier's Encyclopedia*, P.F. Colliers and son, 1960, vol. 9, p. 393.

[43] *Our Yesterday's*, Eastern Custer County Historical Society, Hermosa, SD, 1967-1970, XVI.

[44] Ibid., p. XVI.

[45] Sandoz, op. cit., *The Battle of the Little Bighorn,* p. 108.

[46] "South Dakota," *Collier's Encyclopedia*, P.F. Colliers and son, 1960, Vol 17, p. 326.

[47] Sergeant Windolph, *I Fought With Custer*, University of Nebraska Press, Lincoln, NE, 1947, p. 108. Additional details to this: most but not all of the Seventh Calvary were wiped out. Reno's and Benteen's men lost many, but survived. They built Fr. Meade in 1878, and Reno was its early commander.

[48] David Humphreys Miller, *Custer's Fall*, Bantam Books, NY, 1957, p. 146.

[49] Frazier, op. cit., *On the Rez*, p. 188. The Indian reservations kept shrinking and moving as reflected through several decades by the changing location of agencies. This was where the government Indian Agent who controlled the purse strings lived, where tribal business was done, and was the population center for the tribe. Originally located on the Platte River near Fort Laramie, this site conflicted with Oregon Trail traffic and plans for a railroad, so it was changed to the White River in western Nebraska. But Nebraska did not want an agency within its borders, so the agency was changed again to a site on the Missouri

River in central South Dakota. That site, however, occupied land suitable for white development, and so the fourth and final location was on the White Clay Creek, just north of the Nebraska border and was named Pine Ridge -- an isolated, semi-arid region that no one else wanted. Each of these changes of agency location involved uprooting of thousands of people and was much debated.

Boundaries of the Pine Ridge Indian Reservation also kept moving, and never to the benefit of the Indian. Originally, the southern edge was thirty miles down into Nebraska, but was then moved north to the state line to keep it out of Nebraska. The original western edge of the reservation was to be established along the north-south railroad at the edge of Buffalo Gap, but this would have included all the Cheyenne River country where many white ranchers lived. It was altered to follow the Cheyenne River; but that would have included a number of white ranchers east of the river. Finally moved to its present location running north and south through the Badland terrain, it was thought to be where no one would want to live.

[50] Gagnon, op. cit., p. 20.

[51] Snyder, *Pinnacle Jake*, University of Nebraska Press, Lincoln, NE, 1951, p. 18.

[52] John O Bye, *Back Trailing In The Heart Of The Short Grass Country*, Self Published, 1956, p. 390.

[53] James H. McGregor, *The Wounded Knee Massacre*, Fenske Printing Inc., Rapid City, SD, 1940, p. 37.

Chapter 3: THE BISSONETTE /CUNY FAMILY

[54] John Dishon McDermott, *The Mountain Men*, File CIN-17-1, Fort Laramie, WY, p. 49. Some of the things we were taught in school history classes in the old days have turned out to be oversimplifications or political mis-statements, e.g., did Columbus discover America? And were Lewis and Clark the men who first explored the West? We now realize that men like Bissonette were living there decades earlier.

[55] Fort Laramie File CIN-60, Dr. 3.

[56] Fort Laramie File CIN-60, p. 3. I always thought the Sioux crossed the Missouri river into western Dakota much earlier than this, and I also found it interesting that they simply invaded lands occupied by other tribes and took over their real estate. Which people own the title to any given land? Is it the first one there -- or the last one to invade and dominate it?

[57] McDermott, op. cit., *The Mountain Men*, File CIN-17-1, p. 49. McDermott worked for the National Park Service and at one time was the historian at Fort Laramie. When he later worked in the Denver Regional Office, he contributed several articles for the ten-volume set of *The Mountain Men and the Fur Trade of the Far West*, published by the Arthur H. Clark Company from 1965 to 1972 under the editorial supervision of LeRoy R. Hafen. The Fort Laramie File CIN-17-21 is the biography of Joseph Bissonette, found in Vol. four. The current librarian at Fort Laramie, Sandra Lowry, was unable to find any current CV information concerning the author.

[58] McDermott, op. cit., *The Mountain Men*, File CIN-17-1, p. 49. It was amazing to me that the National Park service had all this information relative to the Cuny family, and the family was apparently unaware that it existed.

[59] McDermott, op. cit., *The Mountain Men*, File CIN-17-1, p. 50. Until I studied the history file, I was unaware of the major role that liquor had with the plains Indians during the early frontier days. Red Cloud's father died an alcoholic. The quarrel between Bull Bear and Smoke in which the former was killed by Red Cloud, apparently took place during a drunken brawl. When U. S. Army generals wanted to discuss a treaty with Indian chiefs, apparently they "loosened them up" with liquor. From the file, it appears that Joseph Bissonette was a major supplier of liquor to all the parties on the frontier: Indian, army officers, troopers, and civilians.

[60] McDermott, op. cit., *The Mountain Men*, File CIN-17-1, p. 58.

[61] There is some question relative to whether the mother of Josephine was his first wife, Julia, or his second wife, Nellie Plenty Brothers. The Wyoming State Archives in Cheyenne differ with those of Fort Laramie National Site. Since Josephine was born in 1835 and Julia did not die until 1855, I accept the fact that Josephine was the oldest daughter of his first wife Julia.

[62] Fort Laramie File CIN-17-5x, *Cuny Family History*, Fort Laramie, WY. Large families were the norm. Joseph Bissonette had eight children with his first wife and fourteen with his second wife. His daughter, Josephine, had seven children. Her son, Charles, had eight with a first wife who died, then married a woman with six children, and together they had four more.

[63] McDermott, op. cit., *The Mountain Men*, File CIN-17-1, p. 60. Joseph Bissonette lived with his second wife, a Brul'e, in Wounded Knee, which was only a few miles from Manderson where his oldest daughter, Josephine Cuny, lived. The family has no information about whether the father and daughter ever had contact again after both ended up on the Pine Ridge Indian Reservation.

[64] McDermott, op. cit., *The Mountain Men*, File CIN-17-1, p. 49. So, when the famous explorer of the West, John Charles Fremont, was "discovering" new places, his guide was Bissonette, who was already living there.

[65] Fort Laramie File CIN-17-23x, Fort Laramie, WY. I am unaware of a stagecoach line over this route, but apparently it followed the Bozeman Trail up through the Powder River country of Wyoming into Montana. It was that route of the white man that disturbed the Lakota, and a decade later led to the Red Cloud War.

[66] Fort Laramie File CIN-17-28, Fort Laramie, WY.

[67] Frazier, op. cit., *Great Plains*, p. 81. Further to this story from the book, Richard G. Hardorff, *The death of Crazy Horse*, University of Nebraska Press, Lincoln, NE. 2001, Appendix A. This contains a letter written in 1934 by Victoria Conroy, who lived near me at the time in Hot Springs, S.D. She was the closest blood relative to Crazy Horse still living. Her grandmother and the father of Crazy Horse were brother and sister. Among the many assertions in the long letter are the following:

(1) Crazy Horse was buried somewhere between Porcupine and the Wounded Knee Creek on the reservation.

(2) She admits that "Crazy Horse took Miss Larrabee for a concubine to his wife" but does not acknowledge they got married; hence that he had two wives at the time of his death.

(3) She states emphatically that Crazy Horse had no offspring. Larrabee married again after his death, her new husband took the name of Crazy Horse, and they had children together who claim to be the descendents of Crazy Horse.

[68] Spring, op. cit., p. 111.

[69] Fort Laramie File CIN-17-10, *Annals of Wyoming*, Fort Laramie, WY, p. 56.

[70] The spelling of the name Ogallala used here in reference to the Indian chiefs is different, and the spelling has varied over time. Today the spelling of the Indian tribe is Oglala. That is also the spelling for the name of the town on the reservation a few miles west of the Pine Ridge agency. However, the spelling for the town south in Nebraska that is located adjacent to the Pine Ridge Indian Reservation is Ogallala, Nebraska. There is also another town spelled Ogallah, Kansas.

[71] Fort Laramie File CIN-17-7x, *Upper Platte Letters*, Fort Laramie, WY. There is certainly a "sugar coated" tone to this letter reporting the successful agreement. See my comments in endnote 59 relative to the use of liquor by the army with Indian leaders during the negotiations leading up to the signing of treaties. One wonders how much of a role liquor may have had in the infamous treaty of 1868 which is still being debated today.

[72] Fort Laramie File CIN-17-7x, *Upper Platte Letters*, Fort Laramie, WY.

[73] Fort Laramie File CIN-17-7x, *Upper Platte Letters*, Fort Laramie, WY.

[74] Fort Laramie File CIN-17-7x, *Upper Platte Letters*, Fort Laramie, WY. According to Agnes Wright Spring in her book, *The Cheyenne and Black Hills Stage and Express Routes*, it was the recession and hard economics of these times in the Fort Laramie area that motivated Ecoffey and Cuny to build their brothel and import girls.

[75] Allen, op. cit., p. X. Allen is now recognized as one of the most authentic and important chroniclers of the Western Frontier, and he certainly had a direct connection with the Cuny family. His first job in the West was working for Adolph Cuny, and he later married Cuny's niece.

[76] Fort Laramie File CIN-17-9, *Medical History*, Fort Laramie, WY.

[77] Fort Laramie File CIN-17-14, *Annals of Wyoming*, Fort Laramie, WY, p. 97.

[78] Fort Laramie File CIN-17-20x, *John Hunton Diary,* Fort Laramie, WY, Vol 2, p. 31. These next several endnotes refer to the Hog Ranches of Fort Laramie. Hollywood may be looking for subject matter to use as a "pre-sequel" to their 2004 TV show, Deadwood. I would suggest they consider a series on the Hog Ranches of Fort Laramie. It would legitimately have all the required elements needed these days to sell a TV plot to the American viewing audience.

[79] Fort Laramie File CIN-17-23x, *by Vaughn*, Fort Laramie, WY.

[80] Fort Laramie File CIN-17-8x, *Letters sent Platte Agency*, Fort Laramie, WY.

81 Fort Laramie File CIN-17-23x, *Daily Rocky Mountain News*, July 12, 1867, Fort Laramie, WY.

82 Fort Laramie File CIN-17-23x, Fort Laramie, WY.

83 Fort Laramie File CIN-17-23x, Fort Laramie, WY.

84 Fort Laramie File CIN-17-7x, *Upper Platte Letters*, Fort Laramie, WY. I graduated from high school in Edgemont, S. D. We used to have school picnics in Red Canyon, and I was never aware until recent years of the history that took place in that area. Of more interest to us at the time was that uranium was discovered in Red Canyon, and it led to better economic times for the struggling community when a processing plant was located in Edgemont.

85 Fort Laramie File CIN-17-7x *Upper Platte Letters*, Fort Laramie, WY.

86 Spring, op. cit., p. 112. Timing is everything and that includes the time to die. Ecoffey's remains were carefully carried by Adolph Cuny to Cheyenne for a funeral and he is buried there in a grave with a headstone placed there by his partner. When Cuny was killed less than a year later, his widow, Josephine, had to flee with her family because she was an Indian. Cuny's remains were placed in an unmarked grave in the Fort Laramie graveyard.

87 Fort Laramie File CIN-17-20x, *John Hunton Diary,* Fort Laramie, WY, Vol 2, p. 159.

88 Ibid., p. 113. The term "oldest" does not mean elderly, but in terms of having been a white man who arrived there almost before any other permanent white residents.

89 Fort Laramie File CIN-17-23x, *Minnequa Historical Bulletin*, Fort Laramie, WY, Christmas 1934, borrowed from Ed Kelley. I considered deleting this quote that is based on a memory from nearly six decades before and I think it is erroneous, but since it was in the Fort Laramie File, I decided that in the interest of full disclosure it should be included.

90 The Seventh Cavalry was under the command of Lt. Col. George Custer when several regiments under his direct command were wiped out in the Battle of the Little Bighorn. Subsequent to that, the Seventh Cavalry was stationed at Fort Meade from 1878 until 1888, at which time it became removed to Fort Riley, Kansas. In the 1930s when I was a boy, the Fourth Cavalry was the unit stationed at Fort Meade, and was there from 1924 to 1942. Cavalry units then became mechanized, and horse operations were gradually suspended with the remaining cavalry mounts joining the remount depot at Fort Robinson, Nebraska.

91 The actual route followed by Josephine Cuny in traveling from Fort Laramie to the Black Hills was not recorded at the time, but it most likely followed the stagecoach trail since it was the only route that could accommodate wagon travel. The route is described in considerable detail by Agnes Wright Spring in her book, *The Cheyenne and Black Hills Stage and Express Routes*. I know this route well and almost every turn and bump in the road, because I traveled it numerous times in a dilapidated Trailways bus on my way from Edgemont, South Dakota to Boulder, Colorado during the years I was a student at the University of Colorado. The stagecoach route was little changed when it was

made into a Wyoming State road; they simply laid asphalt over the prior ruts on the stagecoach trail.

[92] Spring, op. cit., p. 117.

[93] Allen, op. cit., p. 238. Much of the description of Pine Ridge is derived from this account by Allen, who lived there at the time and is considered by many historians as having provided the most accurate description of the early years of Pine Ridge.

[94] Ibid., p. 50.

[95] Frazier, op. cit., p. 186.

[96] Allen, op. cit., p. 239.

[97] Frazier op. cit., p. 186.

[98] Ibid., p. 186.

[99] Allen, op. cit., p. 57.

[100] Ibid., p. 53.

[101] Gagnon, op. cit., p. 20.

[102] Virginia Lautenschlager, *A History of Cuny Table*, South Dakota Humanities Council, 2005, p. 8.

Chapter 4: THE WILSON RANCH EMPIRE

[103] *Our Yesterday's*, op. cit., p. 346. By Owen Wilson, who was the son of Tom Wilson, and submitted this account of the Wilson family for this historical book.

[104] Bud Wilson, *A Wilson Family History*, Phoenix, AZ, 1988, self published, p. 34. Bud Wilson was the son of Edna and Jim, and nephew of Tom Wilson. Much of the history is also included in *Family history of the Wilson's from Buffalo Gap*; a collection by various members of the Wilson family, and much of it is also repeated in *Our Yesterday's*.

[105] Ibid., p. 34.

[106] Ibid., p. 12.

[107] Ibid., p. 38.

[108] Ibid., p. 40.

[109] Ibid., p. 38.

[110] Ibid., p. 59.

[111] Ibid., p. 40.

[112] *Our Yesterday's*, op. cit., p. 347.

[113] Ibid., p. 237.

[114] Ibid., p. 347.

[115] John O. Bye, *Back Trailing in the Heart of the Short Grass Country*, self published, 1956, p. 298.

[116] Ibid., p. 298.

[117] A.B. Snyder, *Pinnacle Jake*, University of Nebraska Press, Lincoln, NE, 1951, p. 131.

[118] *Our Yesterday's*, op, cit., p. 348.

[119] *Wilson Family History*, op. cit., p. 60. Obituary from *Hot Springs Star newspaper*.

[120] Ibid., p. 60.

[121] Ibid., p. 61.

[122] Ibid., p. 59.

[123] *Our Yesterday's*, op. cit., p. 348.

[124] Ibid., pg. 347.

[125] "Blutch," *Our Yesterday's*, Eastern Custer County Historical Society, 1970, pg. 349. The author of the "Blutch" chapter was Alice (Wilson) Pierce who grew up in Hot Springs and attended high school there.

[126] Ibid., pg. 348.

[127] Ibid, pg. 348. When Anita (Degnan) Gallentine and I were reminiscing about this incident, she recalled the deputy sheriff involved was Wes Dalbey, who was often deputized for special events such as the Fair, Rodeo, and the 4th of July dance.

[128] I find no documentation for this event, but Anita Gallentine, Hazel (Bondurant) Krutsch, and I all recall being there at the time, Hazel and I up in the balcony and Anita, being a couple years older, was down on the floor dancing.

[129] Ibid., pg. 352. This account by his daughter, Alice, differs from that by his brother, Owen. In the same document, pg. 348, Owen writes, "I recall that during World War Two, Blutch enlisted in the Merchant Marine. How this happened no one knows because he was a disabled veteran from World War One.... He later received an honorable discharge."

[130] Ibid., pg. 348.

Chapter 5: THE NORMAN RANCH EMPIRE

[131] "Norman family," *Our Yesterday's*, op. cit., p. 260.

[132] "Fallen warrior's history," *Rapid City Journal*, 9-20-04.

[133] *Our Yesterday's*, op. cit., p. 263.

[134] "Norman," *Our Yesterday's*, op. cit., p. 255. This is an adaptation of the chapter the Late Audery Norman, wife of Tom Norman, wrote for the book.

Chapter 6: BUFFALO GAP

[135] Frazier, *On The Rez*, op. cit., p. 141.

[136] Ibid., p. 140.

[137] op. cit., *Our Yesterday's*, p. XVI.

[138] *Our Yesterday's*, op. cit., p. XV1.

[139] Windolph, op. cit., p. 56.

[140] This information comes from the Black Hills historian, Beverly Pechan, who was the Museum Director and Historian at Fort Meade from 1997 to 2000.

[141] Dee Brown, *Bury My Heart At Wounded Knee*, Holt, Rinehart, NY, 1971, p. 297.

Chapter 7: GUS HAASER

[142] Anna Marie (Johnson) Nordstrom, Livingston, MT, 2002, As related to her by Gregg Haaser, Gus Haaser's son.

[143] "Gus Haaser," *Our Yesterday's*, op. cit., p. 243.

[144] Bert L. Hall, *Roundup Years, Old Muddy to Black Hills*, self published, 1936, p. 15.

Chapter 8: GRANDMA SEWRIGHT

[145] "Sewright," *Our Yesterday's*, p. 11.
[146] Paul WarCloud, op. cit., p. 88.

Chapter 9: THE BONDURANT RANCH

[147] *Our Yesterday's*, op. cit., p. 343.
[148] Ibid., p. 343.
[149] Ibid., p. 344.

Chapter 10: MY DAD AND FRONTIER BANKING

[150] The WPA was the Works Projects Administration established by the Roosevelt Administration during the 1930s depression to provide meaningful work to those unemployed and with many of them on public welfare.
[151] A.E. Dahl, *Banker Dahl*, Fenske Book Company, Rapid City, SD, 1965, Appendix.
[152] *Our Yesterday's*, op. cit., p. 4.

Chapter 11: THE WOUNDED KNEE MASSACRE

[153] Gagnon, op. cit., p. 7.
[154] Gagnon op. cit., p. 12.
[155] Ibid., p. 17.
[156] James H. McGregor, *The Wounded Knee Massacre*, p. 41.
[157] McGregor, op. cit., p. 66.
[158] Dee Brown, op. cit., p. 413.
[159] Ibid., p. 417.
[160] Ibid., p. 418.
[161] Ibid., p. 419.
[162] Gagnon, op. cit., p. 20.
[163] Mabel Lange Swanson, *Sauer Kraut on the Pioneer Trail*, Pine Hill Press, Freeman, SD, 1977, p. 96.

BIBLIOGRAPHY

Abbott, E.C., and Helena H. Smith, *We Pointed Them North*, University of Oklahoma Press, Norman, OK, 1939.

Allen, Charles W., *From Fort Laramie to Wounded Knee*, University of Nebraska Press, Lincoln, NE, 1997.

Black Elk DeSersa, Ester, Olivia Black Elk Pourier, Aaron DeSersa Jr., and Clifton DeSersa, *Black Elk Lives*, University of Nebraska Press, Lincoln, NE, 2000.

Brown, Dee, *Bury My Heart at Wounded Knee*, Holt, Rinehart & Winston, Inc., New York, NY, 1971.

Brown, Joseph E., *The Scared Pipe*, University of Oklahoma Press, Norman, OK, 1953.

Bye, John O., *Backtrailing in the Heart of the Short Grass Country*, self published, 1956.

Capps, *The Great Chiefs*, Time Life Books, New York, NY, 1975.

Cochran, Keith, and Dave Strain, editors; Phyllis Gorum, translator, *Buffalo Gap: A French ranch in Dakota, 1887*, Lame Johnny Press, Rapid City, SD, 1981; Originally Mandat-Grancey, Le Baron E.de, Breche Aux Buffles, Librairie Plon, Paris, 1889.

Catron, Marjorie E., editor, *Camp Crook South Dakota Centennial 1883 – 1993*, Camp Crook Centennial Committee, 1983.

Dahl, A. E, *Banker Dahl of South Dakota*, Fenske Book Company, Rapid City, SD, 1965.

Editor, *Buffalo Gap Centennial 1886 – 1986*, Buffalo Gap Centennial Committee, 1986.

Editor, *Our Yesterday's*, Eastern Custer County Historical Society, Hermosa, SD, 1970.

Eli Paul, R, editor, *Autobiography of Red Cloud*, Montana Historical Society Press, Helena, MT, 1997.

Frazier, Ian, *On the Rez*, Farrar, Straus, Giroux, New York, NY, 2000.

Frazer & Hunt, *I Fought with Custer*, University of Nebraska Press, Lincoln, NE, 1947.

Freeman, *Life and Death of Crazy Horse*, Holiday House, New York, NY, 1996.

Gagnon, Gregory, and Karen White Eyes, *Pine Ridge Reservation: Yesterday and Today*, Badlands Natural History Association, Interior, SD, 1992.

Hardorff, Richard G., *The Death of Crazy Horse*, University of Nebraska Press, Lincoln, NE, 2001.

Hoig, Stan, *The Cheyenne (Indians of North America)*, Chelsea House Publications, Emeryville, CA, 1989.

"Indians in America," *Collier's Encyclopedia*, P.F.Collier & Sons, New York, NY, 1960.

Lautenschlager, Virginia Irene (Kain), *A History of Cuny Table, South Dakota: 1890 – 2002*, South Dakota Humanities Council, 2002.

Link, Mike, *Black Hills Badlands: The Web of the West*, Voyageur, Bloomington, MN, 1980.

Mattes, *Great Platte River Road*, Nebraska Historical Society, Lincoln, NE, 1969.

McGregor, James H., *The Wounded Knee Massacre*, Fenske Printing Inc., Rapid City, SD, 1969.

McMurtry, Larry, *Crazy Horse*, Viking published by the Penguin Group, New York, NY, 1999.

Means, Russell, *Where White Men Fear to Tread*, St. Martin's Griffin, New York, NY, 1995.

Miller, David Humphreys, *Custer's Fall*, A Bantam Book, New York, NY, 1963.

Neihardt, Hilda, *Black Elk and Flaming Rainbow*, University of Nebraska Press, Lincoln, NE, 1999.

Neihardt, Hilda, *Black Elk Speaks*, University of Nebraska Press, Lincoln, NE, 1932.

Neihardt, Helda, *Vision Revisited*, University of Nebraska Press, Lincoln, NE, 2001.

Nordstrom, Anna Marie (Johnson), *Gus Haaser*, Private letters to author, 2003.

Rambow, Charles, *Bear Butte*, Pine Hill Press, Sioux Falls, SD, 2004.

Rezatto, *Tales of the Black Hills*, Fenwyn Printing, Rapid City, SD, 1989.

Sandoz, Mari, *Crazy Horse: The Strange Man of the Oglalas*, University of Nebraska Press, Lincoln, NE, 1942.

Sandoz, Mari, *The Battle of the Little Bighorn*, University of Nebraska Press, Lincoln, NE, 1966.

Snyder, A.B., *Pinnacle Jake*, University of Nebraska Press, Lincoln, NE, 1951.

Spring, Agnes Wright, *The Cheyenne and Black Hills Stage and Express Routes*, University of Nebraska Press, Lincoln, NE, 1948.

"South Dakota," *Collier's Encyclopedia*, P.F. Collier & Sons, New York, NY, 1960.

Sundstrom, Jessie Y., *A History of Custer City: the Early Years 1876 - 1925*, Self Published, Custer City, SD, 1998.

Sundstrom, Jessie Y., editor, *Custer County History to 1976*, Custer County Historical Society, Published at Rapid City, SD, Printing Inc., 1977.

Swanson, Mabel, *Sauerkraut on the Pioneer Trail*, Pine Hill Press, Sioux Falls, SD, 1977.

WarCloud, Paul, *Dakotah Sioux Indian Dictionary*, Tekakwitha Fine Arts Center, Sisseton, SD, 1989.

Wilson, Bud, editor, *Wilson Family History*, Self Published, 1982.

Windolph, Sergeant, *I Fought With Custer*, University of Nebraska Press, Lincoln, NE, 1947.

INDEX